Greenhouses for Homeowners and Gardeners

Written by

John W. Bartok, Jr.
Extension Professor Emeritus
Department of Natural Resources Management and Engineering
University of Connecticut

Natural Resource, Agriculture, and Engineering Service (NRAES)
Cooperative Extension
152 Riley-Robb Hall
Ithaca, New York 14853-5701

NRAES–137
June 2000

ISBN 0-935817-51-4

Library of Congress Cataloging-in-Publication Data

Bartok, John W., 1936–
    Greenhouses for homeowners and gardeners / John W. Bartok, Jr.
        p. cm. — (NRAES ; 137)
    Includes bibliographical references (p.).
    ISBN 0-935817-51-4 (pb : alk. paper)
    1. Greenhouses — Design and construction. I. Title. II. NRAES (Series) ; 137.

SB416 .B37 2000
690'.8924—dc21

00-030485

Natural Resource, Agriculture, and Engineering Service (NRAES)
Cooperative Extension • 152 Riley-Robb Hall
Ithaca, New York 14853-5701
Phone: (607) 255-7654 • Fax: (607) 254-8770
E-mail: NRAES@CORNELL.EDU • Web site: WWW.NRAES.ORG

Contents

Figures ix

Tables xiv

Introduction 1
About This Book 1

CHAPTER 1 — Greenhouse Basics: Getting Started

How Does a Greenhouse Work? 3
How Are Greenhouses Used? 4
    Year-round Greenhouses 4
    Season-extender Greenhouses 4
    Conservatories 5
    Sunspaces 6
    Window Greenhouses 6
    Indoor Light Gardens 6
How Much Does a Greenhouse Cost? 7
How Much Time Does a Greenhouse Demand? 7

CHAPTER 2 — Selecting a Greenhouse: Types, Styles, and Sizes

Types of Greenhouses 9
    Attached (Lean-to) Greenhouses 9
    Freestanding Greenhouses 10
    Pit Greenhouses 11
    Solar Greenhouses 12
Greenhouse Styles 12
Selecting a Size 13
SIDEBAR: Greenhouse Aesthetics 13

CHAPTER 3 — Greenhouse Planning: Permits, Building Options, Foundations, and Utilities

Permits 14
    Zoning Permits 14
    Building Permits 14

Contents

CHAPTER 3 — Greenhouse Planning: Permits, Building Options, Foundations, and Utilities *(continued)*

Custom Designs 15

    Reasons for a Custom Design 15

    Services Provided by Architects and Engineers 16

Accommodating the Physically and Mentally Challenged 16

    Access 16

    Layout 17

    Benches 17

    Environmental Control 17

    Watering Devices and Tools 17

Hiring a Contractor to Build a Greenhouse 19

    How to Find a Contractor 19

    The Importance of a Contract 20

Building a Kit Greenhouse 20

    The Instruction Manual 20

    Skill Level Required to Build a Kit Greenhouse 22

    SIDEBAR: Construction Tips for Kit Greenhouses 22

    Tools Required to Build a Kit Greenhouse 23

    Storage of Materials 23

    SIDEBAR: Tools and Equipment for Building a Kit Greenhouse 23

Building a Greenhouse from Plans 23

    Materials 23

Purchasing a Used Greenhouse 24

    Inspection and Evaluation 25

    What Is a Used Greenhouse Worth? 25

    Disassembly and Reassembly 25

The Foundation 25

    Types of Foundations 26

    Foundation Layout 30

Upgrading a Greenhouse 33

Utilities 33

    Electricity 33

    Water Supply 35

Contents

CHAPTER 4 — Framing Materials and Glazing

Framing Materials 37

    Galvanized Steel 37

    Aluminum 37

    Wood 37

    SIDEBAR: Tips for Building Wood Frames 38

Glazing 38

    Light Requirements of Plants 38

    Glazing Basics 39

    Types of Glazing 40

Installation 43

    Glass 43

    Corrugated Fiberglass, Polycarbonate, and Polyethylene 44

    Flat Fiberglass and Polycarbonate 44

    Structured Sheets — Polycarbonate and Acrylic 44

    Film Plastic 45

CHAPTER 5 — Greenhouse Layouts and Equipment for Efficiency

Using Space Inside the Greenhouse 48

    The Layout 48

    Racks and Shelves 49

    Beds 50

    Work Areas 50

    Benches 51

    Space Under Benches 53

    Floors and Walkways 53

Labor-saving Equipment 55

    Growing Media Preparation Equipment 55

    Planting Aids 57

    Materials Handling Equipment 57

    Pesticide Application Equipment and Storage 57

    Personal Protective Equipment 58

    Monitoring Instruments 59

Watering Systems 61

    Mist Systems 61

    Overhead Watering Systems 62

    Trickle Watering Systems 63

    Capillary Mats 64

    Hydroponics and Soilless Culture Systems 65

Contents

CHAPTER 5 — Greenhouse Layouts and Equipment for Efficiency *(continued)*

Fertilizing Systems 67
    Selecting a Proportioner 67
    Proportioner Installation and Use 68
    Adjusting Proportions 69

CHAPTER 6 — The Greenhouse Environment: Heating, Cooling, and Plant Lighting

Heating the Greenhouse 71
    Sizing the Heater 72
    Choosing a Fuel 74
    Cost of Heating the Greenhouse 75
    Heating Units 77
Energy Conservation 87
    Interior Liners 87
    Exterior Covers 88
    Sealing Laps 89
    Thermal Blankets 89
    Permanent Insulation 92
    Management Practices to Reduce Energy Usage 93
Cooling the Greenhouse 93
    Heat Exclusion 93
    Natural Ventilation Systems 96
    Fan Systems 97
    Evaporative Cooling 98
    SIDEBAR: Winter Ventilation 100
Controlling Humidity 100
    Measuring Humidity 100
    Increasing Humidity 101
    Decreasing Humidity 102
Air Circulation 102
Environmental Control 103
    Thermostats 104
    Controllers 104
    Computers 104
Supplemental Lighting 105
    Lighting Basics 105
    Light Sources 106

Contents

Measuring Light 109

Cost of Supplemental Lighting 110

CHAPTER 7 — Window Greenhouses and Growth Chambers

Window Greenhouses 111

    Selection 111

    Environmental Control 113

    Installation 113

    Operation 114

Germination and Growth Chambers 114

    Germination Cabinet 114

    Growth Chamber 114

    Light-Support Frame 114

    Cart 116

    Rack System 116

CHAPTER 8 — Garden Structures

Cold Frames and Hotbeds 118

    Constructing the Frame 118

    Locating the Frame 119

    Making a Hotbed 119

    Using a Cold Frame or Hotbed 121

    Construction and Operating Costs 122

    Plants to Grow in Cold Frames and Hotbeds 122

Shade Houses 122

    Uses for Shade Houses 122

    Shade House Construction 123

Rowcovers and High Tunnels 123

    Rowcovers 125

    High Tunnels 127

APPENDIX A — Maintaining the Greenhouse: A Checklist

Frame 129

Glazing 129

Heating System 130

Cooling System 130

Water System 130

Contents

APPENDIX A — Maintaining the Greenhouse: A Checklist *(continued)*

Lighting 130
General Cleanliness 130
Winter Maintenance 130

APPENDIX B — Greenhouse and Equipment Suppliers

Greenhouse Manufacturers and General Suppliers 131
Greenhouse Replacement Part Suppliers 133
Suppliers of Specific Equipment 133

APPENDIX C — Greenhouse Plans

8' x 12' Lean-to Greenhouse 135
8' x 16' Curved-eave, Lean-to Greenhouse 140
8' x 8' Freestanding Greenhouse 145
10' x 10' A-frame Greenhouse 147
12' x 15' Gothic Greenhouse 151
10' x 12' Slant-leg Greenhouse 156
14' x 21' Vertical-leg Greenhouse 163
10' x 16' Pit Greenhouse 169
10' x 12' High Tunnel 173
3' x 6' Cold Frame 177

APPENDIX D — Useful Conversions 179

Glossary 183

References 191

Other Publications from NRAES 193

Index 197

About the Author 200

Figures

CHAPTER 1 — Greenhouse Basics: Getting Started

Figure 1-1   The parts of a greenhouse 3
Figure 1-2   Attached solar greenhouse 4
Figure 1-3   Season-extender greenhouse 5
Figure 1-4   Conservatory 5
Figure 1-5   Attached sunspace for heat gain and living space 6

Figure 1-6   Window greenhouse 7
Figure 1-7   Basement light garden 7

CHAPTER 2 — Selecting a Greenhouse: Types, Styles, and Sizes

Figure 2-1   Attached greenhouse designs 9
Figure 2-2   Freestanding greenhouse designs 11
Figure 2-3   Pit greenhouse 12

CHAPTER 3 — Greenhouse Planning: Permits, Building Options, Foundations, and Utilities

Figure 3-1   Sample plot plan showing the location of a proposed greenhouse 15
Figure 3-2   Greenhouse ramp specifications for accommodating the physically challenged 17
Figure 3-3   Wheelchair-accessible bench layouts 17
Figure 3-4   Adjustable-height bench design 18
Figure 3-5   Plant bench design 18

Figure 3-6   Planting aids for the physically challenged 19
Figure 3-7   A good installation manual can reduce greenhouse erection time and make
              assembly easier 21
Figure 3-8   Form for making a conduit arch 24
Figure 3-9   Cross-section of greenhouse foundation 26
Figure 3-10   Concrete slab foundation (cross-section) 26

Figure 3-11   Poured concrete wall (cross-section) and brick or stone-faced concrete block
              wall (cross-section) 27
Figure 3-12   Concrete pier foundations 28
Figure 3-13   Wood post foundation 28
Figure 3-14   Pipe foundation 29
Figure 3-15   Ground surface mounting and lap joint construction for ground timbers 29

Figure 3-16   Wood deck installation (including method of leveling) 30
Figure 3-17   Kneewall designs 30
Figure 3-18   Squaring an attached greenhouse 31
Figure 3-19   Procedure for squaring the foundation 31
Figure 3-20   Ridge flashing options for attached greenhouses 32

Figures

CHAPTER 3 — Greenhouse Planning: Permits, Building Options, Foundations, and Utilities *(continued)*

Figure 3-21   Distribution box for small greenhouse with no electric heat or supplemental lighting 34
Figure 3-22   System transfer switch 35
Figure 3-23   Basic alarm system with a battery-operated warning device, thermostat, and power failure relay 35
Figure 3-24   Water filters 36
Figure 3-25   Backflow prevention 36

CHAPTER 4 — Framing Materials and Glazing

Figure 4-1   Types of framing materials 37
Figure 4-2   Types of double-pane glass 41
Figure 4-3   Extrusions for attaching polycarbonate and acrylic structured-sheet glazing 42
Figure 4-4   Single-layer glass installation 43
Figure 4-5   Double-pane glass installation 44

Figure 4-6   Corrugated fiberglass or polycarbonate installation 44
Figure 4-7   Structured-sheet polycarbonate or acrylic glazing installation 45
Figure 4-8   Structured-sheet polycarbonate installation 45
Figure 4-9   Aluminum extrusions for attaching film plastic 45
Figure 4-10   Installation of blower for inflating a double-layer polyethylene cover 46

Figure 4-11   Homemade manometer for measuring static pressure 47
Figure 4-12   Common methods of anchoring polyethylene 47

CHAPTER 5 — Greenhouse Layouts and Equipment for Efficiency

Figure 5-1   Bench system layouts for a 14-foot-by-18-foot greenhouse showing alternate arrangements and amount of bench space 49
Figure 5-2   Wooden stairstep bench 49
Figure 5-3   Brackets and hangers to support shelves or baskets 50
Figure 5-4   Greenhouse bed construction 51
Figure 5-5   Portable potting bench 51

Figure 5-6   Construction of a greenhouse bench with a wooden top 52
Figure 5-7   Construction of a greenhouse bench with a wire fabric or expanded metal top 52
Figure 5-8   Floor and aisle material options 54
Figure 5-9   Types of floor drains 55
Figure 5-10   Soil shredder 56

Figure 5-11   Homemade soil screen 56
Figure 5-12   Concrete or soil mixer 56

Figures

Figure 5-13   Electric soil sterilizer placed over a homemade wooden soil cart 56
Figure 5-14   Storage bins for growing mix 57
Figure 5-15   Carts and wheelbarrows for moving materials 57
Figure 5-16   Pesticide applicators 58
Figure 5-17   Store chemicals in a locked cabinet to keep them away from children and animals ... 59

Figure 5-18   Use an appropriate respirator when working with soil, growing mixes,
               fertilizers, and pesticides 59
Figure 5-19   Common types of thermometers used in a home greenhouse 59
Figure 5-20   Sticky trap (yellow or blue) for monitoring insect activity 60
Figure 5-21   Time clocks and interval timers can control lighting or watering systems 60
Figure 5-22   Typical mist bed setup 61

Figure 5-23   Automated irrigation system 62
Figure 5-24   Layouts for automatic watering systems 63
Figure 5-25   Drip-tube irrigation systems 63
Figure 5-26   Low-flow tape and emitter watering systems 64
Figure 5-27   Capillary mat irrigation system 65

Figure 5-28   Typical hydroponic and soilless culture systems 66
Figure 5-29   Fertilizer proportioner installation 68
Figure 5-30   Fertilizer proportioner with a water-operated piston pump 69

CHAPTER 6 — The Greenhouse Environment: Heating, Cooling, and Plant Lighting

Figure 6-1   Winter design temperature map for estimating heat loss 74
Figure 6-2   Cross-section of a through-wall gas heater 77
Figure 6-3   Gas-fired unit heater 78
Figure 6-4   Gas-fired hot water heater 78
Figure 6-5   Counter-flow gas wall furnace 79

Figure 6-6   Gas-fired nonvented heater 79
Figure 6-7   Electric utility heater with fan 80
Figure 6-8   Electric baseboard heater 80
Figure 6-9   Infrared heater 80
Figure 6-10   Portable kerosene heater 81

Figure 6-11   Oil-fired furnace 81
Figure 6-12   Extension of the home heating system 81
Figure 6-13   Wood or coal stove 82
Figure 6-14   Pellet stove 82

Figures

CHAPTER 6 — The Greenhouse Environment: Heating, Cooling, and Plant Lighting *(continued)*

Figure 6-15   Reduction in solar gain as the face of the greenhouse is located east or west of true south 83

Figure 6-16   Slope of glazing to get maximum solar gain 83

Figure 6-17   A propagation heat mat can provide the ideal temperature for seed germination 85

Figure 6-18   Electric heating cables are available in many lengths 85

Figure 6-19   Agritape root zone heaters are easy to install and use 86

Figure 6-20   A typical warm water root zone heating system contains tubing, a circulating pump, a source of hot water, and a control system 87

Figure 6-21   Methods for supporting poly liners or blanket materials on cables or clothesline 88

Figure 6-22   Low-cost blanket support for a sloped roof or wall 90

Figure 6-23   Method of supporting blanket material on conduit or tubing 90

Figure 6-24   Track-supported system for hanging blanket material 91

Figure 6-25   Woven blanket materials 91

Figure 6-26   Thermal blanket system for an attached greenhouse; side blanket is attached to top blanket 91

Figure 6-27   A thermal blanket that stores against one endwall works well for freestanding greenhouses 91

Figure 6-28   Edge seals keep heat inside the thermal blanket 92

Figure 6-29   Shade cloth installation over individual bench 94

Figure 6-30   Shade fabric is available with different levels of shading 95

Figure 6-31   Wood or aluminum slat roll-up external shade 95

Figure 6-32   Wind has a significant influence on the ventilation rate; open eave and leeward vents to get uniform cooling 96

Figure 6-33   Hinged vents can be opened by hand or powered with a thermostatically controlled vent motor 96

Figure 6-34   Nonelectric, solar-powered vent opener (lifting force = 15–35 pounds) 96

Figure 6-35   Fan ventilation 97

Figure 6-36   Locate thermostats at plant height; provide shade over thermostats 98

Figure 6-37   Effect of relative humidity of outside air on evaporative cooling 98

Figure 6-38   An electric humidifier will increase the moisture level and cool the greenhouse 99

Figure 6-39   Evaporative cooler (swamp cooler) 99

Figure 6-40   Fan-and-pad evaporative cooling system (best for larger greenhouses) 99

Figure 6-41   Instruments for measuring humidity 101

Figure 6-42   Horizontal airflow in a greenhouse 103

Figure 6-43   The ceiling fan forces air from the ridge down to the floor 104

Figure 6-44   Thermostats should be shaded from the sun to prevent false readings 104

Figures

Figure 6-45   Typical step environment controller 104
Figure 6-46   Equipment staging for the controller in figure 6-45 105
Figure 6-47   The light spectrum 105
Figure 6-48   Comparison of lamp efficiency 106
Figure 6-49   Types of lighting common for supplemental greenhouse illumination 107

Figure 6-50   Photometer (measures in foot-candles) 110
Figure 6-51   Quantum meter (measures in micromoles/square meter-second) 110

CHAPTER 7 — Window Greenhouses and Growth Chambers

Figure 7-1   Types of window greenhouses 112
Figure 7-2   Germination cabinet construction 115
Figure 7-3   Light-support frame construction 116
Figure 7-4   Portable germination/light cart 117
Figure 7-5   Plant rack system 117

CHAPTER 8 — Garden Structures

Figure 8-1   Locate a cold frame or hotbed where it will receive good sunlight and is
              protected from wind 119
Figure 8-2   Hotbed with electric heating cable for plants grown in flats or pots 120
Figure 8-3   Hotbed with heating cable for growing crops in soil 120
Figure 8-4   Types of heating cables 121
Figure 8-5   Retain heat by covering on cold nights 121

Figure 8-6   Lath-covered frame for shade 123
Figure 8-7   A-frame shade house 124
Figure 8-8   Shade shelter with a pipe frame 124
Figure 8-9   Hoop-supported rowcover or low tunnel 125
Figure 8-10   Low-cost PVC pipe rowcover 126

Figure 8-11   Floating rowcover 126
Figure 8-12   High tunnel 127
Figure 8-13   Roll-up side construction 127

Tables

CHAPTER 1 — Greenhouse Basics: Getting Started
Table 1-1   Approximate greenhouse costs 8

CHAPTER 3 — Greenhouse Planning: Permits, Building Options, Foundations, and Utilities
Table 3-1   Desirable ranges of specific elements in irrigation water 36

CHAPTER 4 — Framing Materials and Glazing
Table 4-1   Comparison of common glazing materials 39

CHAPTER 5 — Greenhouse Layouts and Equipment for Efficiency
Table 5-1   Preparation of fertilizer stock solutions 70

CHAPTER 6 — The Greenhouse Environment: Heating, Cooling, and Plant Lighting
Table 6-1   Estimated heat requirements, in Btu/square foot of floor area 72
Table 6-2   Overall heat transfer coefficients 73
Table 6-3   Fuel cost comparison 75
Table 6-4   Degree-days (55°F base) 76
Table 6-5   Solar heat storage 84

Table 6-6   Approximate heat loss reduction 87
Table 6-7   Comparison of greenhouse blanket materials 89
Table 6-8   Chart for the selection of shade fabric 95
Table 6-9   Typical fan performance 97
Table 6-10   Relative humidity chart for interpreting sling psychrometer readings 101

Table 6-11   Fan sizes for air circulation 103
Table 6-12   Photoperiod of some common plants 106
Table 6-13   Comparison of light sources 108
Table 6-14   Conversion factors — photometric/quantum 109

APPENDIX D — Useful Conversions
Table D-1   Conversions between Fahrenheit (°F) and Celsius (°C) temperature 179
Table D-2   Useful conversions 181

Introduction

Stepping out of the snow into a greenhouse on a cold winter day is like walking into a jungle on a tropical island. The warm, humid air quickly warms your body, prompting you to remove your coat and gloves. Radiant energy from the sun, trapped by the greenhouse glazing, creates an environment that makes plants respond as if it were the peak of summer. The smell of the flowers, plants, and soil reminds you of the joys of summer gardening and fills you with anticipation for spring.

Greenhouse gardening appeals to many people for many different reasons, and it can be a very fulfilling, lifelong activity. A greenhouse can help garden enthusiasts get through the cold part of the year, both physically and mentally. It fills a void during winter, when it is too cold to grow plants outdoors in the garden.

Home greenhouses are an ideal way to introduce children to nature and show them how seeds develop into beautiful flowering plants or tasty vegetables. The experience of growing and tending to plants can lead to a fruitful career as a horticulturist, florist, or garden-center operator. With the rapid increase in commercial greenhouse and nursery ventures over the past few years, there is an increasing need for people trained to lead these industries.

Many home greenhouses blossom into full-fledged businesses. With enough interest and a "green thumb" for plants, a greenhouse gardener can soon find his or her greenhouse bulging at the seams, and then either more space must be added or the plants must be given away or sold. This situation often leads to the purchase of a more sizeable poly-covered hoop house and the start of a part-time business.

Retirees often adopt greenhouse gardening as a hobby to enjoy during their retirement years. Many of them are avid gardeners during the summer, and they are looking for an activity to fulfill their gardening needs during the long winter months.

About This Book

Greenhouses for Homeowners and Gardeners will help readers select and design the most appropriate size and style of greenhouse to fit their needs, find the best place to locate a greenhouse, and decide whether to build a greenhouse themselves or hire a contractor to do it. After reading this publication, aspiring greenhouse operators will be able to make informed decisions about glazing and framing materials, space utilization, interior design, heating and cooling systems, supplemental lighting, watering and fertilizing systems, and other greenhouse design and construction issues. Window greenhouses, growth chambers, cold frames and hotbeds, shade houses, and rowcovers and tunnels are also discussed in the book in chapters 7 and 8.

Nearly 150 line drawings are included in the book to help readers visualize the way greenhouses are built; evaluate alternative methods of construction; select labor-saving equipment; and understand the skills involved in designing, building, and operating a greenhouse.

Ten diverse do-it-yourself plans for home green-houses and other structures that can extend the growing space are included in appendix C beginning on page 134. Each plan includes diagrams, materials lists, and construction details. A maintenance check-list, lists of greenhouse and equipment suppliers, and useful conversions are included in three additional appendixes. A glossary of terms that might be unfamiliar to readers begins on page 183, and an index is included on page 197.

Greenhouses for Homeowners and Gardeners is written as a reference to update similar publications that have become obsolete due to changes in materials and construction techniques. The author, John W. Bartok, Jr., extension professor emeritus at the University of Connecticut, has over thirty years of experience working with hobbyists, commercial growers, institutions, and manufacturers.

CHAPTER 1

Greenhouse Basics: Getting Started

How Does a Greenhouse Work?

The sun's energy is transmitted to the earth in the form of short-wave radiation. When this radiation passes through the atmosphere and strikes objects on the earth, it is converted to heat. Outdoors, the heat is lost back to the sky. Clouds and smog act like an insulation blanket, slowing the heat loss. This is why frosts seldom occur on cloudy nights.

The glazing on a greenhouse, like clouds in the atmosphere, traps heat within the structure. Some glazings retain heat better than others. For example, adding a second layer of plastic or glass reduces heat loss by about 35%. Placing insulation blankets on a greenhouse can reduce heat loss even further. On cloudy days, supplemental heat may be needed in a greenhouse to maintain a good growing environment for the plants.

Energy from the sun is intense. On a clear winter day, the

temperature inside a closed greenhouse can reach 90–100°F when the temperature outside is only 0°F. In the summer, the temperature inside a closed, empty greenhouse can climb to more than 140°F. All greenhouses should have some means of venting to cool the structure when it gets too hot for the plants.

Figure 1-1 shows some common terminology associated with greenhouses. Basic frame materials include steel, aluminum, and wood. The pros and cons of

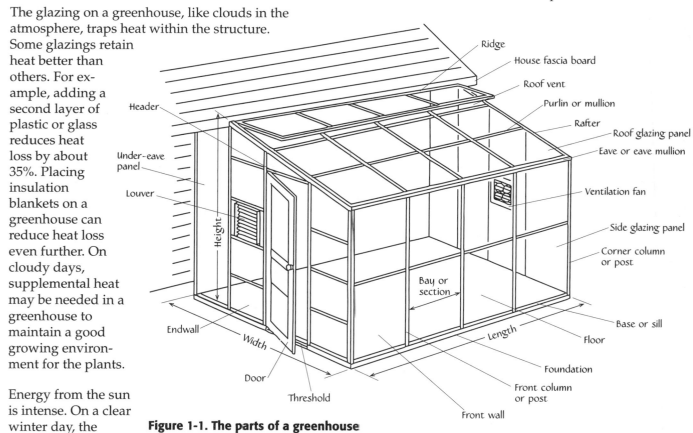

Figure 1-1. The parts of a greenhouse

each should be considered before making a choice. The same is true of glazing options. Historically, glass is the preferred material, but plastics are continually being improved and offer some special qualities that may make them a better choice. Framing materials and glazing are discussed in much more detail in chapter 4.

How Are Greenhouses Used?

Year-round Greenhouses

The year-round greenhouse is designed to provide optimum growing conditions all year. It has a heating system to warm the structure on cold winter nights and a ventilation system to cool it on warm summer days. It may have a solar design (figure 1-2) to reduce the energy needed for heating and cooling. (Solar designs are discussed in more detail in chapter 2, beginning on page 12.)

The year-round greenhouse is ideal for housing a collection of orchids or tuberous begonias or for maintaining a conservatory of decorative plants to provide a changing array of colors throughout the year. It might also be used to provide fresh vegetables and fruits for your table when you cannot pick them from the garden. If your interest is in propagating woody ornamentals or perennials, then the greenhouse can provide the necessary humid climate.

A year-round home greenhouse is usually covered with a more permanent glazing—such as polycarbonate, acrylic, or double glass—to reduce heating costs during the winter. These glazing materials do not require as much maintenance as a plastic film cover. Glazing options are discussed in more detail in chapter 4.

Season-extender Greenhouses

A season-extender greenhouse is used primarily to lengthen the outdoor growing season. It generally contains limited supplemental heat—perhaps a small electric heater to keep the temperature above freezing on cold nights. Usually, it is a low-cost structure made with a wood or pipe frame and covered with film plastic glazing (figure 1-3).

In early spring, lettuce and cole crops can be planted in a season-extender in containers or beds. These crops do best at temperatures between 45° and 55°F but can withstand occasional temperatures below freezing. Seedlings are usually started indoors and then moved to the greenhouse when they are transplant size. Warm, sunny days will push the crops ahead, and you can be eating salads before you would have been able to plant seed outdoors.

A second and equally important use for season-extenders is starting transplants for the garden. You can grow varieties from a seed catalog that are not available at the local garden center. One method is to start crops such as corn, beans, and peas, which are normally seeded directly in the garden, in cell trays in the greenhouse and then transplant them into the rows in the garden. Besides gaining three to four weeks on the season, you will end up with garden rows without skips. It is best to start the seed in a

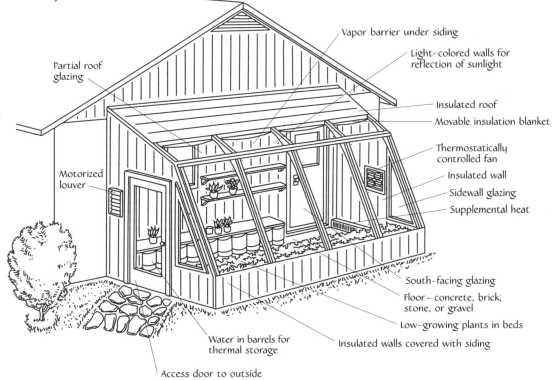

Figure 1-2. Attached solar greenhouse

germinator and then prick the seedlings off into flats for the greenhouse. (See chapter 7 for more information on germinators.) Unless you have a very large garden, a home greenhouse will provide plenty of space for the quantity of plants you need.

In late August or early September, lettuce, spinach, and cabbage can be replanted in the greenhouse for harvest through December in northern climates or all winter long in milder climates.

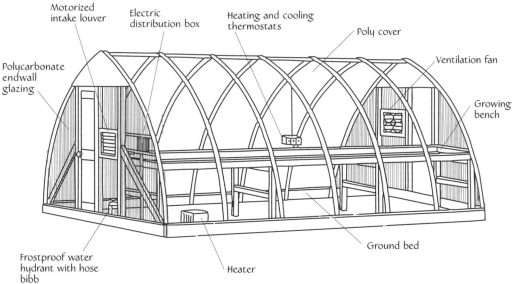

Figure 1-3. Season-extender greenhouse

During winter, the season-extender greenhouse is a great place to store bulbs and plants that need wind protection and temperature modification. It can also be used to store yard and garden equipment out of the weather. So even though they are called season-extenders, these greenhouses are useful year-round.

Cold frames, hotbeds, and high tunnels are other low-cost structures that can extend the growing season. These structures are discussed in chapter 8.

Conservatories

In the nineteenth century, English architects allowed their imaginations to run free, and so began the Victorian tradition of designing ornate greenhouses with arches, flowing curves, and decorative embellishments (figure 1-4). Known as conservatories, these elaborate structures are still in use today.

Today, conservatories of the traditional design are available only from English manufacturers. A more common type of conservatory consists of naturally lighted living and growing space designed as part of the home by an architect and built by a contractor. Although the structure may be separated from the home by walls, it is more frequently an integral part of the living space.

Glassed-in areas filled with wicker or patio furniture convert living rooms into relaxing, more informal retreats. Conservatory greenhouses also make great dining rooms or kitchens. The view of the outdoors and the smell and feel of the plants provide year-round contact with nature. Shading may be needed on bright sunny days, and shades can be drawn to reduce heating needs on cold winter nights.

If you are looking for a place for inspiration and creativity, a glazed area filled with plants may be just what you need. A northern exposure is best when uniform room lighting is required for activities like painting, sewing, or writing.

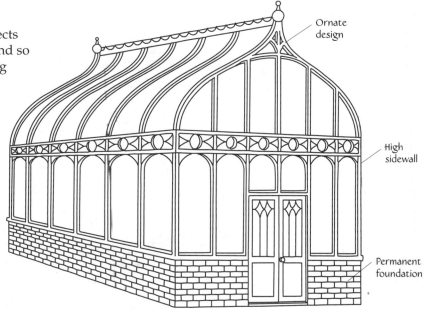

Figure 1-4. Conservatory

A conservatory built around a pool will provide the high humidity and temperature needed for tropical plants. Tiled floors are best around pools to handle any splashed water.

Exposed wood framing, usually cedar or redwood, adds warmth to the conservatory space. Double-glass glazing reduces condensation drips and energy usage. Today's improved environmental controls help maintain an environment well-suited to both plants and people.

Sunspaces

If designed and located properly, sunspaces can become part of the living space in a home. Commonly referred to as sunrooms, these glazed areas of the home are enjoyed primarily for their warmth and brightness (figure 1-5).

Sunrooms can be built as an extension of the kitchen, living room, or dining room or as an enclosure to a swimming pool or hot tub. They are great places to enjoy breakfast or lunch, perhaps overlooking a lawn, garden, or pond.

Many modern sunrooms are designed to collect and transfer excess heat to the home during the cooler seasons of the year. This requires a small fan located near the roof of the sunroom and an air return duct near the floor. When the air inside the sunroom becomes too warm, the fan is activated to transfer the excess heat into the home.

Plants can be grown in sunrooms, but they must be carefully selected. Most houseplants adapt readily to sunrooms, and garden plants such as begonias and geraniums will bloom in them all winter. Because the air is drier in a sunroom, the plants tend to require more frequent watering. Unless a shade system is used during the summer, temperatures inside can reach over 100°F.

If you plan to use the sunspace for

collecting heat to supplement the home heating system, it is best to limit the number of plants grown in the room. In a greenhouse with many plants, as much as 50% of the heat is used to evaporate moisture transpired by the plants.

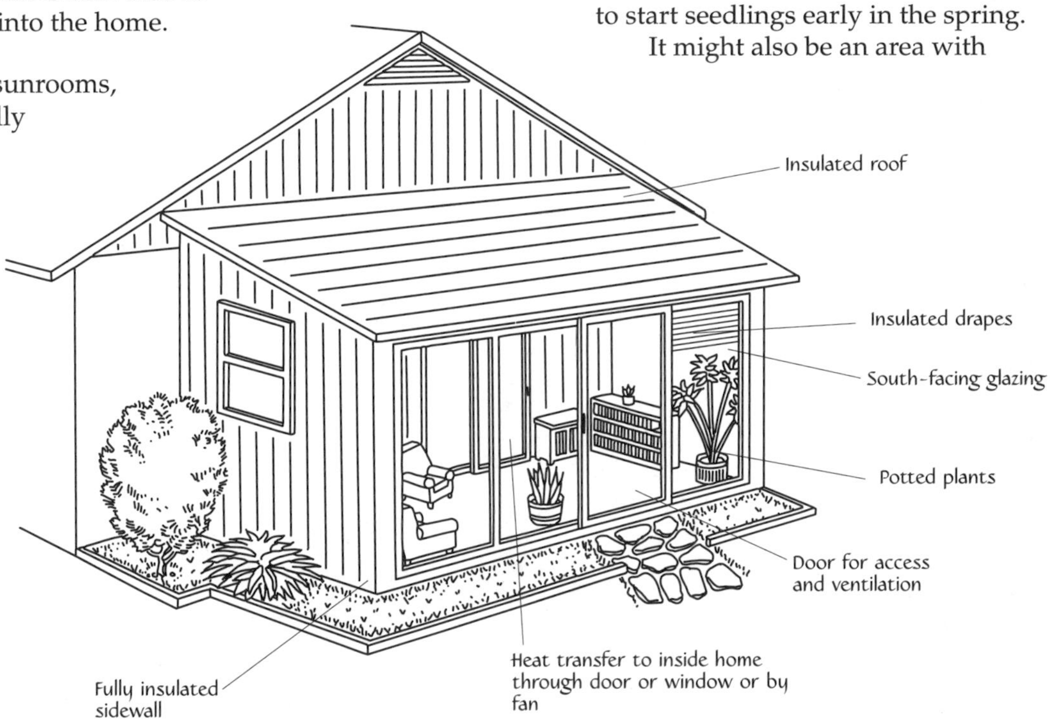

Window Greenhouses

Many reasons exist for choosing a window greenhouse—limited yard space, too many obstructions to building a structure, or limited time to devote to gardening. Window greenhouses attach to the outside wall of the home over a window area (figure 1-6). Although a southern exposure is desirable, any orientation will work.

Window greenhouses use heat from the home, and they are low in cost and easy to install. Disadvantages are that they tend to quickly fill with plants, and they require more attention, as they heat up and cool down rapidly. Window greenhouses are discussed in more detail in chapter 7.

Indoor Light Gardens

Artificial light can be used to grow plants. In fact, with a proper design, you can achieve optimum growing conditions for plants. When a greenhouse is not feasible, an indoor light garden is a good alternative. An indoor light garden can be a small area under a two-tube fluorescent fixture used to start seedlings early in the spring. It might also be an area with

Insulated roof

Insulated drapes

South-facing glazing

Potted plants

Door for access and ventilation

Heat transfer to inside home through door or window or by fan

Fully insulated sidewall

Figure 1-5. Attached sunspace for heat gain and living space

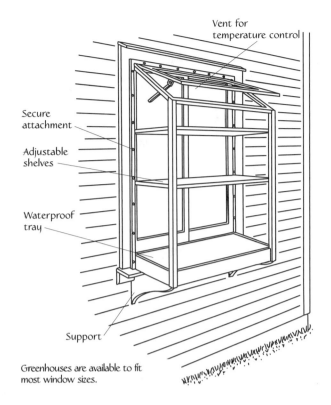

Figure 1-6. Window greenhouse

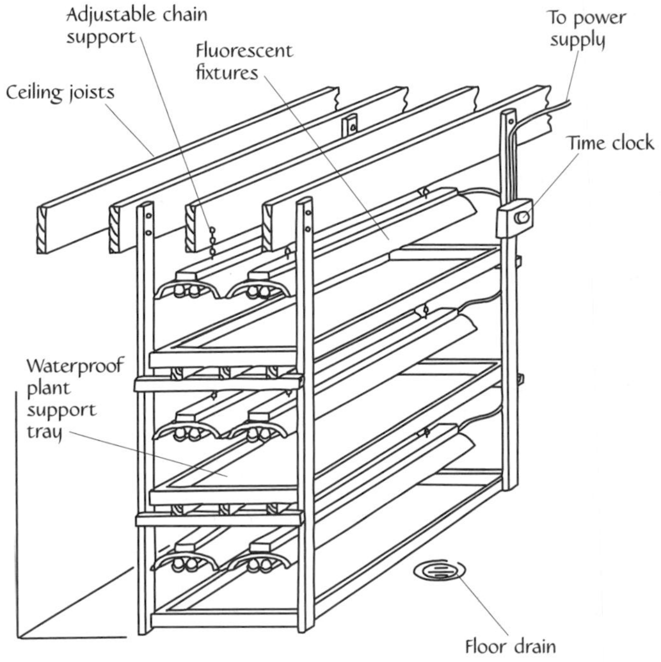

Figure 1-7. Basement light garden

many shelves in the basement for growing African violets (figure 1-7). Construction costs for this type of growing space are less than those of an equivalent area of greenhouse space, but operating costs (for energy to run the lights) are greater.

Light gardens must provide adequate lighting, or plants will grow leggy and not flower. Excess moisture given off by plants in a large setup must be vented to prevent mildew problems in the house.

How Much Does a Greenhouse Cost?

One of the first questions that comes to mind when considering a home greenhouse is What will it cost? Many variables affect the cost, including the style of greenhouse, site preparation, water and electricity needs, access, and heating systems. Table 1-1 (page 8) gives some estimates to help you determine the costs for a project. The figures assume a typical greenhouse size of 100–200 square feet of floor area. Hiring a

contractor to do the construction will approximately double the cost. A heater will add from $200 to $800, and a fan system will add about $500.

How Much Time Does a Greenhouse Demand?

Operating a home greenhouse takes as much time as caring for a pet cat or dog. Greenhouses need some attention every day. Watering, feeding, pruning, repotting, and other tasks need to be done. If you devote enough time to it, greenhouse gardening can be relaxing and very rewarding. However, if the greenhouse becomes a burden, then it is no longer fun.

Unfortunately, greenhouses often end up empty and abandoned due to changes in the owner's lifestyle or a lack of time. Before you start construction, make sure you are ready to commit to the demands of greenhouse gardening. You will be amply rewarded for your time!

Table 1-1. Approximate greenhouse costs

Type of greenhouse	Costs	
	Per square foot	10'x12' greenhouse
Metal frame Steel pipe or tubing, lumber endwalls, poly cover, anchor stakes, aluminum door	$3–4	$360–480
Wood frame Treated posts, construction-grade lumber, poly cover, aluminum door	$3-3.50	$360–420
Wood frame Same as above but with corrugated fiberglass reinforced plastic or polycarbonate glazing	$6–7	$720–840
Wood frame Same as above but with polycarbonate or acrylic structured-sheet glazing	$9–10	$1,080–1,200
Kit greenhouse Aluminum extrusion frame, double-wall polycarbonate or single tempered glass glazing, concrete piers	$25–30	$3,000–3,600
Kit greenhouse Same as above but with double-wall tempered glass glazing	$40–50	$4,800–6,000

Note: Table reflects 1999 prices. Costs do not include delivery charges, site preparation, floor covering, benches, electricity, water, heat, or fans. Costs also do not include labor. The figures assume a typical greenhouse size of 100–200 square feet of floor area. Hiring a contractor to do the construction will approximately double the cost. A heater will add from $200 to $800, and a fan system will add about $500. Local building code requirements or conditions may also affect costs.

CHAPTER 2

Selecting a Greenhouse: Types, Styles, and Sizes

Choosing a greenhouse can be an exciting and challenging process. Although you may already have a location in mind, it is important to evaluate several options. Many types and styles of greenhouses are available, so you should be able to find one that matches the aesthetics of your house or creates a focal point on your property. You can build a greenhouse to any size, but the most common size is 100–200 square feet in floor area. This chapter will review some options to help make your selection easier.

Types of Greenhouses

Attached (Lean-to) Greenhouses

The most common type of home greenhouse is one that is attached to a building—usually the home, but it could also be a garage, shed, or other building (figure 2-1). There are several advantages and disadvantages to this.

Advantages of Attached Greenhouses

1. Easy access — A door to the outside is important for moving in plants and materials, but an entry door from the home or garage makes it convenient to tend to plants no matter what the weather is like. Making frequent checks on greenhouse conditions, especially before retiring at night, is important to having healthy plants. With an attached greenhouse, you can spend a few minutes of free time in the greenhouse without having to bundle up and go outside.

2. Extended living space — A home greenhouse can be one of the most beautiful rooms in your home. Some homeowners use the greenhouse for meals or entertaining. If it is large enough, it can include chairs and a table. Greenhouses can even include a spa, a waterfall, or an office.

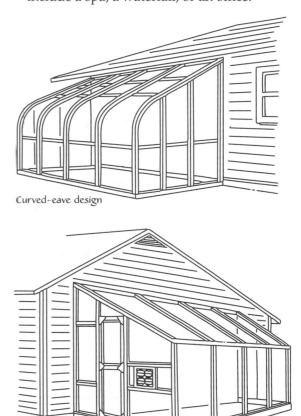

Curved-eave design

Straight-eave design

Figure 2-1. Attached greenhouse designs

3. Insulation for the house — An attached building provides a buffer between the outside and inside. It keeps the wind from conducting heat away from the wall area that it covers. It also adds about 15% to the insulation value of the wall.

   If the greenhouse is oriented properly, some of the heat gained on a sunny day in the winter can be transferred to the home, thus reducing the heating bill. This is the basic principle under which sunspaces and solar greenhouses operate. On a sunny March day, an attached greenhouse on a home located in a latitude of 40° north will capture about three times the amount of heat needed to maintain a 60°F nighttime temperature.

4. Lower cost — Because it has one less wall, an attached greenhouse usually costs less than a comparable freestanding design. The wall to which it is attached provides support for the roof bars. If your home heating system has enough extra capacity, you can connect the greenhouse to the furnace or boiler with an extra zone and thus save on the heating system cost. Either a hot water or hot air system will work.

5. Integral part of the home design — If you are planning a new home or major renovation, you can integrate a home greenhouse into the design. A greenhouse can add aesthetic appeal and functionality to a home without looking like an add-on. It is important to consider orientation, adjacent living space, storage of materials, and heating and cooling systems during the design phase.

Disadvantages of Attached Greenhouses

Several disadvantages of an attached greenhouse need to be considered:

1. Size limitations — You are generally limited in the size and shape of structure that can be attached to your home or other building. This relates mainly to the exterior wall area available.

   If the greenhouse is attached under the eaves of a ranch home, there may be height limitations (and therefore width limitations). This will vary somewhat with the design and slope of the greenhouse roof. Also, it is almost impossible to expand an attached greenhouse if you need more growing space.

2. Moisture — Plants transpire a lot of moisture. If this moisture is not controlled, it can permeate the house wall insulation or enter the home. Moisture always travels from a warm area to a cooler area, so at some times during the year, its movement is into the house. A good vapor barrier on the greenhouse side will stop moisture from entering the insulation. Moisture can be controlled by venting the high-humidity air and replacing it with drier outside air.

3. Summer overheating — A common complaint of owners of attached greenhouses located on the south side of the home is overheating. This can be offset somewhat with shading and a good ventilation system.

4. Dirt and insects — The proximity of the greenhouse to the living area means that dirt and insects may be brought into the home. Good housekeeping in the greenhouse will minimize this problem. Also, odors from pesticides and fertilizers can permeate the home. Another reason why housekeeping is important is that the growing area and plants are more visible from inside the house.

Freestanding Greenhouses

A freestanding greenhouse stands apart from other structures (figure 2-2). It can fit into spaces where an attached greenhouse is not possible, and many more design options are available. Below are some other advantages and disadvantages to consider.

Advantages of Freestanding Greenhouses

1. More flexibility — Many sizes, shapes, and configurations of freestanding greenhouses exist to fit almost any need. Besides the standard "A" roof, there are hoop, Gothic, and dome designs.

   With a freestanding model, you are not limited in size to what will attach to a building. It can be any width and length, depending on your particular needs. Although an 8-foot-by-10-foot or 10-foot-by-12-foot size is common, both larger and smaller sizes are readily available.

2. Location — Choosing a location is easier with a freestanding greenhouse. The greenhouse can be placed where trees, buildings, or other obstructions will have a minimum effect. It can also be placed to intercept maximum sunlight, especially during the short days in the winter.

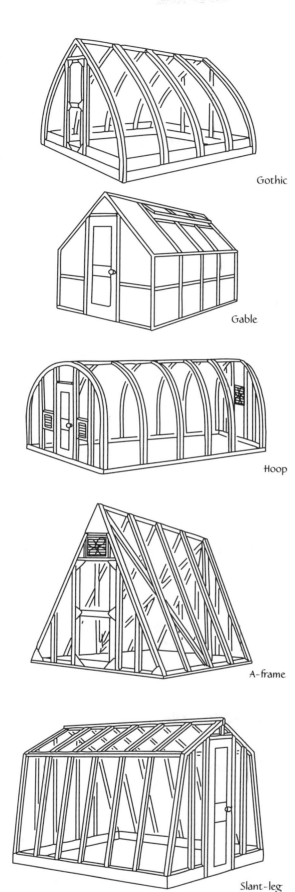

Figure 2-2. Freestanding greenhouse designs

Gothic

Gable

Hoop

A-frame

Slant-leg

3. Easy expansion — If you outgrow the growing space in a freestanding greenhouse, you can easily expand it. Usually, the endwall can be removed, the foundation expanded, and new intermediate sections added. Although it is best to build the structure large enough in the first place, changes in the plants you grow or the resources available to you may prompt you to add more space.

4. Private getaway — A greenhouse is a great place to unwind after a busy day. It can also be a place to get away from the phone or other annoying things in our lives.

Disadvantages of Freestanding Greenhouses

Several disadvantages of a freestanding greenhouse should be noted.

1. Access — If you live in an area where heavy snowfall occurs and the greenhouse will be used year-round, you may have to shovel a path to get to it.

2. Utilities — You will need to bring water and electricity to the greenhouse. This may mean digging a trench below the frost line to prevent pipes from freezing in the winter. A heating system separate from the home system is necessary. This will require a fuel supply, electricity, and a vent system to remove flue gases.

3. Energy — Heat loss is greater with a freestanding type due to the increased wall area and the greater exposure to wind. This results in a higher heating cost.

Pit Greenhouses

A pit greenhouse, built partially below ground, uses earth to keep it cool during the summer and warm during the winter (figure 2-3 on page 12). The ground temperature 3–4 feet below the surface remains fairly constant, around 50°F most of the year. This means that only a small amount of heat is needed to raise the temperature to the desired growing temperature. Usually, a small electric heater will do the job.

These advantages are offset by some disadvantages. Pit greenhouses are more expensive to build, as the soil around the pit has to be supported by concrete walls. Drainage is also important. Water from irrigation and ground sources has to be removed. Exterior drains around the footing wall and an interior drain

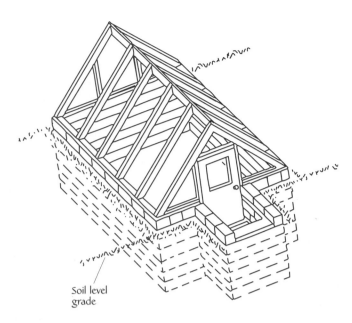

Soil level
grade

Figure 2-3. Pit greenhouse

are necessary. For greenhouse access, steps need to be cut into the soil.

If you have a south-facing hillside, you can use a semi-pit greenhouse design. This design incorporates a partially or fully glazed south wall to get more light to the plants. Drainage is easier to install to a downslope location. Access is also much easier, as the door can be placed in the front glazed wall at floor level. The slight increase in heat loss with semi-pit designs is more than offset by the easy access and increased light.

Solar Greenhouses

The solar greenhouse design attempts to duplicate the attributes of the pit house, but it is built at ground level. Solar greenhouses differ from conventional greenhouses in that they are designed to both collect and retain solar energy and thus reduce the use of fossil fuels for heating. Areas of the greenhouse that don't receive direct sunlight, such as the north wall and roof and the foundation, are insulated to retain heat. Insulated interior walls and framing members are painted white to reflect light.

The solar greenhouse usually contains a large thermal mass, usually water or stone, to absorb and store excess daytime heat. At night, the heat is released to keep the greenhouse warm. Night insulation systems using blankets, panels, or shutters are often used to reduce heat loss through the glazing.

During the summer, solar radiation is fairly uniform throughout the United States—about 2,000–2,400 British thermal units per square foot per day (Btu/sq ft/day) in July. During the winter, however, the northern part of the United States receives less than half of the solar radiation received in the Southwest (5–600 versus 1,100–1,200 Btu/sq ft/day). Solar radiation values for your area can be obtained from a state climatologist or local weather station.

Orientation of the Glazing

For maximum heat gain, the glazed area of a solar greenhouse should be orientated within a 20° angle of true south. A slightly eastern orientation is better than west of south, as it allows the morning sun to clear any condensation earlier.

The maximum amount of energy passes through glazing when it is perpendicular to the sun's rays. With most greenhouse designs, this occurs only for a short time during the spring and fall. The rest of the year, more of the light is reflected off the surface.

If the greenhouse is to be used all winter, the slope of the south-facing glazing should be located to intercept the maximum sunlight during January and February, when the combined effects of low temperatures and reduced solar radiation are most severe. There are several "rule-of-thumb" guidelines for determining the slope of the south-facing glazing. For winter production and maximum heat gain, add 15° to your latitude to get the angle between glazing and a horizontal pane. For spring and fall operation, the angle in degrees should approximate the latitude. A vertical glazed wall is best for summer operation, as it reduces overheating. It is also easier to construct and seal. For more information on solar heating, see page 82.

Greenhouse Styles

The style of greenhouse you select is usually a matter of personal preference. There are several choices, although some have limitations as to where they can be installed (see figures 2-1 to 2-3).

1. Gable — This style has sloping, flat roof panels and vertical sides. It can be attached to the home at its endwall or designed as a lean-to by using only half of the structure.

2. Slant-leg — With this style, flat, sloped roof panels are attached to a sloping sidewall. Added floor space is gained using the same amount of materials as the gable style.

3. A-frame — This is an easy-to-build style, but it is limited in width.

4. Hoop — Usually formed by covering bent pipe or tubing with a flexible plastic cover, this style is less expensive than other styles.

5. Gothic — In the Gothic style, the roof and walls form a continuous shape. Because of the steep slope of the roof, snow slides off easier than with a hoop design.

6. Dome — The dome shape is limited to a free-standing design. It is made by connecting triangles together. It is more expensive to build, as each triangle has to be covered with glazing separately.

When contemplating placing a greenhouse on the second floor, a roof, or an elevated deck, it is best to have an architect or engineer do the design. These situations require special designs and engineering related to safety, support, and watertightness of the installation.

Selecting a Size

Usually, available space and construction costs dictate greenhouse size more than need or desire. In northern climates, the heating costs for a year-round structure may also have an influence. Size restrictions placed by a local zoning commission may be a factor in some communities.

When choosing a size, consider how the greenhouse will be used—year-round, seasonally, or mainly as a sunspace. If you are an avid gardener and need space for an extensive collection of houseplants, then design a structure that is slightly larger than your present space requirements. Greenhouses tend to quickly fill with new acquisitions.

Typical home greenhouses have 100–200 square feet of floor area. This provides room for bench and bed space and a central work aisle. Common widths are 8 feet, 10 feet, or 12 feet or some dimension near that, depending on the size of the framing members and the width of the glazing. Length depends on the space available, but 10 feet is usually a minimum.

GREENHOUSE AESTHETICS

Although home greenhouses are not generally beautiful, with a proper design and location, they can be an attractive addition to your home or yard. Results from a number of surveys show that greenhouses can enhance the value of your property. To do so, they have to look like they belong there.

If you are building a new home, then the greenhouse should be designed into the plans. A proper exposure and orientation can be selected at that time, and access to utilities can be prearranged.

If you are adding on a greenhouse, then select a style and size that will complement your home. For example, a gable-roof design may be more appropriate than a hoop shape to match the architecture of your home.

When locating a freestanding greenhouse, a couple of factors should be considered. From an aesthetics standpoint, the greenhouse should be parallel to the house, any accessory buildings, the road, or a property line. From a light- and heat-gathering standpoint, the greenhouse should have an east–west-oriented ridge if you are located above 40° latitude or a north–south ridge if you are in the southern United States below 40° latitude.

How you landscape the immediate area around the greenhouse can have an impact on aesthetics. Gardens, border plantings, or beds can do a lot to improve appearance and help blend the structure into the area. Be careful not to plant shrubs or trees that will create shade on the greenhouse.

Most greenhouses are sized in increments of 3–4 feet, depending on the glazing.

Other considerations include:

- Adequate head room. The minimum space should be 5½ feet at the eave. Taller houses are easier to heat and ventilate, as the air has greater buffering capacity.

- Bench access. Bench width should be limited to about 30 inches for access from one side and 5 feet for access from both sides.

Greenhouse Planning: Permits, Building Options, Foundations, and Utilities

After you decide what style and size of greenhouse will fit your needs and where to best locate it, the next step is getting it built. If you are handy with tools and understand basic construction techniques, then you may want to make it a do-it-yourself project from plans or a kit. If you don't have the time or aren't comfortable doing the work, then it is best to contract the job out.

Before beginning any construction, consider the location and the type of foundation that will be required. Sources of electricity and water can also affect how the greenhouse is built and the cost.

Permits

All states and most communities have building and zoning regulations. Before beginning any construction, you must determine whether a permit is needed. Check with the building or code enforcement department in the town hall or community administrative office.

Zoning Permits

Zoning commissions exist to ensure environmental protection and orderly community growth. Zoning regulations are promulgated by the zoning commission and enforced by a zoning enforcement officer.

Zoning deals with land use. Zoning regulations can define setback distances from nearby property lines,

the maximum area of the lot that can be covered by a structure, and buffers to nearby property.

To obtain a zoning permit, you might need a plot plan that shows the location of the proposed greenhouse in relation to your home or other structures, the property lines, and well and septic system or sewer lines (figure 3-1). This plan will be used to determine compliance with the regulations. If you cannot meet the setback requirements, you can apply for a variance. This may require a public hearing, where neighbors will have the right to support or oppose the application. Zoning approval is required before you can apply for a building permit.

Building Permits

Building codes were established to provide minimum safety standards for construction and for heating, plumbing, and electrical systems. The local code is usually based on a national or regional code but includes variations to meet local conditions. Enforcement of the code is handled by a building official or inspector. Your project may be inspected at key points during the construction process—usually prior to the placement of any concrete, after the frame has been erected, and after the electrical and plumbing systems have been installed. A Certificate of Occupancy (CO) is issued after the final inspection. Plans for the greenhouse are usually required so the building inspector can determine the strength of frame members.

Things that building inspectors look for with home greenhouses include the method by which the frame is attached to the ground (concrete, piers, or ground anchors), glazing attachment, and installation of the electrical and heating systems. A small fee may be required to cover the inspection process.

Most building officials are very helpful in getting you through the code process. Their job is to see that your greenhouse is a safe place to work.

Custom Designs

A number of situations might prompt you to hire a professional to help in designing your greenhouse. An architect can provide a design that fits your location and your needs. An engineer can provide plans that will meet the building code and can be followed by a builder.

Reasons for a Custom Design

Standard Design Does Not Fit

Manufacturers use a modular design when building greenhouses. Designs are usually based on glass or plastic panel sizes. If you want to locate your greenhouse in a courtyard between two wings of your home or if a standard attached greenhouse cannot fit under the eave overhang on your home, then a custom design may be required.

Problem Sites

Steep slopes or groundwater problems may necessitate special designs or construction techniques. If retaining walls or drainage systems need to be installed, you may need to hire an engineer. Locating the greenhouse on a deck usually requires a special floor construction to handle water drainage.

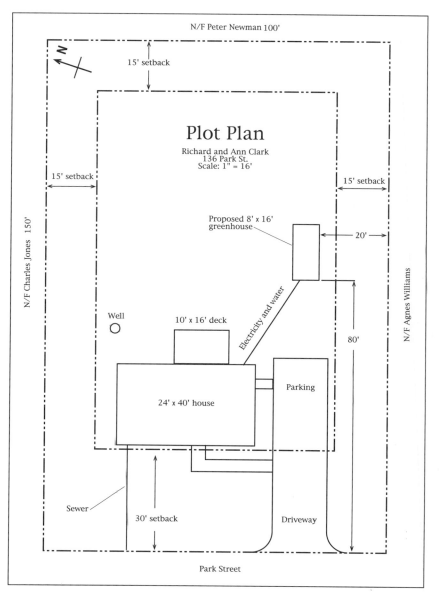

Figure 3-1. Sample plot plan showing the location of a proposed greenhouse

Architectural Appearance

A well-designed, aesthetically pleasing greenhouse that blends into the surroundings can add value to your property. An architect can create an innovative design that may require nonstandard materials.

Developing plans for a greenhouse that will be connected to a headhouse or other accessory building frequently requires the help of an engineer. Access and space utilization are important considerations that need to be addressed.

Remodeling

If you are planning to expand or remodel an existing greenhouse, you may need to hire a professional. The condition of the existing structure should be evaluated for deterioration, such as rotted or rusted framing members, leaks in the glazing, or a settled foundation. Locating replacement parts or additional materials for a greenhouse expansion can be difficult if the manufacturer is no longer in business.

Services Provided by Architects and Engineers

Architects generally deal with the appearance and aesthetics of a building. Some architects can also provide engineering expertise. An engineer handles the structural and code aspects of a job and, if necessary, determines how the greenhouse will be attached to a building. Some building inspectors require a seal from a professional engineer (PE) on the plans.

Most people have trouble visualizing what a completed greenhouse will look like and how it will fit into the proposed location. An architect or engineer can provide sketches that show a perspective and some possible alternatives. These can be simple hand-drawn sketches that show little detail and therefore do not cost very much.

The sketches are usually modified to come up with a final design and appearance. If possible, have the architect sketch out a couple of views. If the design is complex, the architect can create a model of the project, but this can be expensive.

The next step is the preparation of working drawings and specifications. Most projects are based on a style or model available from a manufacturer, and most manufacturers can help with modifications to fit special situations.

An estimate of the job cost is usually provided to see if costs are in line with your budget. If the design is complex, it might be best to write up a set of specifications for the plans and then put the job out for bid to several manufacturers or erectors. If necessary, you can modify the design at this time to lower the cost.

An architect or engineer can also help you select a contractor. It is important to hire someone with previous greenhouse experience, as construction techniques for greenhouses are different from those for conventional buildings. Greenhouse manufacturers usually have a list of acceptable contractors.

You may want to ask the architect or engineer to obtain any required permits. They know where to get permits and what kind of documentation is necessary.

Sometimes the architect or engineer oversees construction to ensure that the plans are being followed and the quality of work is acceptable. A final inspection should be conducted at the completion of the project.

The cost of architectural and engineering services will be about 10–20% of the construction costs. You may want these services for just the design phase or for the total project. If the project is complicated or if you have no construction experience, hiring a professional is money well-spent.

Accommodating the Physically and Mentally Challenged

A greenhouse can be of great therapeutic, rehabilitative, recreational, and vocational value to people who are physically and mentally challenged. It allows them the opportunity to interact with nature year-round, even when the weather is bad.

The joy of planting seeds and watching them grow into flowering or fruiting plants is universal. A greenhouse can be designed to accommodate seniors who have become less mobile and allow them to continue gardening. It can also introduce physically and mentally challenged people of various ages to the field of horticulture.

The greenhouse should be designed to accommodate the particular disability that the person has. Below are some guidelines for overcoming the most common barriers.

Access

The walkway should be accessible in all weather. Concrete or pressure-treated lumber provides a level surface. A minimum width for wheelchairs is 36 inches.

The aisle width between benches should be a minimum of 32 inches for wheelchairs or people who use walkers or canes. A 60-inch-square area is needed to turn a wheelchair.

Doors should have a clear opening of 32 inches. Lever-type door hardware is better than knobs.

Thresholds should be ¼ inch or less in height with a beveled edge.

Ramps can be used to access raised areas (figure 3-2). The desired ramp slope is a 1-inch rise to a 12-inch run. A level, 60-inch-square landing at the top will aid in opening the door. Ramps should have a nonslip surface such as brushed concrete, self-adhesive grit strips, or indoor-outdoor carpeting.

Layout

Benches should be arranged to allow as much freedom of movement as possible but still maximize space utilization. Sketch some sample layouts on graph paper before deciding on a design. Figure 3-3 shows three possible layouts.

Benches

The workbench height should be convenient for the person who will use it. If the person is in a wheelchair, provide a 27- to 30-inch clearance under the work surface for leg space. Bench designs are shown in figures 3-4 and 3-5 on page 18.

Environmental Control

Vents for cooling the greenhouse should be motorized. The thermostat for heating and cooling equipment should be located at plant height in a convenient location away from an outside wall for easy adjustment. It should also be shaded from the sun.

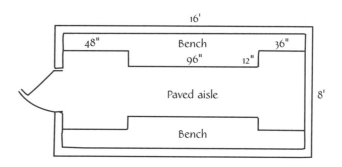

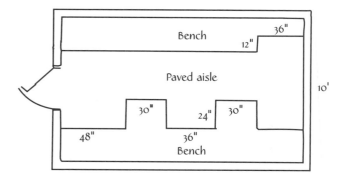

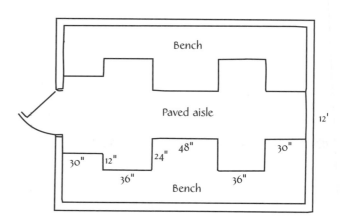

Figure 3-3. Wheelchair-accessible bench layouts

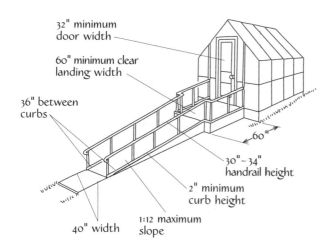

Figure 3-2. Greenhouse ramp specifications for accommodating the physically challenged

Watering Devices and Tools

A lightweight hose or cable hose carrier makes watering easier. Lever faucets and hose shutoffs are easiest to operate.

Planting aids and equipment help reduce the effort needed to do tasks. Growing seedlings in plug trays helps in singulating the plants. A hand dibble, bulb planter, cultivator, ice cream scoop for filling pots, plastic squeeze bottle for watering, and cell trays for planting make tasks easier (figure 3-6 on page 19). It might be a good idea to provide a bench or chair for relaxation. Storage for soil, containers, and tools should be readily accessible.

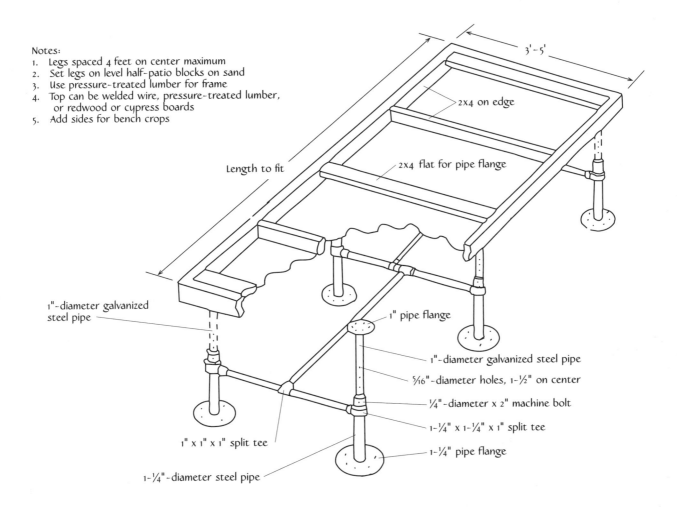

Notes:
1. Legs spaced 4 feet on center maximum
2. Set legs on level half-patio blocks on sand
3. Use pressure-treated lumber for frame
4. Top can be welded wire, pressure-treated lumber, or redwood or cypress boards
5. Add sides for bench crops

3'-5'

2x4 on edge

2x4 flat for pipe flange

Length to fit

1" pipe flange

1"-diameter galvanized steel pipe

1"-diameter galvanized steel pipe

5⁄16"-diameter holes, 1-1⁄2" on center

1⁄4"-diameter x 2" machine bolt

1-1⁄4" x 1-1⁄4" x 1" split tee

1" x 1" x 1" split tee

1-1⁄4" pipe flange

1-1⁄4"-diameter steel pipe

Figure 3-4. Adjustable-height bench design

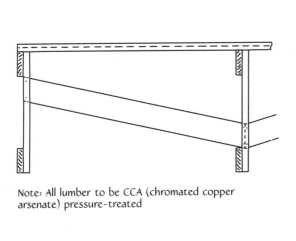

Note: All lumber to be CCA (chromated copper arsenate) pressure-treated

Figure 3-5. Plant bench design

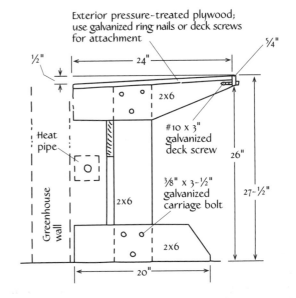

Exterior pressure-treated plywood; use galvanized ring nails or deck screws for attachment

24"

5⁄4"

1⁄2"

2x6

#10 x 3" galvanized deck screw

26"

Heat pipe

27-1⁄2"

3⁄8" x 3-1⁄2" galvanized carriage bolt

Greenhouse wall

2x6

2x6

20"

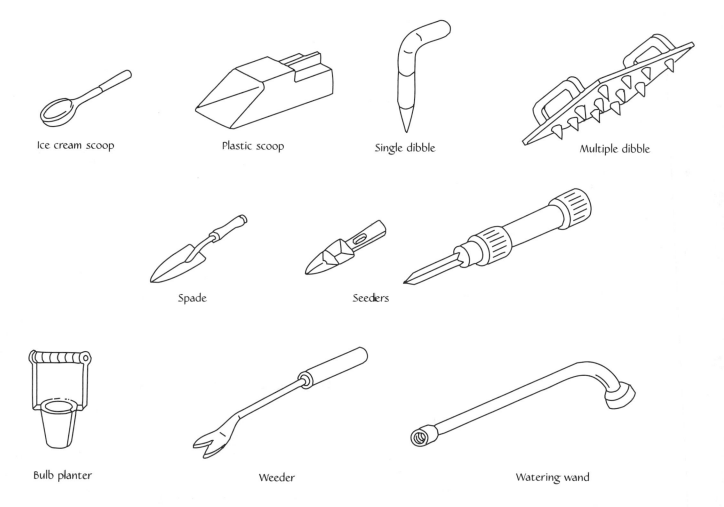

Figure 3-6. Planting aids for the physically challenged

Hiring a Contractor to Build a Greenhouse

Not everyone has the time or skill needed to build a greenhouse. The simplest design can take a weekend to assemble. If you need a concrete foundation or have to modify your home, assembly will take much longer.

The amount of skill needed to build a greenhouse varies. A simple wood or pipe-frame greenhouse can be constructed with just a few hand tools and a minimum skill level. If the instruction manual is good, a kit greenhouse is not much more difficult once the foundation is done. If the manual is poorly written, the project can be a real challenge. Most custom-designed greenhouses should be built by a professional.

Before taking on a greenhouse project, assess how much time and skill you will need and determine what you can do yourself. Hire a professional to do the rest.

How to Find a Contractor

If you are purchasing a greenhouse, the manufacturer or distributor may be able to provide a list of contractors. It is best to select a contractor who has experience in greenhouse installation. It is also better to deal with someone who is familiar with local soils and drainage and who knows how to obtain the necessary permits.

To check on the reputation of a builder, ask for a list of prior clients and call a few of them. Also contact the local building official to see whether there have been problems with the builder's previous jobs.

If you will be hiring subcontractors for foundation or finish carpentry work, you may want to check on their reputations as well.

The Importance of a Contract

When hiring a contractor, it is important to have a contract signed by both parties. A contract provides a legal framework within which the rights and obligations of both parties are defined and protected. If the materials or workmanship is not satisfactory, you will have a legal claim against the contractor. If you fail to make the agreed upon payments, the contractor will have legal recourse against you. Before signing a contract, you should review a number of items. The following checklist covers the major ones:

- What will the builder provide? What do you have to provide?

  Building and zoning permits: Are they needed?

  Site work: Do shrubs or other obstructions need to be removed?

  Foundation: Who will remove the topsoil, place the wall or piers, install drainage? Will the walls be insulated?

  Erection: If the greenhouse is attached, who will be responsible for modifications to your home?

  Floor: Concrete, brick, or gravel? Is drainage included?

  Benches and growing beds: Are these included?

  Water: Who will provide the plumbing for the hose bibbs?

  Electricity: Will outlets and lighting needs be met?

  Alarm: Is a high/low temperature alarm included?

  Heat: What type of heating system will be provided?

  Cooling: Will vents or fans be manual or automatic?

  Shading: Is it included?

  Waste removal and cleanup: Whose responsibility is this?

  Landscaping: Is this part of the contract?

- Are detailed plans and specifications included in the contract?

- What are the starting and completion dates?

- Does the contractor have liability and performance insurance?

- Does the contract specify the manufacturer, model number, and other pertinent greenhouse information?

- How and when will payments be made? Does the contract contain a payment "hold back" clause that allows you to retain the last payment until the work is completed to your satisfaction? Does the lender (if you need one) require a Certificate of Occupancy (CO)?

- Does the contractor provide a warranty on the quality of materials and workmanship?

A detailed contract will generally result in fewer problems during construction. However, it may increase the price, because the builder will have fewer options with regard to material purchases and erection procedures.

Building a Kit Greenhouse

Assembling your own greenhouse can be a fun project that involves the whole family. All you need are some basic mechanical skills and a small assortment of tools.

Most greenhouse kits are like a giant erector set. The parts come in large boxes and have to be identified and sorted. Then you follow the instruction manual and assemble the greenhouse step-by-step. Most kits come with predrilled holes, so you don't have to do much marking and drilling.

Building your own greenhouse can save money. As labor is usually about half the cost of construction, you can save a lot if you do the project yourself. If you do not have all the skills needed, then draw on the expertise of family members, friendly neighbors, or good friends. A greenhouse-building party might be a good idea.

The Instruction Manual

Before ordering a greenhouse, it is important to look at a copy of the instruction manual. Some manufacturers take the time to develop a detailed set of instructions that guide you one step at a time through the erection process. A good manual will include a listing of the parts needed for the steps, pictorial assembly drawings, and techniques that will make the job easier.

A good manual will also include alternate methods for constructing the foundation or attaching the greenhouse to the home (figure 3-7). This is important, as every installation is a little different.

The manual should also have a list of materials that are included with the kit and a list of materials you will have to provide. Items like foundation materials, trim boards, flashing, insulation, and paint may be your responsibility.

An instruction manual should explain alternatives for the heating system and discuss how to size a system for your location. Some manufacturers can provide heating equipment.

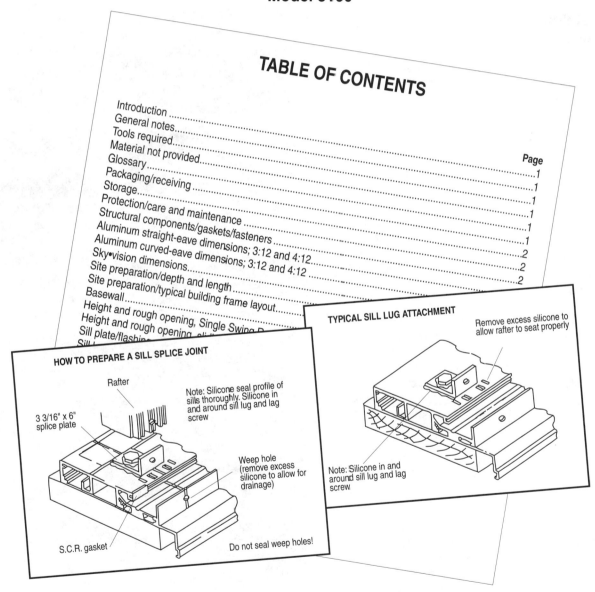

Greenhouse Systems

Installation Manual
Model 3100

TABLE OF CONTENTS

Page

Introduction 1
General notes 1
Tools required 1
Material not provided 1
Glossary 1
Packaging/receiving 1
Storage 1
Protection/care and maintenance 1
Structural components/gaskets/fasteners 1
Aluminum straight-eave dimensions; 3:12 and 4:12 ... 2
Aluminum curved-eave dimensions; 3:12 and 4:12 ... 2
Sky•vision dimensions 2
Site preparation/depth and length
Site preparation/typical building frame layout
Basewall
Height and rough opening, Single Swing
Height and rough opening,
Sill plate/flashing
Sill

HOW TO PREPARE A SILL SPLICE JOINT

Rafter

3 3/16" x 6" splice plate

Note: Silicone seal profile of sills thoroughly. Silicone in and around sill lug and lag screw

Weep hole (remove excess silicone to allow for drainage)

S.C.R. gasket

Do not seal weep holes!

TYPICAL SILL LUG ATTACHMENT

Remove excess silicone to allow rafter to seat properly

Note: Silicone in and around sill lug and lag screw

Figure 3-7. A good installation manual can reduce greenhouse erection time and make assembly easier
Adapted by permission from TRACO Skytech Systems, Inc.

Information on the operation and maintenance of the greenhouse might also be included. This can help you get better service from your purchase.

To supplement the instruction manual, some manufacturers provide a video that shows construction techniques. This can be valuable, as assembly techniques are sometimes difficult to explain in words. A toll-free phone number may also be provided to get technical assistance if you are short on materials or if you cannot figure out how to assemble a certain part.

If the instruction manual is not well-written and illustrated, you may be in for a real challenge trying to figure out which screw to use or which frame member should be attached first.

Skill Level Required to Build a Kit Greenhouse

A number of skills can make a greenhouse project easier. The ability to read blueprints and technical drawings is important if the greenhouse requires much assembly. However, if the instruction manual is well-written and illustrated, you may not need these skills.

Most greenhouse projects require site work and landscaping. This may be as simple as removing the topsoil in the area where the greenhouse will be placed and filling the area with gravel or stone. In other situations, it may involve moving shrubbery, building retaining walls, installing drainage, or leveling the site. Sometimes it is better to contract out this part of the project.

All greenhouses must be anchored to the ground to resist wind loads. This may require placing screw-type ground anchors through the foundation boards or driving metal posts into the ground. It could also require the placement of concrete piers or a concrete wall poured to below the frost line. Again, you could hire a contractor to do the more extensive foundation work.

If you need to modify your home to attach the greenhouse, you may need some carpentry skill. Most of the materials required are available at a local lumberyard or home center.

You might need plumbing to bring water to the greenhouse. This could be as simple as running a hose from a nearby hose bibb, or it could involve placing a supply line below the frost line to have water available year-round.

CONSTRUCTION TIPS FOR KIT GREENHOUSES

- Clean and level the site and remove stones, piles of soil, and foundation form materials before starting the erection process.

- Gather the parts needed for each assembly before starting. This will save time and make it easier to follow the instructions.

- When assembling the parts, work in a protected area to avoid scratching painted frame members. Covering the area first with canvas, plastic, cardboard, or an old blanket works well.

- You may need the help of a second person for erection of the frames and installation of glazing panels.

- Endwall frames are usually installed first. Then snap a chalk line to locate the position of intermediate frames.

- Install all purlins or mullions before inserting the glazing panels. This makes the frame square and rigid.

- Install all screws and bolts called for in the instructions. Do not leave any out. Do not overtighten the screws, as this could collapse tubing or extrusions.

- Rubber gaskets are used on many greenhouses to provide a watertight seal. Wipe the surface where the gasket will be attached with a cloth dipped in rubbing alcohol to remove any oil residue.

- Caulking is a good material for filling in small holes, gaps, and cracks to prevent water or air leaks. Use a 100% rubber silicone caulk with a 35- or 50-year durability. The caulk should be compatible with the material it will adhere to. Match the colors or use a clear caulk. Be sure to keep any weep holes open to allow water drainage.

- Install aluminum flashing where the greenhouse meets the house, accessory building, or foundation to shed water. Sheet flashing is available in rolls in the roofing section of a home center.

- Paint or stain any exposed wood to protect it.

Many greenhouses need power for lighting, fans, and heaters, so electricity must be supplied. Unless you have skill with electricity, this job is better left to a licensed electrician.

If you are uncertain about construction techniques or site preparation, refer to a construction reference manual in your local library or home center.

Tools Required to Build a Kit Greenhouse

Most manufacturers of kit greenhouses provide a list of tools needed to assemble their greenhouses. Usually, these are the basic hand tools most homeowners have around the house, such as a screwdriver, wrench, hammer, handsaw, level, tape measure, and square. You may need a battery-operated or electric drill and circular saw for some construction. If a concrete foundation is necessary, you may need a shovel, pick, and concrete tools. You can rent specialized tools if you do not want to purchase them. See "Tools and Equipment for Building a Kit Greenhouse" at right for a list of tools that you may need.

Storage of Materials

When the cartons containing the greenhouse arrive, open the boxes and check for damaged parts. Then store the cartons off the ground, under cover, and in a safe place until you need the materials.

Building a Greenhouse from Plans

Generally, the lowest cost greenhouse is one that you build from plans using locally available materials. You may use plans as a guide to design a greenhouse for a location where a prefab greenhouse will not fit.

Most plans are for designs that can be easily constructed using basic hand and power tools along with basic carpentry skills. They also use materials that are readily available at local home centers or greenhouse suppliers.

Appendix C (page 134) contains plans that will fit the needs of many homeowners who want to garden in a controlled environment. Most of the designs are relatively easy to build. They all can be lengthened easily to provide more growing area. A list of materials is included with each plan to simplify purchasing and to make it easier to get quotes from several suppliers.

TOOLS AND EQUIPMENT FOR BUILDING A KIT GREENHOUSE

- ☐ Electric or battery-powered drill/driver — ⅜-inch
- ☐ Handsaw or electric circular saw
- ☐ Twist drills
- ☐ Flat-head and Phillips-head screwdrivers
- ☐ Pliers
- ☐ Adjustable wrench
- ☐ Claw hammer
- ☐ Rubber mallet
- ☐ Line level
- ☐ Torpedo level
- ☐ Framing square
- ☐ Chalk line
- ☐ Tape measure — 25-foot
- ☐ Tin snips
- ☐ Chisel
- ☐ Awl
- ☐ Hacksaw
- ☐ Rasp
- ☐ Metal file
- ☐ Staple gun
- ☐ Caulking gun
- ☐ Stepladder
- ☐ Sawhorses
- ☐ Shovel/post-hole digger
- ☐ Trowel
- ☐ Mortar mixing box
- ☐ Wheelbarrow
- ☐ Safety glasses
- ☐ Gloves

Sections later in this chapter discuss alternative construction techniques for the foundation and utilities.

Materials

Lumber and steel tubing are the most common materials used to build greenhouses from plans. They are easy to work with using tools found in most homes.

Lumber

Shopping for lumber can be difficult because of the large number of species and the complex grading system. Fir, spruce, hemlock, and pine are softwoods used in construction. Dimension lumber in select, structural, or construction grade will give the best results for greenhouses. Construction grade is good for general framing applications. Select structural is best if you will be finishing the surface with a clear coating for a fine appearance. To prevent warping, the lumber should be kiln-dried (KD) to below 15% moisture content. The pieces you select should be straight-grained and free of loose knots or checks.

Plywood is used for gusset plates and benches. It comes in 4-foot-by-8-foot sheets in several thicknesses, the most common being ¼-inch, ⅜-inch, and ½-inch. Plywood used in greenhouse construction should be labeled as "exterior," which means the plywood has a water-resistant bond between the plies and is designed for outdoor and high-moisture conditions. "Exposure 1" plywood, commonly referred to as "CDX," is bonded with an exterior glue but does not have resistance to long-term exposure to high moisture.

Wood that will be used for benches or placed in contact with the ground should be rot-resistant. Untreated construction lumber will give only 5–10 years of service when in contact with the soil. Species such as redwood and cedar have a longer life but may be very expensive. Most commercial greenhouses use pressure-treated lumber, which is available in most lumberyards and home centers. This type of lumber is generally warranted for 20–40 years. The most common preservative is copper chromated arsenate (CCA).

Avoid lumber treated with creosote or pentachlorophenol, as these chemicals may be toxic to some plants. These preservatives are no longer available to homeowners, but railroad ties, telephone poles, and road guardrail posts are treated with them.

Steel Tubing

Steel tubing is available as round tubing, water pipe, or conduit. It can also be purchased with a square or rectangular cross-section. Material that has been galvanized both inside and outside will provide the best service.

Water pipe and conduit in ½-inch, ¾-inch, and 1-inch sizes are available in home centers and can be bent to shape with a pipe bender or wood block form. You

may be able to rent a bender from a local plumber, electrician, or rental center for a day. Plans for a wood block bending form are shown in figure 3-8.

Square and rectangular tubing can be purchased from a greenhouse manufacturer or welding shop. They will also have the equipment to bend the tubing to shape.

Other materials for completing the greenhouse are available from greenhouse suppliers. These include bench materials, fans, heaters, thermostats, growing mixes, containers, fertilizers, and so on. Most suppliers will sell to the hobbyist.

Purchasing a Used Greenhouse

Used greenhouses become available for a number of reasons. Frequently, when a property with a greenhouse changes hands, the new owners have no need for or interest in the greenhouse, and rather than let it deteriorate, they sell it.

Greenhouses are sometimes abandoned by schools, prisons, and other institutions. Sometimes greenhouse programs are discontinued. Sometimes a greenhouse is not maintained and falls into disrepair.

Although a classified ad in a local newspaper may bring results, you may have better luck finding a used greenhouse by contacting local garden clubs, plant societies, or greenhouse suppliers. Town assessors or local contractors may also have leads.

Sometimes you can get a good buy in a used greenhouse. Other times, you simply inherit a lot of work.

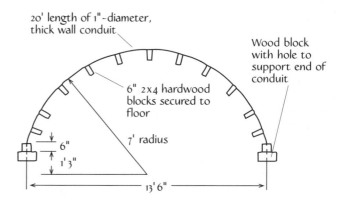

1. Set up the jig on a wood floor.
2. Make end bends with a pipe bender.
3. Use a 3-foot length of steel rod or pipe to make the final bend.

Figure 3-8. Form for making a conduit arch

Inspection and Evaluation

Once you locate a used greenhouse, you need to conduct a thorough inspection and evaluation. Does it meet your needs? The greenhouse should be large enough for your present plant collection and provide additional space for expansion.

Does the greenhouse fit your location? If it is a lean-to, will it fit under the eaves of your home or building? How much modification will be necessary?

Next, consider the condition of the greenhouse. Are wood members rotted or broken? Is the paint peeling? Can the connectors be removed easily? If you know who the manufacturer is, you may be able to get replacement parts. If not, some manufacturers may have standard parts that will work.

You should also check the condition of the equipment inside the greenhouse. Benches may be rotted or made of asbestos-cement board. The cost of new benches is $3–4 per square foot. Heaters and fans that have been sitting idle for a while may be rusted and need replacement.

The glazing may be in poor condition or may be difficult to remove. In older glass greenhouses, caulking was used to hold the glass in place, and it is frequently difficult to remove without breaking some of the panes. Most plastic materials have a limited lifespan and may have to be replaced with a new material.

What Is a Used Greenhouse Worth?

Considering the amount of labor needed for disassembly and reconstruction and the materials needed for rebuilding, a used greenhouse is never worth more than 50% of a new greenhouse. If extensive work is needed to scrape and repaint the structure, then its value will be considerably less.

You might find someone willing to give you a used greenhouse if you remove it from their property. This could very well be a bargain, but some free greenhouses are in very poor condition and require extensive work and materials to return them to usable growing space. Sometimes a free greenhouse is no bargain.

Disassembly and Reassembly

Suppose that you find a used greenhouse that is in good condition and that will fit your needs and

location. How do you proceed to move it? If plans for the greenhouse are not available, it is best to first take all the dimensions that you can. This includes foundation size, bolt locations, door and vent openings and locations, and so on. A good set of photos or a videotape can also aid in rebuilding.

Second, label all parts with a permanent marker. Include frame members, door parts, vent pieces, bolt sizes, and other parts that are removed piece by piece. A diagram on which you can label the parts is very helpful. Try to keep the parts separated by type.

When you get all the parts home, clean them by scraping and wire brushing off all loose dirt and paint. Paint scrapers and a wire brush in a drill work well if the paint does not contain lead.

CAUTION! Many older greenhouses were coated with paint containing lead. Flaking lead paint can be a serious health problem. If ingested, low levels can lead to learning and behavioral problems in children. High levels may cause damage to the nervous and reproductive systems in adults. Do-it-yourself kits to test for lead are available at home centers. If the paint is not flaking, it may be best to encapsulate it with a watertight paint seal. Contact your local paint store for the best choice of paint. If the paint is flaking, it may be best to use a chemical paint remover. Any removed lead paint should be disposed of safely. Contact your local transfer station or building inspector for advice. Be sure to wear safety goggles, a dust mask, and protective clothing when removing paint or caulking.

If the glass is held in place by caulking, remove the old caulking so a new bed of caulking can be applied. You may need to apply heat to soften it.

After preparing the site and placing the foundation, you can begin erecting the greenhouse frame and applying the glazing.

The Foundation

The foundation is the link between the greenhouse and the ground. It provides a level surface on which to mount the frame. It also anchors the structure to the ground so it will not blow away in heavy winds.

After selecting the greenhouse site, you should first determine the final floor level of the greenhouse. Floor level should be above the surrounding terrain so drainage will flow away from the structure. Avoid having the floor lower than the outside ground, as rainwater from the roof may seep into the greenhouse, wetting or even flooding the floor.

Next, grade the site so that it is level in the area of the greenhouse and sloped around the edges to carry rainwater away from the area (figure 3-9). On steep sites, you may need to build a retaining wall.

The next step is to remove the topsoil, unless you will be growing crops directly in the ground. Remove soil, stones, and debris to at least 6 inches below grade to get a good base.

Types of Foundations

Next, install the foundation. Many types of foundations can be used. Base your selection on the style and location of the greenhouse, whether the greenhouse is permanent or temporary, and the amount of money you want to spend. Some typical systems are discussed below.

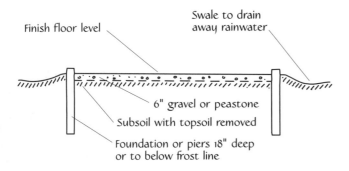

Figure 3-9. Cross-section of greenhouse foundation

The mounting surface on top of the foundation should be level so frame members and glazing panels fit squarely into place. Deviations of more than ½ inch in 12 feet are generally not acceptable.

Concrete Slabs

A concrete slab makes a convenient base for a greenhouse. For an attached structure, the finish floor is generally placed level with or one to two steps below the house floor. For a freestanding greenhouse, the floor should be several inches above the finish outside grade.

A 3-inch-thick floor is adequate for home greenhouses. The outside edges should be thicker to give support and resist cracking from frost action (figure 3-10).

Compacted gravel or stone at least 4 inches thick on top of the subsoil will provide drainage. A 6-mil (0.006-inch) polyethylene moisture barrier on top of the gravel or stone will keep the slab dry. Avoid puncturing the plastic during concrete installation.

Build a form out of 2-inch-thick lumber around the perimeter. The top of the form should be at the finish floor height. It can act as a screed board to level the concrete as it is placed. Reinforcing wire or fiber can be added to increase the flexure strength of the slab.

Once the concrete has set (in about 24 hours), the forms can be removed. Polystyrene or polyurethane insulation board 1 or 1½ inches thick can be installed vertically around the outside of the foundation to a depth of 1–2 feet to keep the floor warmer in the winter.

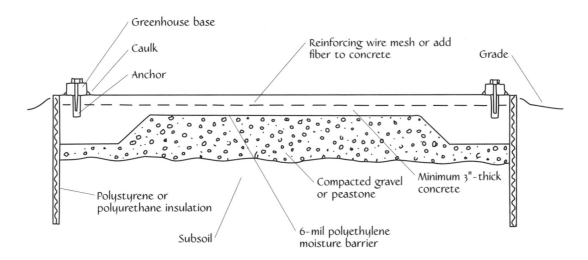

Figure 3-10. Concrete slab foundation (cross-section)

The greenhouse base can be attached to the slab using screw anchors, which are available at most home centers.

Poured Concrete or Concrete Block Walls

A poured concrete or concrete block wall is frequently used for permanent glass-glazed greenhouses (figure 3-11). The wall is set on a footing below the frost line and gives good support for heavier structures. The greenhouse can also be set on a kneewall to raise the height of the greenhouse above grade.

To build the wall, first dig a trench in the soil to below the frost line and place forms for the footing. Check with the local building inspector to determine what this depth is and to see if an inspection is required before the footing is poured. The footing is usually twice as wide as the wall and equally as thick. For example, if you are installing a 6-inch-thick wall, the footing will be 6 inches high by 12 inches wide.

After the footing hardens, place the wall forms on top to pour the walls. An alternative is to build a concrete block wall. The wall height should be a minimum of 6 inches above grade. Walls can be built to about 3 feet above grade or bench height.

At this point, you should install footing drains around the perimeter to drain groundwater and roof water away from the site. Place a 4-inch-diameter perforated pipe at the outside base of the footing and cover it with peastone or trap rock. The stone should be brought up along the side of the wall to near ground level.

You can finish the outside wall several ways. You can leave it plain or paint it with a concrete paint. You can also face it with brick or stone, in which case you need to build a ledge into the wall to support the facing when the wall is built.

To reduce heat loss, attach an inch or two of insulation board to the surface, either outside or inside.

Now you are ready to backfill soil against the foundation, grade, and seed. If you place a solid concrete floor inside the greenhouse, you should position a strip of isolation joint material between the wall and the floor to keep the floor from cracking when it shrinks.

Concrete Piers

Concrete piers, a low-cost method of providing support for a greenhouse, are cylinders of concrete located under the corners of the greenhouse and at intermediate points under the walls.

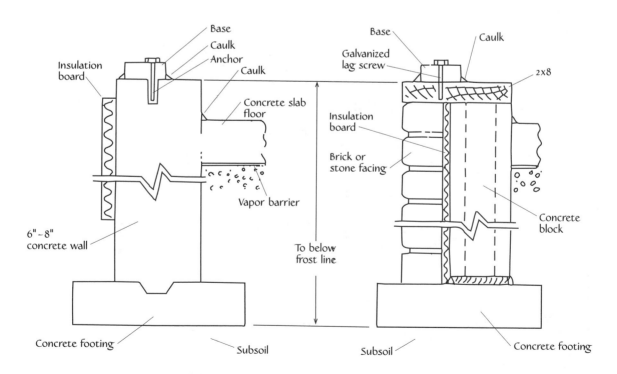

Figure 3-11. Poured concrete wall (cross-section) and brick or stone-faced concrete block wall (cross-section)

After preparing the site, follow the manufacturer's recommendations or the plans to determine the location and size of piers. Use a post-hole digger to remove the soil to below the frost line. If the soil is firm, it can be used as the form for the concrete. If not, purchase cardboard tubes (Sonotubes) or make wooden forms.

You can place L-bolts into the top of the pier before the concrete hardens or drill in concrete anchors later (figure 3-12). The size and length of the anchors will depend on whether you place wooden beams on the piers or just attach the frame members.

You can dig a trench between the piers to a depth of 12–24 inches for foam insulation.

Wood Post Foundation

Wood-frame greenhouses frequently have pressure-treated posts as a foundation (figure 3-13). They are low-cost and easy to work with and provide a good connection to the ground. Most plans specify a post size of 4 inches by 4 inches or 4 inches by 6 inches, both of which are available at most lumberyards.

Follow the plans for the number and location of posts. Set posts to below the frost line or to a hard subsoil base. Use a post-hole digger to dig the holes. Use a string line to determine the posts' locations and a level to ensure that they are vertical in the holes. Once the posts are set, backfill them with the removed soil. You can leave the posts a couple of inches longer than needed and then cut them off to a level line with a power or hand saw.

Once the posts are cut off and level, nail a plate in place and attach the frame. If you will be using the greenhouse year-round, place board-type foam insulation around the outside of the posts to a depth of 18 inches to reduce heat loss.

Pipe Post Foundation

Metal pipe or tubing is commonly used to attach conduit or tubing greenhouses to the ground. Ground posts, as they are called, are 30–42 inches long (figure 3-14).

After staking the pipe locations, drive the posts into the ground with a hammer or maul. Place a steel or wood cap over the end that will be hammered to prevent it from being damaged.

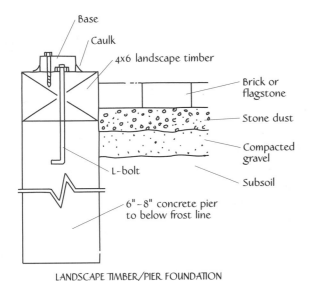

LANDSCAPE TIMBER/PIER FOUNDATION

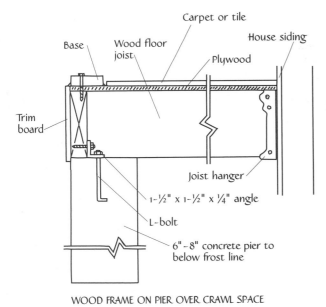

WOOD FRAME ON PIER OVER CRAWL SPACE

Figure 3-12. Concrete pier foundations

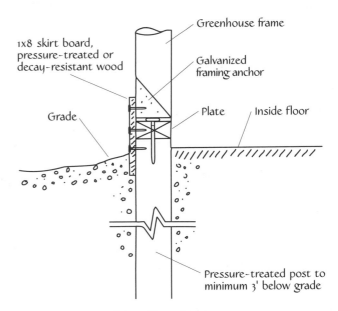

Figure 3-13. Wood post foundation

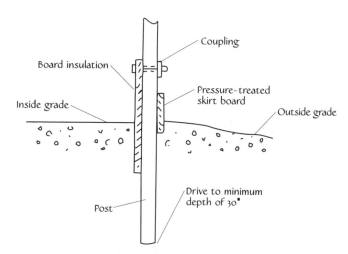

Figure 3-14. Pipe foundation

To get accurate spacing, drill slightly oversized holes in a scrap piece of board at the exact post spacing. Then put the board on the ground and drive the posts through the holes. If you encounter stones, dislodge them with a crowbar. For a more permanent foundation, set the posts into post holes and surround them with concrete. An easy way to do this is to pour in dry sand-cement mix and then add water.

Posts are normally left about 6–8 inches above the ground so a foundation board can be attached. This pressure-treated board gives rigidity to the posts. It seals the greenhouse at ground level to prevent rodents from entering and forms an attachment for the bottom of the glazing. You can bury insulation board along the post line and attach it to the foundation board. This will reduce heat loss and give a warmer soil temperature.

Once the posts and the foundation are in place, attach the greenhouse frame. In some designs, the frame slides into or over the ground posts. In others, a coupling is used to connect the two.

No Foundation

A lightweight greenhouse such as one made from tubing or wood can be placed on a smooth ground surface without using a foundation. This is a good option for temporary structures or for greenhouses that might be moved.

Landscape timbers work well as a base to attach the frame. It is a good idea to remove grass and loose topsoil from the site to get a level surface. The structure still has to be anchored to the ground so it does not move or blow away in the wind. This can be done using ground anchors as shown in figure 3-15.

Mounting a Greenhouse to a Deck

Kit greenhouses are frequently attached to a deck. With easy access from the home through a sliding glass door, these structures are ideal areas to grow plants or to add recreational space to the home. The greenhouse adds weight to the deck, so it is important to ensure that the posts and carrying beams will support the load.

Most decks are sloped away from the house to provide drainage. To make the base for the greenhouse level, use 2x4 or 2x6 pressure-treated planks with shims underneath (figure 3-16, page 30). Fill any space between the shims with foam-in-place insulation.

The deck surface can be covered with ½-inch pressure-treated plywood attached with galvanized ring nails. Fill gaps with caulking. Depending on its use, the floor can be painted, tiled, or covered with carpet or other flooring material.

To reduce heat loss during the winter, glue or nail 2-inch-thick polystyrene insulation (blueboard not beadboard) to the underside of the deck.

A kneewall can be used to add extra height to the greenhouse. A simple wall construction such as that

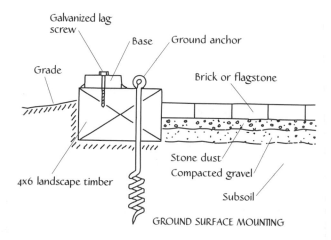

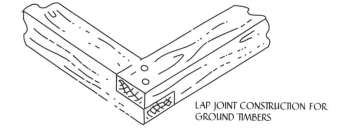

Figure 3-15. Ground surface mounting and lap joint construction for ground timbers

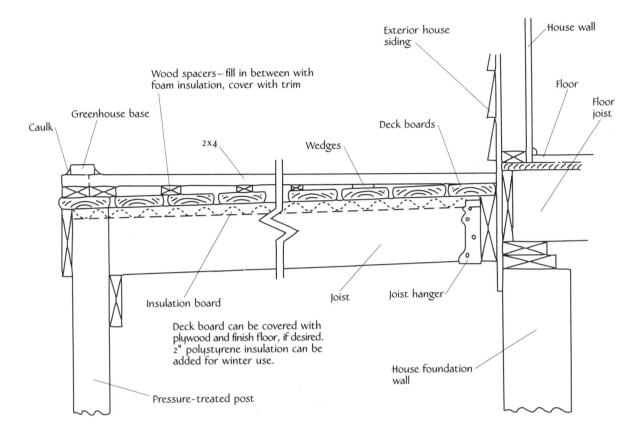

Figure 3-16. Wood deck installation (including method of leveling)

Labels in figure: Caulk; Greenhouse base; Wood spacers—fill in between with foam insulation, cover with trim; 2x4; Wedges; Deck boards; Exterior house siding; House wall; Floor; Floor joist; Insulation board; Joist; Joist hanger; Deck board can be covered with plywood and finish floor, if desired. 2" polystyrene insulation can be added for winter use.; House foundation wall; Pressure-treated post

shown in figure 3-17 works well. A U-shaped galvanized channel attaches the wall to the deck and acts as a cap. It can be fabricated at a sheet metal shop.

Foundation Layout

Review the plans or kit instructions to determine the exact dimensions of the foundation. Once you have determined these dimensions, go back and check them again, as they are critical to getting a good start. Sometimes it is best to lay out the base pieces on a garage floor or other level surface to doublecheck the dimensions.

Next locate the foundation on the ground. If you are building an attached greenhouse, the foundation should be perpendicular to the house wall (figure 3-18). Check to see where the ridge will be located. Will it fit under the overhang? Will it attach to the overhang? Will it miss the doors and windows?

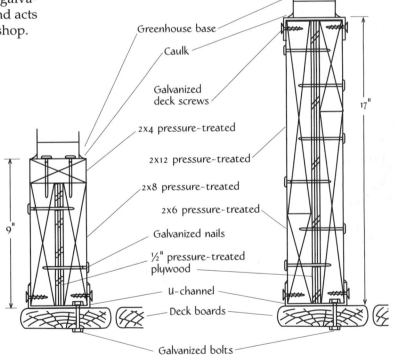

Labels in figure: Greenhouse base; Caulk; Galvanized deck screws; 2x4 pressure-treated; 2x12 pressure-treated; 2x8 pressure-treated; 2x6 pressure-treated; Galvanized nails; ½" pressure-treated plywood; U-channel; Deck boards; Galvanized bolts; 9"; 17"

Figure 3-17. Kneewall designs

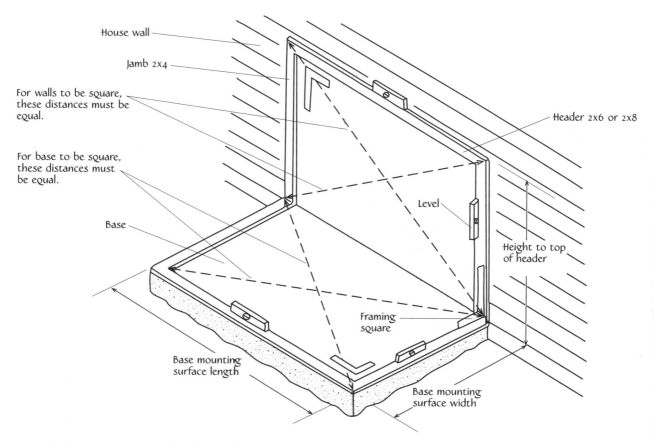

Figure 3-18. Squaring an attached greenhouse

When locating the corners of a freestanding greenhouse, be sure that you have adequate space to work around the structure. Also make sure it is not located over your well or septic system if you have one.

Several methods can be used to square a foundation. A large framing square will give approximate lines. A better method is to use the 3-4-5 right angle Pythagorean Theorem (figure 3-19). From a corner stake, measure 3 feet towards the second corner; mark this spot. Next, measure 4 feet at an approximate 90° angle towards the third corner; mark this spot. The distance between the two stakes should be 5 feet. Make some adjustments if it is not. You can also use 6 feet, 8 feet, and 10 feet as dimensions. If you have access to one, a surveyor's level could speed the layout process.

To check whether the building is square, measure the opposing sides and diagonal distances. The diagonals should be equal if the opposing sides are equal.

Batter boards and string lines set back from the greenhouse corner locations will help you locate the exact corner once you start digging for the foundation. To get the string lines level, use a straight edge and line level or a surveyor's level.

A wood header is usually required for attachment of the rafters or top mullion (figure 3-20, page 32).

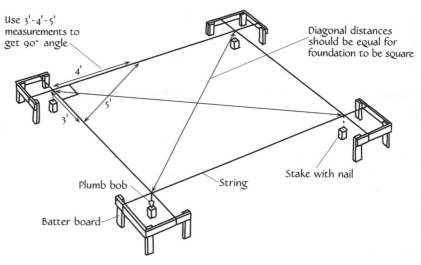

Figure 3-19. Procedure for squaring the foundation

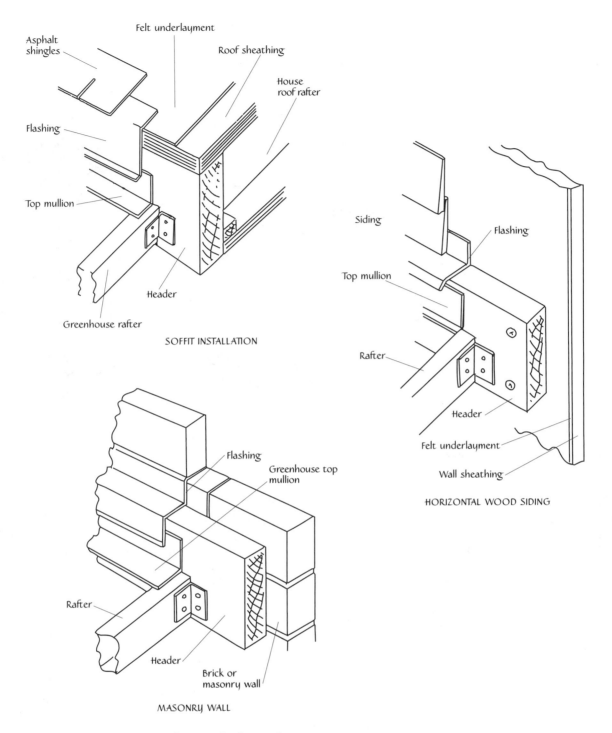

Figure 3-20. Ridge flashing options for attached greenhouses

Using a chalk line, mark a horizontal line to designate the location of the top of the rafters. The distance from the base to the top of each rafter may vary and have to be adjusted.

If the greenhouse will be attached to the overhang, the rain gutter and fascia board will have to be replaced by a header. The width of a kit greenhouse is usually measured from the front of the header. You

will need to fill in the area under the overhang with framing and siding to match the house or with clear glazing panels made to size.

Proper preparation of the house wall surface is also important. The mounting surface must be level, square, and perpendicular to the base. If the wall is a flat surface, such as texture 1-11 plywood, stucco, or brick, you may be able to mount to it without any modification. If the surface is uneven, such as clapboards or shakes, you will have to notch it out to attach the jambs and header to the sheathing.

For wood surfaces, attach the jambs and headers with galvanized deck or lag screws that are long enough to penetrate into the frame of the house. For masonry or brick walls, use appropriate anchors. Countersink the attaching hardware to provide a level surface.

Upgrading a Greenhouse

Besides routine maintenance, greenhouses require upgrading from time to time to take advantage of advances in technology. Discussed below are areas where significant new developments have been made in the past few years. Additional information can be found in the other chapters.

Older greenhouses frequently have cypress or redwood roof framing and glazing bars. These woods require maintenance every few years. The glazing and caulking must be removed, the wood scraped and painted, and the glass reset into a new bed of glazing compound. Aluminum bar caps are available to protect the top of the bar and extend the time between reglazing. Aluminum bars with rubber gaskets are standard on most glass greenhouses today. An older greenhouse could be retrofitted with aluminum bars to reduce maintenance. At the same time, wider, tempered glass panes could be installed to reduce breakage and increase the light level.

A second glazing option is to remove the existing glass and wood bars and replace them with a system of aluminum extrusions and large-sheet polycarbonate or acrylic plastic material. Besides increasing light levels, this will reduce heating costs by 35–50%.

Because most plants are grown in containers today, closed-bottom benches are no longer necessary. Plastic or metal benches with an expanded metal top allow more air circulation around the plants, which reduces disease potential. A new bench layout could be considered to increase the amount of growing space. See chapter 5 for more information on benches and layouts.

Some of the aluminum bar configurations incorporate support for shade screens or energy blankets. New aluminum foil-faced shade material is more effective than older woven polypropylene material, as it reflects the light back through the glass. These materials are also designed to reduce heat loss by reflecting heat back into the growing area.

Other energy-conserving measures include installing foil-faced, board-type insulation around the perimeter kneewall and using a silicone seal between the laps on the glass to reduce air infiltration.

Some types of heating systems have become more efficient in the past few years. Using root zone heating systems on top of the benches, under benches, or in ground beds can reduce heating costs, as the heat is supplied where it is needed most. Air temperature can then be lowered 5–10°F, thus reducing heating costs. Radiant heat also lowers heating costs, because the plants are heated and not the air. Both electric and gas-fired systems are available.

Many older greenhouses are still cooled by manually opened roof and side vents. Installation of vent motors or a more efficient fan system can improve temperature control.

Air circulation is important for uniform heating, leaf moisture removal, and replenishment of carbon dioxide in the crop canopy. Installing one or more small circulating fans to provide a horizontal airflow pattern (racetrack pattern) will improve air circulation.

Utilities

Electricity

Electricity makes greenhouse operation much easier and more efficient and gives better environmental control. Usually, the power source is the distribution panel in the home. Only in rare cases and for large greenhouses should a separate service entrance and meter be considered.

Check the panel in the home to see that it has enough extra capacity and circuit breakers or fuse space for the power needed in the greenhouse. For most small home greenhouses of less than 200 square feet, a single 20-amp, 115-volt line is adequate to power the fan, louver motors or a vent motor, a room light, and the controls for a gas heater (figure 3-21, page 34). For larger greenhouses, you need to determine the wattage of each piece of electrical equipment. The watts for all equipment are added together to get the total electric supply needed. On some pieces of equipment, such as an electric heater, wattage is listed on the nameplate. If the electric heater has more than one heat range, use the largest value.

Operating wattage is usually not listed on fans and other motor-driven units. Calculate the wattage by multiplying the voltage by the amperage, which can be found on the nameplate. For example, a ¼-horsepower fan unit may operate on 120 volts and use 4.5 amps. The wattage is 120 volts x 4.5 amps = 540 watts.

If you are installing electric heat or artificial plant lighting, then you will need additional capacity. Calculations for these items are shown in the sections on heating and plant lighting in chapter 6.

Usually the supply comes from the main panel in the home. A single breaker or fused circuit supplies power to a distribution box located in the greenhouse. The cable between the two should be of adequate size to carry the power load.

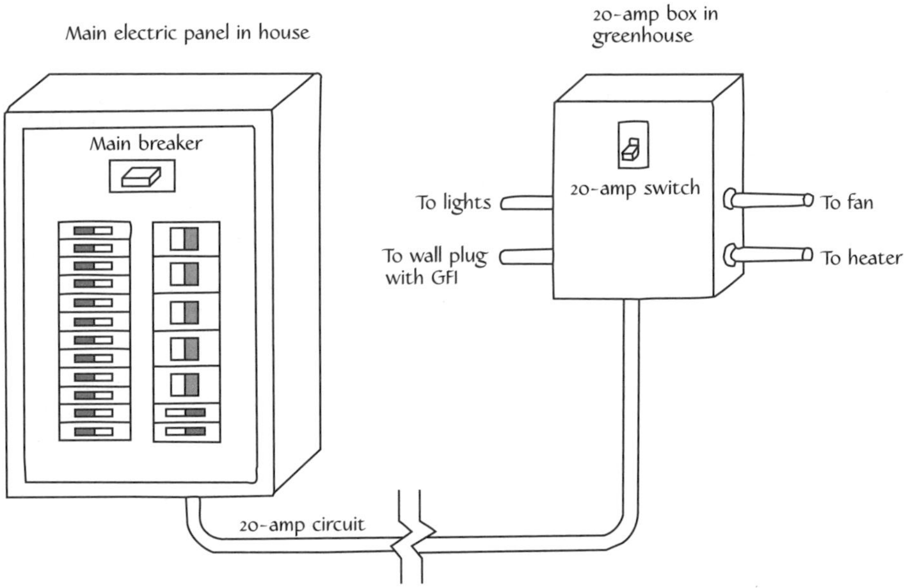

Additional circuits are needed where more equipment is used.

Figure 3-21. Distribution box for small greenhouse with no electric heat or supplemental lighting

If the greenhouse is located some distance from the house, you will need larger wires to prevent excessive voltage drop. From the distribution box, run individual circuits with properly sized breakers or fuses to the different pieces of electrical equipment and lights. Unless you have experience with electrical installations, you should call in a licensed electrician. Most communities require a building permit for this type of work.

If you do the work yourself, obey all the safety rules. Be sure that the power is shut off before working on any circuit. Avoid standing on a damp floor; wear rubber-soled shoes and stand on a rubber mat. Be sure that installation of any electrical circuits or equipment meets the National Electric Code.

All electric circuits should be grounded. Attach the ground wire at the electrical box in the greenhouse, and make sure that there is a continuous circuit back to the ground terminal in the panel in the home.

Use waterproof outlet and switch boxes in the greenhouse, as humidity levels are very high and water from irrigation could be splashed onto something. Outlet circuits should be ground-fault-interrupter-protected (GFI-protected). One GFI can protect a whole circuit if it is installed in the first box.

The supply wire from the home to a freestanding greenhouse should be placed below ground. Locate it

at least 18 inches below the ground in a bed of sand to protect it from rocks. It may be located in the same trench as the water supply pipe if it is separated by at least 12 inches. Use direct burial waterproof cable. To make it easy to replace (if ever necessary), the cable could be run through a plastic pipe or conduit.

Within the greenhouse, wires should have "W" (for *waterproof* insulation) in their type designation, such as THW. Either attach wires to the purlins or a backer board or place them in conduit. Use waterproof electrical boxes, as greenhouse conditions are usually damp. Mount them securely to the frame.

Install a minimum of one light fixture with a 100-watt bulb for room lighting. A watertight and dustproof fixture is best. Lighting is discussed in much more detail in chapter 6.

Backup Power

If you will have valuable plants or plants that you cannot afford to lose in your greenhouse, you will need a backup power supply. This will provide power to fans or heaters if the power is interrupted. The auxiliary generator should be large enough to start the largest motor or piece of equipment. For a small greenhouse, a 5-kilowatt (5,000-watt) unit should be sufficient. This size is not large enough to power electric heat or supplemental plant lighting.

For a larger greenhouse with more equipment, determine what equipment must remain operational in a power outage. Consider both summer and winter conditions. List each piece of equipment and its horsepower, voltage, and amperage. Take this list to a supplier of generating equipment for suggestions on the type and size of unit needed to handle the electrical load.

A better approach may be to get a unit large enough to handle essential equipment as well as appliances in the home and greenhouse. It is convenient to have lights, water, and heating equipment operating during a winter storm or after a hurricane.

Devices are usually plugged directly into small generators. Larger generators should be connected to the electric distribution system through a transfer switch (figure 3-22). This prevents generator power from being fed back through power company lines and injuring linemen who are making repairs.

Develop an operating procedure for use during an emergency. Before starting the generator, shut off all electrical equipment. Place the transfer switch in the position to operate the generator. After the generator is started, place essential equipment into operation, starting with the largest motor first.

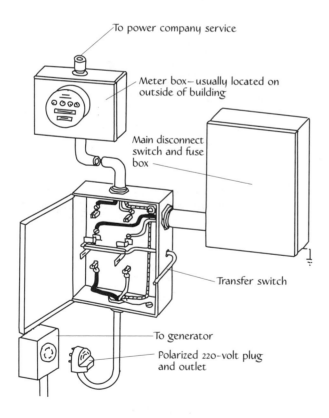

Figure 3-22. System transfer switch

Alarm System

An alarm system is an inexpensive form of insurance that can protect your greenhouse and its valuable plants. It will indicate when a power failure or equipment failure has occurred.

The basic alarm consists of a warning device, a power supply, and sensors. A simple alarm is a battery-operated doorbell that uses a thermostat as a sensor (figure 3-23). When the temperature in the greenhouse falls below the desired minimum level, the bell goes off. The bell is usually located in the home, where it will be heard. Additional sensors can be added to detect power failure, pump failure, intrusion, or fire.

Water Supply

A dependable source of clean water is needed to operate a greenhouse. The source can be a municipal supply, a well, a spring, or surface water.

If the water contains sediment, which is common with pond or stream water, then filtration will be needed. Screen or fabric filters are sized in gallons per minute for the quantity of water used (figure 3-24, page 36).

Water quality can affect plant growth. Excessive levels of some elements, such as calcium, boron, iron, magnesium, and chlorine, can reduce plant growth. If you suspect high levels of any of these, or if you are having problems growing plants, then get a chemical water test. Desirable ranges are given in table 3-1 on page 36. High or low pH can be easily adjusted.

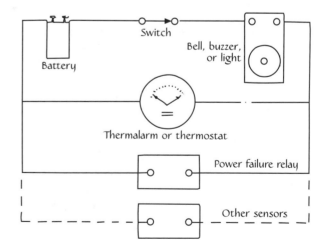

Figure 3-23. Basic alarm system with a battery-operated warning device, thermostat, and power failure relay

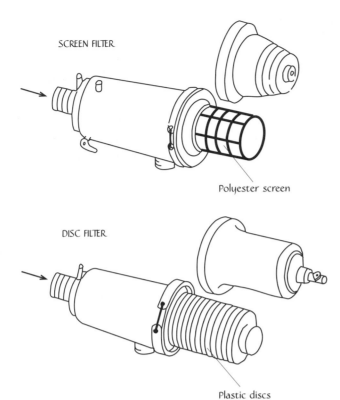

SCREEN FILTER

Polyester screen

DISC FILTER

Plastic discs

Figure 3-24. Water filters

Table 3-1. Desirable ranges of specific elements in irrigation water

Parameter	Desirable range
pH	5–7
Soluble salts	0–1.5 mS/cm
Phosphorus (P)	0.005–5 mg/l
Calcium (Ca)	40–120 mg/l
Sodium (Na)	0–5 mg/l
Boron (B)	0.2– 0.8 mg/l
Fluoride (F)	0–1.0 mg/l
Magnesium (Mg)	6–24 mg/l
Chlorine (Cl)	0–80 mg/l
Potassium (K)	0.5–10 mg/l
Iron (Fe)	2–5 mg/l
Copper (Cu)	0–0.2 mg/l
Manganese (Mn)	0.5–2.0 mg/l

Source: Adapted from *Florist Facts*, The Pennsylvania State University, April 1988.

mS/cm = millisiemens/centimeter

mg/l = milligrams/liter; mg/l is equal to parts per million (ppm)

The quantity of water needed to irrigate plants depends on the crops grown, the square footage of growing area, and the time of year. A rule of thumb is to size the water supply to provide about 0.4 gallon per square foot of growing area on the hottest day in the summer. For example, a greenhouse with 200 square feet of bench space will need about 80 gallons of water on the hottest day in the summer. This formula is based on evapotranspiration rates from the plant leaf surfaces, evaporation from the soil surface, and leaching.

A ¾-inch-diameter supply pipe is adequate for most small home greenhouses. This will yield about 5–6 gallons per minute (gpm) — enough to operate one hose. If the distance from the supply is greater than 100 feet, or if you expect to install a sprinkler system, then use a 1-inch-diameter line, which will yield about 10 gpm.

For freestanding greenhouses, the water supply line should be buried below the frost line. It should be connected to a dry hydrant in the greenhouse so it can be drained if freezing temperatures occur. A dry hydrant is a hose bibb that drains the aboveground piping to a dry well below ground when it is shut off.

To prevent possibly contaminating drinking water in the home with backsiphoning from the greenhouse, install a vacuum breaker on the hose bibb in the greenhouse (figure 3-25). This is required by most municipal water systems.

If water needs in your greenhouse are relatively modest, collect rainwater from the house or greenhouse roof and direct it into a storage tank for use in hand watering. Most home greenhouses can be watered with a single hose. The hose should be of good quality—one that is flexible and does not kink. A water breaker or wand with a breaker attached to the end will reduce the force of the water applied to the plants.

Other types of application equipment such as sprinklers, drip systems, mist systems, and hydroponics are discussed in chapter 5.

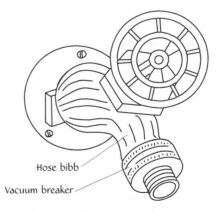

Hose bibb

Vacuum breaker

Figure 3-25. Backflow prevention

CHAPTER 4

Framing Materials and Glazing

Framing Materials

The greenhouse frame supports the glazing, some equipment, and hanging plants. It must be able to withstand snow and wind loads. Galvanized steel, aluminum, and wood are common framing materials (see figure 4-1).

Hoop and Gothic-style houses are generally made using galvanized steel tubing, which is low in cost and easy to bend. Most kit greenhouses use extruded aluminum members that may be painted or left bare. Plans are available for many wood frame structures. These are easy to build for the do-it-yourselfer.

Galvanized Steel

The best steel members are hot-dipped in galvanizing solution *after* the frame is bent and drilled. This ensures a more complete coverage and reduces the potential for rusting. If the tubing is galvanized *before* cutting and drilling, a galvanizing spray or rust-resistant paint can be used to protect uncoated areas.

Aluminum

Aluminum is particularly well-suited for greenhouse frames, as it can be formed into complex shapes to fit the glass and provide drip edges and support for shade or blanket systems. These frames are usually protected with a good grade of paint—either white to reflect light or brown to blend with the surroundings.

Wood

A wood frame is often the first choice for those who build their own greenhouses. Wood is easy to work with; costs less than other materials; and has a warm, traditional look. It provides more insulation than metal. Standard wood frame material shapes are available from several manufacturers; these materials will support glass glazing.

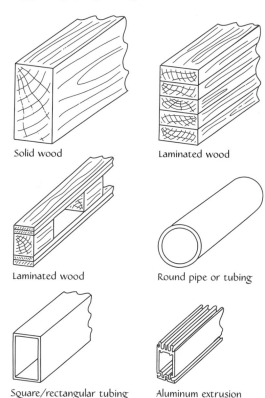

Solid wood   Laminated wood

Laminated wood   Round pipe or tubing

Square/rectangular tubing   Aluminum extrusion

Figure 4-1. Types of framing materials

Wood that is not in contact with the ground can be construction grade or better—hemlock, spruce, pine, or fir. It should be painted to repel moisture and reflect light. Redwood and cypress are more resistant to rot and insect and moisture damage; however, their cost may be prohibitive.

Wood that is in contact with the ground or used for benches should be pressure-treated with a preservative. This will extend its life to 20–40 years, as compared to 5–10 years for untreated material. Copper chromated arsenic (CCA) is the standard preservative used in pressure treating today. Although CCA is approved for use in contact with plants by the U.S. Environmental Protection Agency (EPA), some independent tests have shown that some leaching does occur, although not at a level above standard limits.

Creosote and pentachlorophenol, commonly used on lumber such as railroad ties in the past, may be toxic to some plants and should not be used.

The heartwood of some woods is very decay-resistant. Cedar, redwood, black cherry, and white and chestnut oak are examples that may be available in some areas. Most of these have a shorter service life than pressure-treated material.

Another preservative material is copper naphthanate, which is sold under the trade name Cuprinol. It can be used as a brush or soak treatment to lengthen the useful service life of untreated lumber. Two or three brush coatings or a 24-hour soak is required. This material is commonly used to treat foundation material, benches, flats, planters, or wood used in the garden.

"Lumber" made from recycled plastic is becoming more readily available. Although more expensive, it appears to have a long service life.

Glazing

Before choosing what type of glazing to use, it is important that you understand the light requirements of plants.

Light Requirements of Plants

Light is needed for photosynthesis and for photomorphogenesis. Photosynthesis combines carbon dioxide from the air with water from the soil in the presence of light energy to form sugar and oxygen. This is the way dry matter is formed, energy is stored, and growth occurs. Photosynthesis utilizes visible light from the blue through the red part of the light spectrum (see chapter 6, page 105 for more information on the light spectrum).

Photomorphogenesis is the use of light energy to produce a plant's shape, stem and leaf orientation, and flowers. Ultraviolet and blue light are needed to keep the stems short and the leaves from elongating too much. The red and far-red wavelengths help keep the plant from being too short. The balance of red and far-red controls the flowering and germination of some plants.

Sunlight provides all the wavelengths needed for photosynthesis and photomorphogenesis. The problem is that during the late fall and winter, the total light energy in the northern part of the United States is inadequate to provide the energy needed for optimum plant growth. Light then becomes the limiting factor in plant growth. Cloudy weather, haze, and smog also reduce light levels.

On the other hand, during the summer and at other times in the southern United States, the problem is too much sunlight, which may cause leaf burn and excessive temperatures. This problem is discussed further in chapter 6.

Glazing Basics

The search for the ultimate glazing material is neverending. The introduction of plastics in the 1950s started a progression of many new materials, both flexible and rigid, that continues today.

What type of glazing is best for a home greenhouse? The answer is not simple, as there are many materials to choose from, and each has its advantages and disadvantages. Criteria such as solar transmission, thermal losses, durability, and cost need to be considered. From a plant's perspective, the light spectrum and diffusion are important.

When sunlight strikes a glazing material, some of it is reflected, a small percentage is absorbed and converted to heat, and the remainder is transmitted into the greenhouse. A comparison of the light transmittance (the ratio of the light passing through a material to the light beaming upon it) is helpful when examining different materials.

Table 4-1 shows that visible light transmission varies from 78% to 93% for the common materials used. One rule of thumb states that, during the winter, for every 1% reduction in light that a plant receives, there will be a 1% reduction in plant growth.

Sunlight passing through glazing can be either direct, which causes shadows, or diffuse, which creates a more uniform light pattern. In areas that have a significant amount of cloudy weather, the sunlight is already diffused when it reaches the greenhouse, and the type of glazing is not as critical. Some researchers have reported improved production and flower quality with diffused light.

Table 4-1. Comparison of common glazing materials

	Visible light transmission	UV light transmission	Shade coefficient	Winter U-value
Glass				
Single/clear/float—1/8"	88%	80%	0.94	1.13
Single/clear/tempered	90	70	0.99	1.11
Single/clear/low-iron/tempered	93	n.a.	1.03	1.11
Single/bronze/tempered	68	39	0.83	1.11
Double/clear/tempered	82	52	0.87	0.49
Double/clear/tempered/low-iron	86	n.a.	n.a.	n.a.
Double/clear/tempered/low-E	78	32	0.73	0.32
Double/clear/heat mirror/argon	56	0.5	0.36	0.21
Double/clear/heat mirror/kripton/low-E	53	0.5	0.38	0.11
Double/clear/bronze/heat mirror/argon	40	0.5	0.29	0.11
Rigid Plastic				
Single fiberglass reinforced plastic	89	19	n.a.	1.56
Single polycarbonate/clear	90	0	n.a.	1.14
Single polycarbonate/white	42	0	n.a.	n.a.
Double fiberglass reinforced plastic/clear	85	n.a.	n.a.	0.45
Double polycarbonate/clear/8mm	83	18	0.91	0.58
Double acrylic/clear/8mm	86	44	0.98	0.56
Film Plastic				
Single/ag-grade/clear/6-mil	87	60	n.a.	1.0
Single/greenhouse/clear/6-mil	87	60	n.a.	1.0
Single/greenhouse/white/6-mil	40	n.a.	n.a.	n.a.
Double/greenhouse/clear/6-mil	78	48	n.a.	0.70

Source: Adapted from Aldrich and Bartok, *Greenhouse Engineering*, NRAES–33, 1994.

Note: Figures may vary slightly depending on the manufacturer and additives such as wetting agents, infrared inhibitors, and strength enhancers.

n.a. = not available

Stippled (rough-surfaced) glass, double-layer rigid plastic, and fiberglass (the rigid, wavy material in which you can see glass fibers coated with plastic) diffuse light. The greenhouse grade of film plastic also diffuses light, although the amount varies with the manufacturer. If you want to be able to see through the glazing to enjoy the outdoor view, use a material such as clear glass or flat acrylic sheets.

Even when the transmittance of a glazing material is high, the amount of light reaching the plants may be low. For example, in older greenhouses with narrow-pane glass, only 50% of the sunlight that shines on the greenhouse reaches the plants. The support bars, the piping, electrical fixtures, and the angle at which the light strikes the glazing all reduce the light. Today, wider frame spacing, stronger glazing, and fewer overhead obstructions can increase the amount of light reaching the plants to over 75%.

To keep heating costs down, you have to consider the thermal properties of the glazing material. Heat supplied inside the greenhouse is lost through conduction, infiltration, and thermal radiation (see "Heating the Greenhouse," page 71). Single-thickness materials such as glass and fiberglass conduct heat more rapidly than double-walled materials. This is why storm windows are used on homes. The cost of heating a greenhouse will be about 40% less with double glazing. Also keep in mind that the more laps or joints the structure has, the more chance there is for loss of heat from infiltration of cold air. Fiberglass, polycarbonate, and acrylic are available in sheets 4 feet wide and as long as the roof bars.

Some greenhouse materials allow more heat loss by thermal radiation than others. Thermal radiation, the opposite of solar radiation, is the loss of heat by radiation waves transmitted by warm objects in the greenhouse. Glass and fiberglass are the best materials in this respect, having very low heat loss rates. Although most film plastic materials allow more heat to escape, the layer of moisture that condenses on the inside of the glazing on cooler nights tends to reduce heat loss.

Another factor to consider is the useful life of the glazing. Some materials become brittle with age; others discolor, reducing light transmission. Materials can last one year or many years, some up to fifty. Short-lived materials such as polyethylene and copolymers are inexpensive and therefore good for temporary greenhouses, cold frames, and tunnels. Materials that last at least ten years should be used for low maintenance and a good appearance.

Some plastic materials tend to yellow with age, which reduces light transmission. Yellowing occurs when the ultraviolet radiation from the sun (the same rays that cause skin to tan) causes a photo-oxidation process that leads to discoloration and a reduction in strength. Durability tests conducted in several parts of the world help manufacturers evaluate new materials before placing them on the market.

The following sections examine in more detail some of the material characteristics that might lead you to select one type of glazing over another. Two general types of glazings are available: glass and plastic.

Types of Glazing

Glass

Glass is still the most common glazing for home greenhouses and the standard by which other materials are judged. Its clean appearance and transparency are good qualities for today's brightly lit homes. Its light transmission is also high, so it promotes good plant growth.

Most older greenhouses had double-strength panes 16–24 inches wide, but current manufacturing techniques can make glass widths to about 6 feet. Although using wider panes increases the amount of light entering the greenhouse, it also requires stronger support members to carry the extra weight. Larger panes also reduce the amount of air infiltration, resulting in a reduction of heat loss. The glass is tempered, making it three to five times stronger than ordinary annealed glass and allowing it to resist thermal stresses better. Wire-reinforced and laminated glass are available, but they are generally used only in school and other institutional greenhouses. Such glass should be avoided if possible because of light reduction and cost.

Many custom-built greenhouses and sunspaces include used sliding glass door replacement panes. These are low-cost and readily available from window manufacturers and lumberyards. One problem with these panes is getting a tight seal in the support members to prevent rainwater from seeping past the joints. A long-life silicone caulk should be used for sealing.

Proper installation of glass on the greenhouse is important to prevent leaking or cracking. In older greenhouses, the glass was placed in a bed of putty sealant on the support bars. Bar caps were installed to hold the glass in place and shed the water and snow. Today's greenhouses use rubber gaskets, both over and under the glass. See "Installation" on page 43 for more information.

SINGLE GLASS

Double-Pane Glass

Many home greenhouse manufacturers use double-pane glass to reduce heat loss and moisture condensation (figure 4-2). If it is available, welded glass, which has two panes that are fused together, is usually a better choice than fabricated panels, which use a spacer and sealant. Air leaks that allow moisture to become trapped between the panes are more likely to occur with the fabricated panes. However, the insulation value of fabricated panes is slightly greater. Fabricated panels are usually guaranteed for 5–10 years against failure. Hot-to-cold temperature changes can break the seals, allowing moisture to get in, which causes streaks.

Uneven thermal expansion or stress from the frame can shatter the glass. For example, the inner glass on a flat panel in a sunspace might break on a morning when the outside temperature is excessively cold. When it breaks, tempered glass forms small, pebble-size pieces that have no sharp edges.

Because of its insulating properties, double glazing slows snow melt. Where frequent snows occur, this can cause a significant reduction in light.

Impurities within the glass, usually iron, can absorb light, causing a reduction in transmittance. Glass that looks green on the edge has iron impurities. If it is blue, it has a low iron content. Low-iron glass contains about 0.03% iron (as compared to float glass, which has approximately 0.1%) and is now readily available for greenhouse use.

Double-pane glass with interior coatings, a plastic interlayer, or gas filling — although fine for a sunspace where glare, heat gain, and furniture fading are concerns — usually reduce light transmittance to levels too low to get good plant growth in the winter. See the visible light transmission values in table 4-1 on page 39.

Polycarbonate

Polycarbonate structured sheets are one of the most recent materials developed for greenhouses. Their large size and readily available aluminum fabrication systems speed up the glazing of a greenhouse. They can also be adapted for reglazing older glass greenhouses. These materials are lighter in weight than glass, so they require less structural framing.

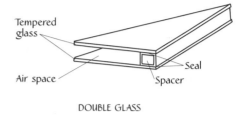

DOUBLE GLASS

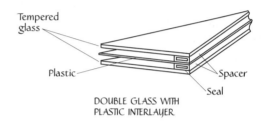

DOUBLE GLASS WITH PLASTIC INTERLAYER

WELDED GLASS

Figure 4-2. Types of double-pane glass

Polycarbonates are less flammable and have a higher impact resistance to hail or vandalism than acrylic materials. For example, a 6-millimeter sheet can withstand a blow from a 10-pound steel ball dropped from a height of 7 feet without cracking. Polycarbonates are used on many school greenhouses, where vandalism might be a problem. They are also fire-resistant, which is required by some building codes.

To ensure long weathering and durability, purchase a coextruded or coated polycarbonate sheet. These show less yellowing over the years than untreated materials.

Polycarbonates are available from several manufacturers. They have ultraviolet protection to extend their useful life to an estimated 15 years. Some brands are coated with a wetting agent or contain an additive to reduce condensation drips.

Polycarbonate structured sheets are available in several thicknesses, from 4 to 16 millimeters ($\frac{5}{32}$ to $\frac{5}{8}$ inch). Normally, the 8-millimeter ($\frac{5}{16}$-inch) thickness is used for home greenhouses.

Acrylic

Acrylic structured sheets are available in 8- and 16-millimeter thicknesses. They have the same formulation used in storm door glazing and have been around for many years. Acrylic yellows slowly with age. It is often used in place of curved pane glass and in areas that might be subject to breakage.

Acrylic material is a little clearer in appearance than polycarbonate, but neither is as clear as glass. Although acrylic has high light transmittance, its distortion will affect your view out of the greenhouse to your yard or garden. Acrylic glazing tends to attract dust more than polycarbonate. It also scratches, so be careful when cleaning it.

Polycarbonate and acrylic sheets have similar installations. Glazing systems consist of an aluminum extrusion base section that attaches to the greenhouse rafter or bar and a cap that holds the sheets in place. One-piece extrusions are also available (figure 4-3).

Fiberglass

Fiberglass reinforced plastic (FRP) is a medium-cost glazing material available in several grades with a 10- to 15-year lifespan. Its large sheet size (4 feet wide by lengths to 30 feet) makes installation easy. It is available in flat and corrugated forms, but the corrugated material provides better edge sealing and strength.

For most applications, specify the "clear" grade when ordering to get maximum light transmission. The material generally needs cleaning only once a year to remove dust and dirt. It may need to be resurfaced with an acrylic liquid sealer every 4–5 years to restore weathered surfaces to near-new condition.

When installing fiberglass, follow the manufacturer's recommendations so you don't void the warranty. Keep joints and laps to a minimum to reduce places where dust can accumulate and air can enter. Place spacers between the fiberglass and the roof purlins to allow space for condensation to drain without causing drips. Place screws or nails at the top of corrugations to prevent water leakage. Seal the ends of the sheets with foam or wood spacers.

Although it is still readily available, fiberglass has largely been replaced by corrugated polycarbonate.

Film Plastic

Improvements in film plastics continue to flow from manufacturers' research centers. Increases in strength, clarity, life, and energy conservation are some of the recent developments. Because most films do not have as long a life as rigid glazings, they are

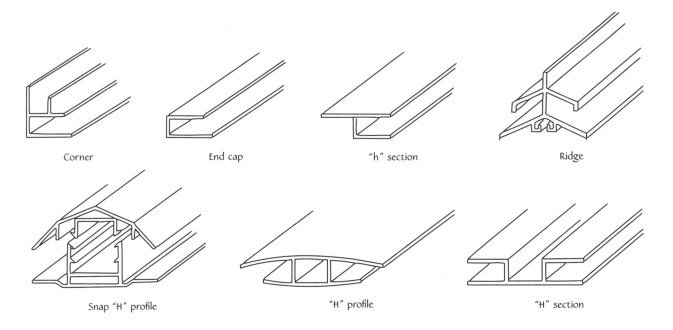

Corner   End cap   "h" section   Ridge

Snap "H" profile   "H" profile   "H" section

Figure 4-3. Extrusions for attaching polycarbonate and acrylic structured-sheet glazing

not used as often for home greenhouses. On the other hand, most new commercial greenhouses are film-covered, mainly due to lower construction costs and lower taxes. Film plastic is a great choice for hoop houses and tunnels, because it is flexible, comes in large sizes, and is easy to attach.

Greenhouse plastics with a life of 2–4 years are stronger than the low-cost construction-grade plastics, which break down in sunlight in about 9 months. Greenhouse plastics combine polyethylene with 1–5% ethyl vinyl acetate. They are also available with an infrared radiation inhibitor, which reduces heat loss from inside the greenhouse by up to 20% on a clear night. You can purchase them through a greenhouse supplier.

Another recent development is the addition of wetting agents, which keep condensed moisture in a film rather than in droplets. The moisture runs freely to the ground or gutter rather the giving you a shower every time you close the door or a gust of wind hits the greenhouse. Most greenhouse suppliers carry one or more brands of these copolymer plastics in a 6-mil thickness.

The latest development in plastic is called "interference films." These films contain additives that block certain portions of the light spectrum. An example of why you might want to do this is to prevent certain fungi from sporulating. By coextruding the films, they can be formed in layers, each with a different feature, such as anticondensate control, infrared retention, light diffusion, dust repellant, and short-wave infrared reflection. Further research between the film manufacturers and plant scientists will determine which parts of the light spectrum can be altered to give optimum growth. These new plastics will most likely be crop-specific.

Film plastics are a good choice for glazing a greenhouse when cost is a major consideration. With a price of $0.05–$0.15 per square foot, you can cover a greenhouse with film many times for what it would cost you to use one of the more permanent materials.

Typically, film plastics work well for greenhouses built to extend the growing season, grow bedding plants in the spring, or provide protection for sensitive woody ornamentals. A light framework of wood, pipe, or conduit can be used, as the plastic weighs almost nothing. However, the frame must be heavy enough to support wind and snow loads.

Installation

Proper installation of the glazing material is important if it is to last a long time, resist wind, and not leak. Each material has a specific installation procedure to get the best results.

Glass

Older greenhouses used lapped glass — small panes (16 by 18 inches to 24 by 30 inches) that are placed in a bed of glazing compound or sealant in the roof bar channels (figure 4-4). The panes are overlapped about ¼ inch to shed water. The glazing compound provides a cushion and seal.

Installation is simple. First, the bars are scraped to remove old compound. Then they are painted with a good grade of white latex paint. Either glazing compound is applied with a caulking gun or a tape of sealant is laid on the bar. The pane of glass is pressed into the compound, and a bead of sealant is placed on top of the glass to seal it. A pair of glazing clips may be used to keep the next pane of glass from sliding. A bar cap is laid over the glass and fastened to the bar with screws.

Lapped glass is not really used on greenhouses manufactured today, so the only time you would use this installation method is when you are rebuilding or reglazing an existing greenhouse.

A different system is used with today's single-pane or double-pane tempered glass (figure 4-5 on page 44). Water and air tightness are achieved with rubber or vinyl gaskets. Either a tape or a cord material can be used. A layer is placed on the glazing bar first, then the glass panel is positioned in place. A bar cap with gasket inserts is then fastened over the top to form the seal. A bead of silicone caulking may be needed in transition areas.

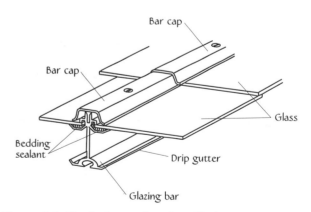

Figure 4-4. Single-layer glass installation

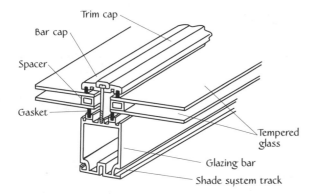

Figure 4-5. Double-pane glass installation

Sliding glass door replacement windows have been used by hobbyists who design and build their own greenhouses. They can be purchased as single or double glazing. These panes are heavy and need a strong frame for support. Pressure-treated 2x4 or 2x6 lumber works well.

The sliding glass panels should be set in a bed of glazing compound or silicone sealant. Wood batten strips can be used to hold the panels in place. Use galvanized or stainless screws so removal will be easy when the caulking needs to be replaced.

Corrugated Fiberglass, Polycarbonate, and Polyethylene

These panels are designed to provide a net coverage in width of exactly 48 inches. Standard lengths are 8, 10, and 12 feet. Other lengths may be available. With long rafters, overlap panels by 6 inches. The corrugations are generally installed parallel to the rafter to allow rain runoff. When joining panels, use an edge overlap of one corrugation (figure 4-6). The upper panel in the overlap should be upwind to reduce rain penetration. A bead of silicone caulk will provide a watertight seal.

The panels are very flexible across the sheet and need to be supported on purlins (roof members) and girts (wall members) spaced about 3 feet apart. The sheets will bend in length but require a minimum bending radius of about 6½ feet.

Sheets can be cut to length with shears, a fine-toothed handsaw, or a circular saw with a plywood blade. Use self-drilling, self-tapping screws (tec screws) with weatherseal washers to attach the panels to the frame. Several types of spacers are available to raise the panel above the purlin to prevent condensation

drip. Place screws through the top of the corrugation. Fastener spacing should follow manufacturer's recommendations. Seal the eave, ridge, vent, and vertical edges with wood or foam closure strips.

Flat Fiberglass and Polycarbonate

This material comes in rolls 3 or 4 feet wide by 50 feet long. It can be used on the roof but is normally used only on the endwalls, where it is easier to install than the corrugated material.

Pieces can be cut to size using shears. Provide overlaps of 1½ inches on framing members. Use self-tapping, threaded screws with rubber washers for attachment. A bead of silicone caulking in the overlap will provide a good seal against rain and wind.

Structured Sheets — Polycarbonate and Acrylic

When installing this material, it is very important to allow for its expansion and contraction, which is eight times greater than that of glass. Allow ⅛ inch for every 4 feet of sheet width or length (figure 4-7). The aluminum extrusions that are supplied with the sheets allow for this.

Sheets can be cut with a fine-toothed handsaw or power circular saw with a plywood blade. Leave protective film in place until just before installation. Remove chips from channels with a vacuum cleaner.

The sheets should be installed with the ribs running vertically to allow any moisture to drain. Place an aluminum tape over the top edge of the sheet to

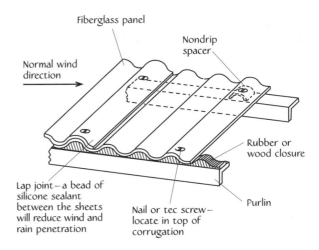

Figure 4-6. Corrugated fiberglass or polycarbonate installation

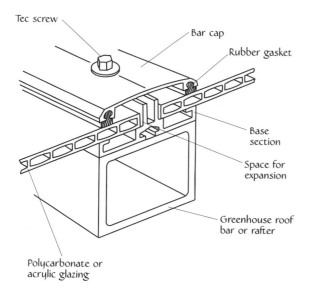

Figure 4-7. Structured-sheet polycarbonate or acrylic glazing installation

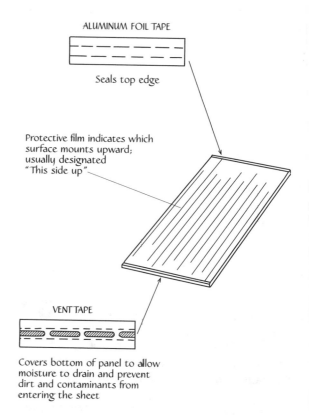

Figure 4-8. Structured-sheet polycarbonate installation

restrict the entrance of dirt (figure 4-8). Use a perforated tape on the bottom to allow any moisture to drain.

Polycarbonate sheets can be bent over a curved eave. The bending radius depends on the sheet thickness. For example, the commonly used 8-millimeter sheet will bend over a minimum radius of 3 feet, 11 inches. Acrylic sheets are rigid and cannot be used over curved surfaces.

Two types of aluminum extrusions are available. The single-piece "H" or "h" extrusion (see figure 4-3, page 42) is less expensive but more difficult to use than the two-piece ones. All are attached to the frame with self-tapping wood or metal screws. A bead of silicone caulk should be placed along the edge of the extrusion after installation to make a weathertight seal.

Although they are more difficult to seal, these materials can be cut to size and used to replace glass glazing. A bed of nonhardening glazing compound will create a watertight seal. Bar caps will hold the pieces in place.

Film Plastic

Film plastic must be attached securely so it won't tear from wind or heavy snow. A number of aluminum extrusions are designed to make the attachment easy (figure 4-9). Wooden furring strips attached with double-headed nails will also work.

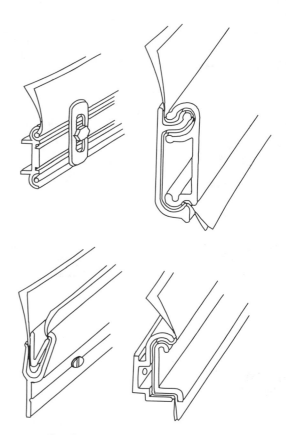

Figure 4-9. Aluminum extrusions for attaching film plastic

A single layer of film is adequate if the greenhouse is located in a mild climate or if it is used only during warm weather. The film is applied over the outside of the greenhouse and attached around the perimeter. In larger wood-frame greenhouses, intermediate wood battens or poly rope could be added to reduce the flapping that occurs on windy days.

A double layer of plastic, which acts similarly to a thermopane window, will reduce heat loss by about 35%. The amount of moisture condensation on the inside surface will be less because the inner surface will be warmer.

Several methods can be used to apply a double layer, depending on the type of frame you have. Both layers can be applied to the outside of a wood frame with a 2x2 wooden spacer in between. First, stretch the inner layer over the frame. Then place the 2x2 spacer on top of each frame and nail it in place. Apply the second layer. Nail furring strip battens over the plastic to each spacer. If you use double-headed nails, future removal will be easier.

Another method consists of applying the first layer over the outside of the frame, holding it in place with batten strips, and attaching the second layer inside the greenhouse frame if there are not too many obstructions. Lath, plastic strapping, or cord will hold the second layer in place.

With a pipe-frame greenhouse, both layers should be applied over the outside of the frame with a small inflation blower connected to the inner layer (figure 4-10). To reduce moisture condensation between the layers, position the blower so the intake can draw air from outside the greenhouse. This air has less moisture than the air inside. The blower should operate continuously to inflate the two layers. Placing a metal plate over the intake on the blower will allow you to adjust the pressure developed to about ¼ inch water static pressure. This pressure can be measured with a home-built manometer made from clear plastic tubing (see figure 4-11).

The following guidelines will help you get a better poly installation:

- Cushion or smooth all sharp edges on the greenhouse frame. Foam insulation tape works well.

- Attach the aluminum extrusions with bolts all the way through the frame member. Furring strips should be attached with #8d nails (figure 4-12).

- Choose a quiet morning when the temperature is at least 50°F to install the plastic. Stretch the film just tight enough to remove the wrinkles. The plastic will tighten more as the weather become cooler.

- On days with high winds, keep the greenhouse doors and vents closed and turn the fan on low speed to keep the plastic from flapping.

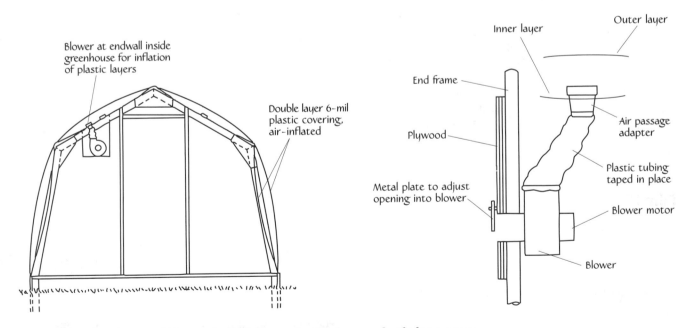

Figure 4-10. Installation of blower for inflating a double-layer polyethylene cover

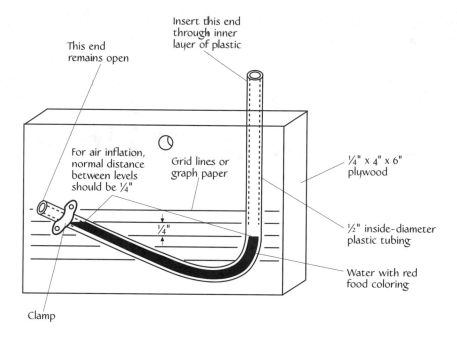

Figure 4-11. Homemade manometer for measuring static pressure

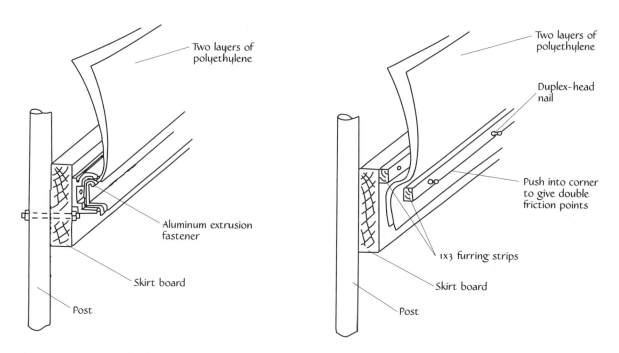

Figure 4-12. Common methods of anchoring polyethylene

CHAPTER 5

Greenhouse Layouts and Equipment for Efficiency

Whether you are planning a new greenhouse or remodeling an older one, efficient use of space is important. One of the most common complaints of home greenhouse gardeners is that they don't have room for all of their plants. This problem can usually be solved by using space more efficiently.

Because new greenhouse space is expensive to build, you should not build a larger greenhouse than you need. Besides, the larger the greenhouse, the greater the operating costs. On the other hand, light is usually the limiting factor in plant growth, especially in the winter. If you fill the greenhouse too full with plants, they will likely not get enough light, which will affect plant growth and result in leggy, weak plants.

You can take advantage of plants' different environmental requirements. Many plants will do well in darker, cooler areas, such as under the benches. Others perform better in brighter, warmer areas closer to the roof. Therefore, your goal should be to design an arrangement of growing space that utilizes the available light and temperature zones and still provides adequate space for walking.

Using Space Inside the Greenhouse

When developing plans for the inside of your greenhouse, you will need to decide how the plants will be grown. You can grow plants directly in the soil or in beds. You can also grow them in containers, either on the ground or on benches.

The Layout

In a well-designed layout, no more than 25% of the space should be used for walkways. As you develop your plans, calculate how much bench, bed, and aisle space you have. You can do this by measuring the benches and calculating their area. Subtract this area from the inside area of the greenhouse to get the amount of walk area.

Use graph paper to try different layouts. Figure 5-1 shows a comparison of bench layouts for a 14-foot-by-18-foot greenhouse. Usable space increases from 61% to 72% when the center bench is shortened and the side benches are connected. Two-foot-wide walkways are adequate in most home greenhouses. Thirty-inch-wide walks may be desirable with some arrangements, and wider aisles are required for wheelchair access (see "Accommodating the Physically and Mentally Challenged," page 16).

The peninsula bench arrangement has become popular with some commercial growers. In larger greenhouses, the narrower side aisles connect to the wider central access aisle. Usable space increases up to 79% in figure 5-1 when peninsula benches are used.

If you grow a lot of potted plants, you may want to consider stairstep benches along the rear wall. This is a good method to use when you want to show off specimen plants. It also results in more sunlight reaching the plants. Construction details are shown in figure 5-2.

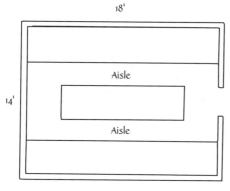

Conventional system – 135 square feet – 61%

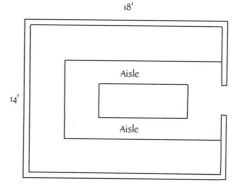

U-shaped layout – 159 square feet – 72%

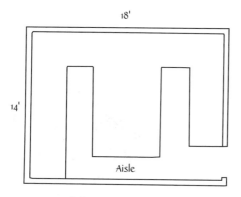

Peninsula layout – 150 square feet – 69%

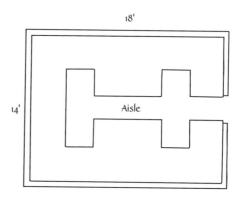

Double peninsula layout – 175 square feet – 79%

Figure 5-1. Bench system layouts for a 14-foot-by-18-foot greenhouse showing alternate arrangements and amount of bench space

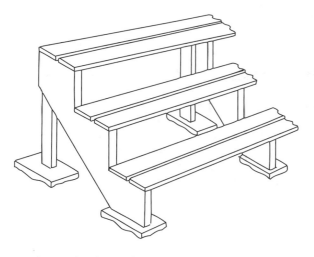

Wooden step benches can be made any size, angle, or height. Besides increasing bench space, they show off plants more effectively.

Figure 5-2. Wooden stairstep bench

Racks and Shelves

The area overhead in the greenhouse offers potential space for plants. Because heat rises, this area is usually warmer than bench level. Overhead plants also receive more light and better air circulation. When utilizing this area, you will need to make provisions for tending the plants. Watering can be done with an extension wand on a garden hose or a permanently installed drip tube irrigation system. (Drip irrigation is discussed in more detail later in this chapter.) Do not place plants so high that they touch the glazing.

By attaching hooks to the glazing bars or attaching pipe or conduit under the bars, you can accommodate hanging baskets. Be careful not to overload the roof.

Most manufacturers offer brackets for attaching shelves or pipes to the greenhouse walls (figure 5-3, page 50). Use long-lasting redwood or cedar for the shelves. Crops grown on shelves may have to be turned frequently to get even growth.

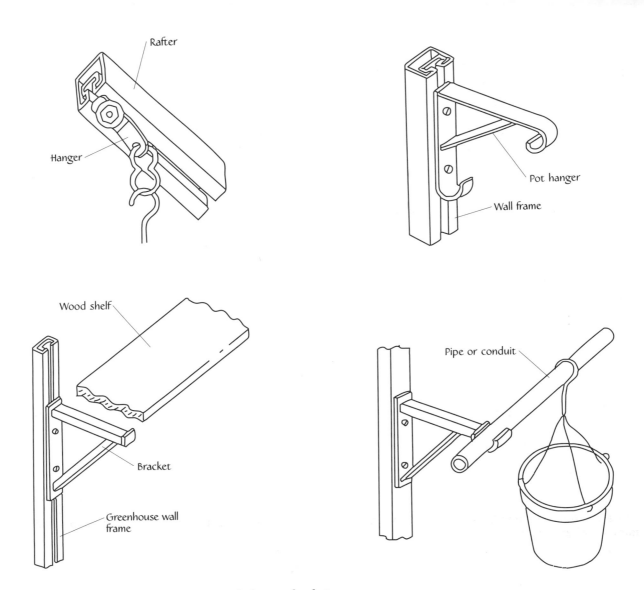

Figure 5-3. Brackets and hangers to support shelves or baskets

Beds

Growing beds can be built as movable boxes, or they can be fixed permanently to the greenhouse floor (figure 5-4). They are often used along the south side glazing to allow more sunlight to reach the plants on the rear benches. Beds work well for tall crops such as tomatoes, cucumbers, or roses, except on the south side, where they will shade the rest of the greenhouse.

A bed worked from one side should be less than 3 feet wide. A center bed can be up to 6 feet wide. Soil should be 8–12 inches deep for good plant growth. Lumber should be decay-resistant so it does not rot. Stakes driven into the ground will support the sides of the bed. The bottom can be lined with a weed mat to keep plant roots from reaching the unsterilized soil below.

Work Areas

Space for potting plants and storing materials and tools must be convenient. If the greenhouse is attached to a garage or shed, you might be able to find work space there. In the greenhouse, you might want to allocate one corner as a potting area. Use an easy-to-clean, solid bench top. Place a rack for tools and pots against the wall behind the bench. Store potting mix in 10- to 20-gallon garbage cans under the bench. You can obtain temporary work space by building a portable shelf that fits between the benches (figure 5-5).

It is convenient to have a sink in the work area for cleaning pots and watering plants. You will need to make provisions to connect the drain to a septic system or sewer line. A sediment trap will help prevent clogging of the plumbing.

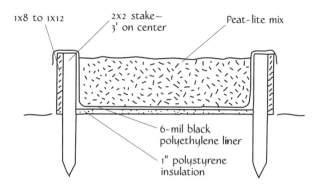

Figure 5-4. Greenhouse bed construction

Labels in figure:
1x8 to 1x12
2x2 stake — 3' on center
Peat-lite mix
6-mil black polyethylene liner
1" polystyrene insulation

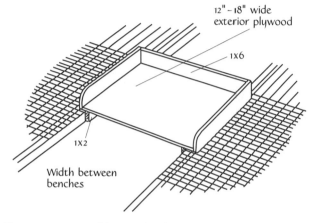

Figure 5-5. Portable potting bench

Labels in figure:
12"–18" wide exterior plywood
1x6
1x2
Width between benches

Benches

Although we seldom think of greenhouse benches as anything more than support for plants, their design can influence how the plants look and grow. Raising the plants up off the floor allows more air movement around them. This increases the carbon dioxide level on the leaf surfaces, which enhances growth, and decreases the moisture that can allow diseases to flourish.

To make it easy to work on plants, build benches so that their surfaces are 30–36 inches above the floor (figure 5-6, page 52). A 30- to 32-inch height is best for benches that will hold flats or pots. Taller benches are better for work areas. The bench width will vary, depending on whether there is an aisle on one or both sides. For one-sided access, a standard width is a normal arm's reach, 32–36 inches. For access from both sides, such as for a bench in the center of the greenhouse, use a width of 60 inches.

Today, most plants are grown in pots or flats. The best bench top material is a galvanized wire mesh or expanded metal that supports the plants and still allows good air circulation (figure 5-7, page 52). A mesh having a 10-gauge or 12 ½-gauge wire thick-

ness will give many years of service without sagging. Mesh is also available with a vinyl coating for a smoother surface and a longer life. Expanded metal is made from a sheet of thin steel that has been slit and then expanded to ten times its original size. A 13-gauge, ¾-inch opening is standard for benches. The diamond-shaped openings give this material better strength and rigidity than the wire mesh. Both materials are available from greenhouse manufacturers or suppliers.

For a temporary bench surface inside the greenhouse, use woven lathing or snow fencing. Available in 4-foot, 5-foot, and 6-foot widths, it can be rolled up when not in use. Reinforced plastic bench tops are also available. Because they cannot corrode or rot, they will last many years.

If you want to grow cut flowers, use a solid-bottom bench with sides. Redwood and cedar are traditional materials that have natural decay resistance. Because of its lower cost, pressure-treated lumber or plywood is commonly used today. Drainage is usually provided by leaving a ⅛-inch to ¼-inch space between the boards or by drilling drain holes in the plywood. The sides that hold the soil in place should be 6–8 inches high and firmly anchored to the bench bottom.

The frame that supports the bench top has to be strong enough to carry the weight of the plants without sagging. Pressure-treated 2x4 lumber, concrete blocks, and pipe are commonly used materials. A maximum spacing of 4 feet between supports is recommended.

Wood frames can be fastened together using exterior plywood gussets and galvanized bolts, screws, or nails. Bracing the benches in both directions or attaching them to the greenhouse frame is necessary for stabilization. The legs should be supported by a concrete walk or concrete patio blocks buried to floor level.

Pipe support frames are easy to build using split pipe clamps and 1¼-inch-diameter galvanized pipe, which is available from greenhouse suppliers. Support for the pipe legs is a concrete pier placed below the floor surface. An easy way to form a pier is to dig a hole large enough for a 10-inch-diameter by 12-inch-long piece of cardboard form tubing. After centering the bench leg, fill the tubing with a dry concrete-sand mix that comes in a bag. Water this with a hose, and in a few hours, the concrete will set. By the next morning, you can attach the cross pipes and then the top.

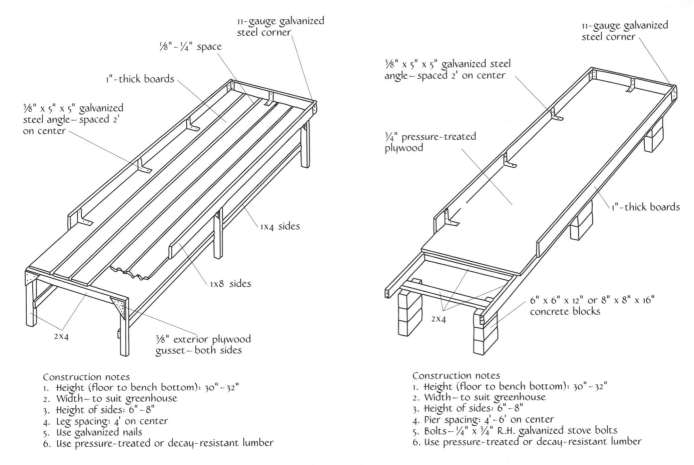

11-gauge galvanized steel corner

⅛"–¼" space

1"-thick boards

⅜" x 5" x 5" galvanized steel angle–spaced 2' on center

1x4 sides

1x8 sides

2x4

⅜" exterior plywood gusset–both sides

11-gauge galvanized steel corner

⅜" x 5" x 5" galvanized steel angle–spaced 2' on center

¾" pressure-treated plywood

1"-thick boards

2x4

6" x 6" x 12" or 8" x 8" x 16" concrete blocks

Construction notes
1. Height (floor to bench bottom): 30"–32"
2. Width–to suit greenhouse
3. Height of sides: 6"–8"
4. Leg spacing: 4' on center
5. Use galvanized nails
6. Use pressure-treated or decay-resistant lumber

Construction notes
1. Height (floor to bench bottom): 30"–32"
2. Width–to suit greenhouse
3. Height of sides: 6"–8"
4. Pier spacing: 4'–6' on center
5. Bolts–¼" x ¾" R.H. galvanized stove bolts
6. Use pressure-treated or decay-resistant lumber

Figure 5-6. Construction of a greenhouse bench with a wooden top

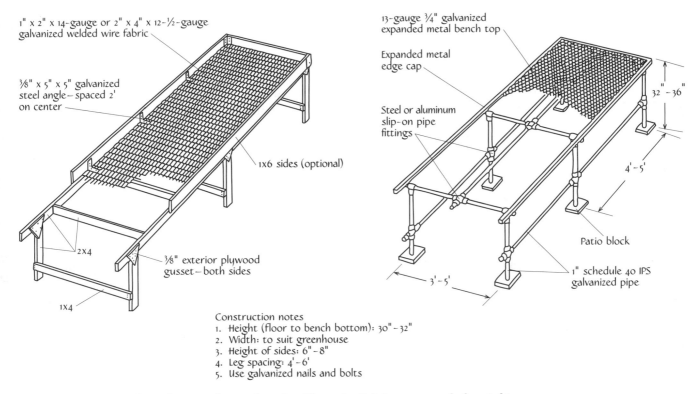

1" x 2" x 14-gauge or 2" x 4" x 12-½-gauge galvanized welded wire fabric

⅜" x 5" x 5" galvanized steel angle–spaced 2' on center

1x6 sides (optional)

2x4

⅜" exterior plywood gusset–both sides

1x4

13-gauge ¾" galvanized expanded metal bench top

Expanded metal edge cap

Steel or aluminum slip-on pipe fittings

32"–36"

4'–5'

Patio block

1" schedule 40 IPS galvanized pipe

3'–5'

Construction notes
1. Height (floor to bench bottom): 30"–32"
2. Width: to suit greenhouse
3. Height of sides: 6"–8"
4. Leg spacing: 4'–6'
5. Use galvanized nails and bolts

Figure 5-7. Construction of a greenhouse bench with a wire fabric or expanded metal top

One system used by many commercial growers consists of a bench top supported on concrete block piers. This system offers flexibility in that the bench can be easily removed for cleaning and the arrangement can be easily changed. To construct a pier, lay one block horizontally on the ground or floor. Set the second block vertically on top of the first one. Place 2x4 lumber across the piers to support the bench top.

As with other parts of the greenhouse, if you want to achieve maximum light inside, use bench materials that are of a light-reflecting color—white or aluminum. Use a good grade of latex or oil paint over a base coat that is compatible with the bench material. It is usually easier to paint wire mesh or expanded metal bench tops with a roller or paint pad.

Space Under Benches

Shade-loving plants, ground covers, and some foliage plants can be grown under benches. This area is characterized by low light levels, high humidity, and cool temperatures. It must be well-drained and kept weed-free. To get better heat and air circulation, the plants can be raised off the floor on pallets or boards placed on patio blocks.

If you want to use the space under benches for growing plants that require high light levels, you will need to install supplemental lighting. Attaching single- or double-tube fluorescent fixtures to the undersides of benches works well. Provisions should be made to keep the fixtures dry.

The amount of supplemental light needed will depend on the type of plants you grow. Experience indicates that you will need about 20 watts per square foot for plants requiring low light levels and 30 watts per square foot for high-light plants.

You can determine the number of fixtures needed by multiplying the area to be lighted by 20 or 30 watts per square foot. Then divide the total by the bulb wattage. For example, if the area under a 3-foot-by-8-foot bench is to be lighted to 20 watts per square foot using 4-foot-long, 40-watt fluorescent tubes, then the number of tubes needed is:

$$\text{No. tubes needed} = \frac{\text{bench area (square feet)} \times 20\text{–}30 \text{ watts/square foot}}{\text{bulb wattage}}$$

$$\text{No. tubes needed} = \frac{(3 \text{ feet} \times 8 \text{ feet}) \times 20 \text{ watts/square foot}}{40 \text{ watts/tube}} = 12 \text{ tubes}$$

This amount can be provided by six double-tube strip fixtures spaced evenly underneath the bench.

When installing artificial lighting, be sure that the electrical circuits are not overloaded and the fixtures are properly grounded. One 20-amp circuit will supply electricity for up to forty 4-foot tubes or twenty 8-foot tubes. Use cool white or warm white bulbs or grow lamps. Place a time clock in the circuit to control the daylength. One added benefit to this system is that it provides heat to the bench above and may provide a good area for propagation. Supplemental lighting is discussed in much greater detail in chapter 6.

Floors and Walkways

Soil Floors

Many options exist for the floor of your greenhouse. Factors to consider when selecting the floor material include use, drainage, appearance, smoothness, and cost.

If you are planning to grow crops directly in the soil, then a soil with high organic content and good drainage is desirable. Most soils can be amended to achieve these qualities, but starting with a loam or sandy loam makes it easier. If you have a light clay soil or a very sandy soil, it may be better to remove the soil to a depth of 8–12 inches and replace it with good-quality garden loam.

To increase the organic matter in the soil, add materials such as peat moss, rotted animal manure, compost, leaf mold, or bark. Drainage can be improved by adding sand, perlite, or vermiculite.

Before growing your first crop, have a soil test done to determine nutrient levels. Most cooperative extension offices and land-grant university plant science departments provide this service.

Other Floor Surfaces

If you are not growing plants in the soil, then the floor surface—at least where you walk—should have good footing. Drainage is important to handle excess water from irrigation. The base should be dug down to 6–8 inches below final grade. Remove topsoil and subsoil.

Install a layer of weed barrier to separate drainage material from the subsoil and to keep weeds from growing into the soil below. This material is perforated so water can percolate through. It is available from most garden centers and greenhouse suppliers. Fill the area over the weed mat with gravel or small stone, leaving enough room for the floor surface material.

The floor surface material can be placed over the whole floor area or just in the walkways, leaving the area under the benches with gravel or stone for better drainage.

The following floor and walkway surface materials are used in home greenhouses (figure 5-8). Each has its own advantages and disadvantages.

1. Peastone and trap rock — These are low-cost materials that give good drainage. They may become dislodged over time and require reshaping.

2. Brick — Bricks are very durable and come in several colors and textures. Used bricks may be available. Avoid glazed bricks, as they may become slippery when wet or covered with algae. Interesting patterns can be obtained when the bricks are installed. A compacted base of sand or stone dust underneath will keep the surface level.

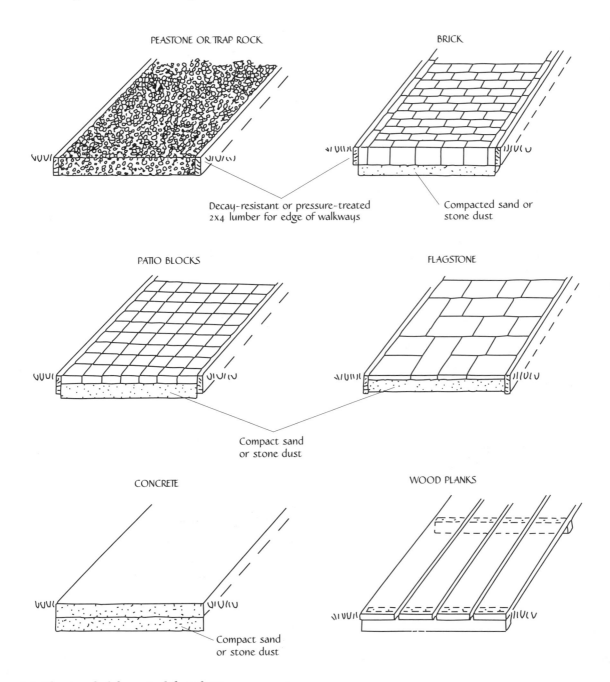

Figure 5-8. Floor and aisle material options

3. Patio blocks — Available in square, rectangular, or decorative shapes, these make a good surface. Lay out the pattern on graph paper before purchasing the materials. A good base of compacted sand or stone dust is needed.

4. Flagstone — Mined from quarries, this material is available in rectangular or random shapes. Use a minimum thickness of 1 inch to prevent shifting of the stone. A compacted base is needed. Areas between stones can be filled with sand or stone dust.

5. Concrete — Concrete can be placed in the walkways or over the whole floor surface. A 4-inch thickness is recommended for strength. Use an isolation joint around the perimeter and control joints about every 6 feet. The surface should be wood-floated or brushed to prevent slipping.

Because such small quantities are needed for a home greenhouse (less than 2 cubic yards), this material is difficult to obtain from concrete suppliers, as most have trucks that carry 7 yards or more. In some areas of the country, contractors have on-site mixers that will provide just the quantity you need.

You can rent a power mixer to mix your own concrete. A mix consisting of one part cement, 2½ parts sand, and 3½ parts ½-inch to 1-inch stone by volume will give a watertight floor with a good wear surface. Add enough water so the mix "flows" easily but is not too "soupy," which will reduce its strength. Unglazed ceramic tile could be adhered to the surface of the concrete once it is dry. Use a waterproof mastic.

If concrete is installed over the whole floor area, then install a floor drain (figure 5-9). This will allow removal of excess water. The floor should be sloped to the drain, and the drain should have a settling basin to collect soil and other solids. The drain can be piped to the outside or to a dry well.

6. Wood — Walkways can be made of decay-resistant or pressure-treated wood. Use 2x6 or 2x8 lumber and allow ⅛ inch between boards for drainage. Crosspieces of 2x4 lumber spaced 3 feet apart under the boards will give good support.

Labor-saving Equipment

The basic tools needed to operate a greenhouse include a trowel, a knife, pruning shears, pails, a watering can, and a hose. Hand tools and mechanized equipment can be added to save time and handle specialized jobs. Greenhouse suppliers sell most of the equipment described below. You can find them listed under "Greenhouse Equipment and Supplies" in the yellow pages of the telephone directory. A partial list of suppliers is provided in appendix B on page 131.

Growing Media Preparation Equipment

Ready-to-use growing media is available in many mixes. Today, most growers use a soilless mix. Soilless mixes contain peat, vermiculite, perlite, polystyrene, bark, lime, fertilizers, and a wetting agent. They come in 3- or 4-cubic-foot bags, either compressed or loose. A 4-cubic-foot bag will fill about 350 4-inch pots, 120 6-inch pots, or 35 standard flats.

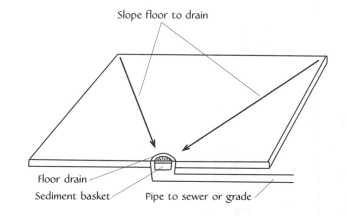

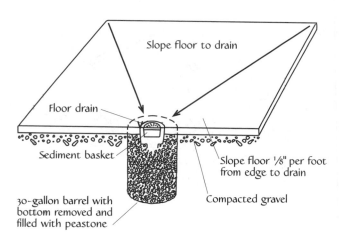

Figure 5-9. Types of floor drains

Some growers still prefer a soil mix. One common mix is ⅓ soil, ⅓ sand, and ⅓ peat. The soil component must be prepared and pasteurized before it is used. A soil shredder (figure 5-10) can be used to prepare topsoil, loosen baled peat, and mix the components. Small shredders are available with electric motors or gas engines.

If you do not have a shredder, a homemade screen will work well to remove stones, clumps, and roots (figure 5-11). It can be made from a 2x4 lumber frame covered with ½-inch-by-½-inch galvanized wire mesh. Use fence staples to hold the screen in place. It can be designed to fold for storage when not in use.

A small portable concrete mixer (figure 5-12) makes an excellent soil and peatlite mixer. A ½-horsepower electric motor or 2-horsepower gas engine can be used to power it.

Pasteurize soil before using it to kill disease organisms, pests, and weeds. Heating is the most common and effective method used. Maintaining a soil temperature of 140–180°F for 30 minutes will destroy most disease organisms and weeds. The best results are obtained when the soil or mix is loose and slightly moist at the time of pasteurization. To conserve energy, pasteurize only the soil. The soil can then be mixed with peat, vermiculite, perlite, or other disease-free components. An electric oven or microwave works well for pasteurizing small amounts of soil. Small commercial soil pasteurizers process ⅛ and ¼ cubic yard per batch (figure 5-13). They operate on electricity and use from 6 to 12 kilowatt hours per cubic yard.

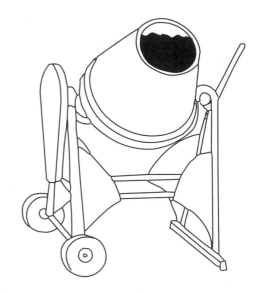

Figure 5-12. Concrete or soil mixer

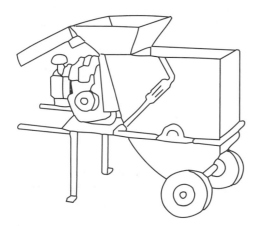

Figure 5-10. Soil shredder

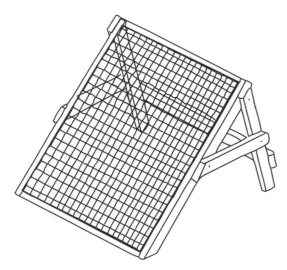

Figure 5-11. Homemade soil screen

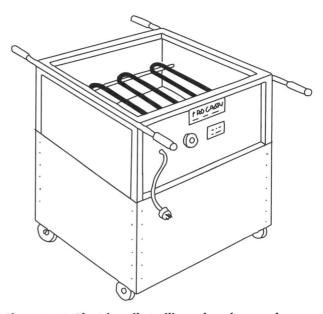

Figure 5-13. Electric soil sterilizer placed over a homemade wooden soil cart

It is important that soil or mix be stored in containers or in an area where it will not be recontaminated. Plastic garbage containers, especially those with wheels (figure 5-14), are convenient to handle and can be stored under the work bench. Commercially prepared peat-vermiculite mixes are usually stored in their shipping containers. Keep the bags closed when not in use to keep the mix from drying out. A mix that has dried out can be easily rewetted with warm water.

Planting Aids

Battery-powered and electric seeders aid in seeding (see figure 3-6, page 19). Seed is poured into the seeder scoop, and the scoop is held over the bed or flat. The unit vibrates to feed the seed evenly. Some seeders have different drums that fit in the bottom of the seed hopper to accommodate different seed sizes.

A dibble can speed transplanting (see figure 3-6, page 19). A single peg will make one hole at a time. Dibble boards that fit over a flat and punch multiple holes at a time are available from greenhouse suppliers. You can also make your own from a piece of plywood and wooden dowels.

Materials Handling Equipment

Carts are handy in the greenhouse when materials need to be moved (figure 5-15). Look for large wheels for easy rolling, and make sure the cart is narrow enough to go through the door and between the benches. A wheelbarrow is handy for moving soil and materials around the garden and yard.

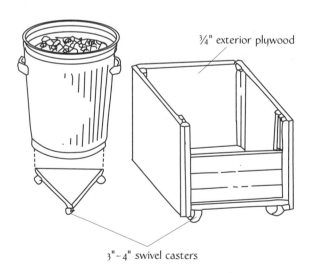

Figure 5-14. Storage bins for growing mix

Pesticide Application Equipment and Storage

The effectiveness of an insecticide or fungicide depends to a large extent on the thoroughness of the application. A hand atomizer (figure 5-16, page 58) is commonly used to apply insecticides to small areas. They are available in capacities from ½ pint to 2 quarts. This type of sprayer is inexpensive, so you can purchase several, one for each type of spray material. Many materials are available in applicator-type containers.

Compressed air sprayers (figure 5-16, page 58) provide better atomization and spray coverage, especially to the undersides of leaves. They are available in capacities from 1 to 5 gallons. These sprayers are not equipped with an agitator, so you must shake them frequently when applying wettable powders.

A knapsack sprayer (figure 5-16, page 58) is used for larger areas. It is made from lightweight polyethylene and holds about 4 gallons of spray material. The

Figure 5-15. Carts and wheelbarrows for moving materials

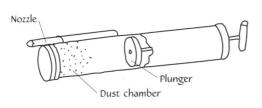

PLUNGER DUSTER

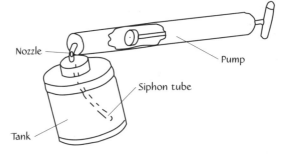

INTERMITTENT HAND SPRAYER

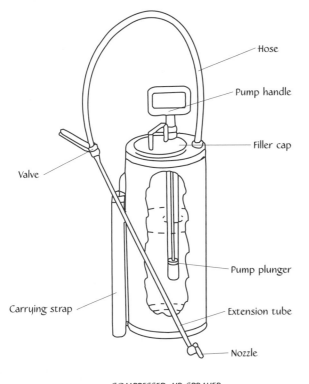

COMPRESSED AIR SPRAYER

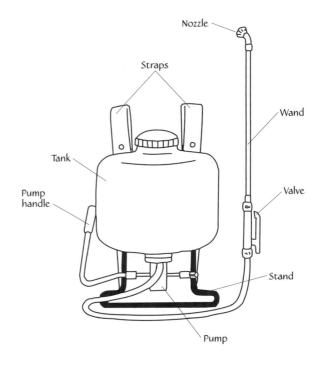

KNAPSACK SPRAYER

Figure 5-16. Pesticide applicators

hand-operated pump maintains pressure, and the spray pattern is easily adjusted.

Pesticides available to the hobbyist have a low toxicity to humans and a short persistence (the length of time they are effective when applied to crops). Still, they should be stored in a locked cabinet to keep them away from children and animals. A small, locked utility cabinet is generally sufficient (figure 5-17). The cabinet should be located where liquid materials will not be subject to freezing or high temperatures.

Personal Protective Equipment

The peat and vermiculite in soilless mixes can be very dusty. Pollen and dry fertilizer can cause irritation. A disposable mechanical filter respirator that covers the mouth and nose will provide protection from irritants (figure 5-18). Models approved by NIOSH (National Institute of Occupational Safety and Health) have two elastic straps in back for a better seal and are assigned a number preceded by a "TC." *These should not be used with pesticides.* Nuisance dust masks, usually distinguished by their single strap, should not be used because of the poor seal obtained around the face.

Figure 5-17. Store chemicals in a locked cabinet to keep them away from children and animals

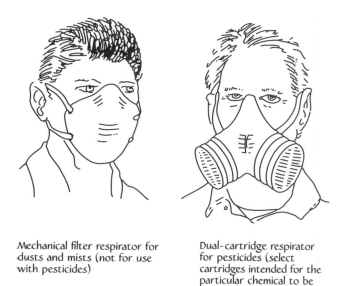

Mechanical filter respirator for dusts and mists (not for use with pesticides)

Dual-cartridge respirator for pesticides (select cartridges intended for the particular chemical to be used)

Figure 5-18. Use an appropriate respirator when working with soil, growing mixes, fertilizers, and pesticides

The label on some chemicals specifies that a respirator be used during mixing and application. Chemical cartridge respirators provide protection against harmful gases and vapors (figure 5-18). The cartridge should be designed for the particular hazard you are facing. The cartridges screw onto the front of the mask and should be replaced based on the manufacturer's recommendations. These respirators can also be equipped with particulate filters for dusts and mists.

Use safety goggles when you need protection from liquid chemical splashes or spray materials.

Gloves will protect your hands from chemicals and soil and when using tools. Disposable plastic gloves are good for handling fertilizers and pesticides. Leather gloves are necessary when working with tools.

A lightweight apron will keep your clothes clean when you are working in the greenhouse. A disposable TYVEK protective suit will prevent chemicals from saturating your clothing when you are spraying.

Monitoring Instruments

You should have several thermometers as part of your equipment supply (figure 5-19). An accurate wall thermometer should be located out of direct sunlight to indicate the greenhouse temperature and to check thermostat accuracy. Select a maximum-minimum thermometer when you would like to

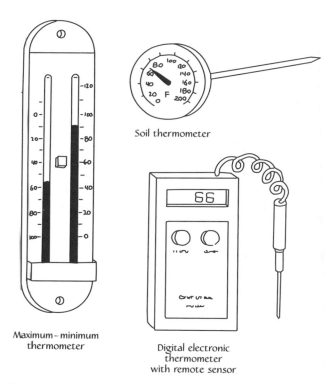

Soil thermometer

Maximum–minimum thermometer

Digital electronic thermometer with remote sensor

Figure 5-19. Common types of thermometers used in a home greenhouse

know what happens in the greenhouse overnight. It indicates the highest and lowest temperatures recorded since the last time it was reset.

A soil thermometer is handy if you are doing propagation or heating a root zone. The sensor is at the end of a probe that is placed in the soil.

Electronic thermometers are available from a number of sources. They operate on a small battery and give a digital display of the temperature reading. Some come equipped with interchangeable sensors for both air and soil readings.

A pocket magnifier is handy to check for the presence of insects or disease. Magnification powers from 5X to 20X will suffice in most situations.

Insect monitoring cards (sticky cards) are used by most commercial growers to indicate the insect population level (figure 5-20). These 3-inch-by-5-inch cards should be placed in the plant canopy. Inspect cards and count insects on a regular basis, and keep a record of the results. Yellow cards are best for attracting winged aphids, fungus gnat adults, leaf miners, and leaf hoppers. Blue cards work well on thrips.

An accurate scale is necessary for weighing fertilizers and pesticides. A 32-ounce-capacity scale is adequate for most home greenhouse operations.

Soil testing for nutrient levels is a job best left to professionals who have accurate equipment. County cooperative extension offices or a plant science department in the nearest land-grant university can usually provide this service for a small fee. They will also make recommendations based on the crop you plan to grow. Reasonably accurate home test kits for pH (acidity) and electrical conductivity (nutrient salt level) are available.

Time clocks and timers are needed to operate lighting and watering equipment (figure 5-21). Both mechanical and electronic models are available. Intervals of 7 days, 24 hours, 1 hour, or 1 minute are common. Equipment can be operated for any part of the

interval or for several cycles within the interval. Often a timer and time clock are needed to get the right sequence. They should have an electric ground wire for use in the greenhouse.

An example of a single timer installation is a 24-hour time clock set to turn supplemental lighting on at

Low-cost 24-hour timer with two on-off settings; unit should have ground wire for use in greenhouse

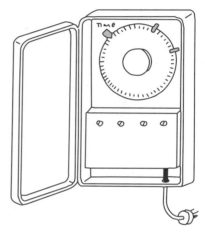

24-hour or 7-day time clock or interval timer

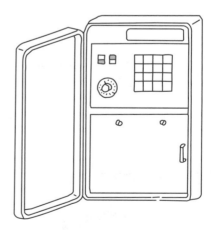

Electronic programmable timers are more accurate and have additional features

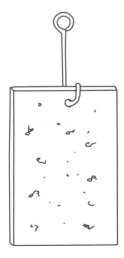

Figure 5-20. Sticky trap (yellow or blue) for monitoring insect activity

Figure 5-21. Time clocks and interval timers can control lighting or watering systems

6 P.M. and off at 10 P.M. to provide 4 hours of extra light during the winter. Low-cost appliance timers work well for this purpose, as they have a capacity up to 15 amps and have intervals of 15 minutes.

Watering Systems

If you operate a small home greenhouse with a variety of plants and containers, automatic watering is neither necessary nor desirable. On the other hand, if you grow blocks of the same size plant and you work away from home all day, an automated irrigation system may be necessary.

The area of greenhouse technology with the greatest amount of innovation over the last few years is watering systems. Most advances are due to a greater use of plastics. If you look through a greenhouse supplier's catalog, you will see many pages of nozzles, drippers, hydroponic equipment, and controls.

A brief discussion of each type of system follows. Details on individual components are not included. For more information, see *Water and Nutrient Management for Greenhouses*, NRAES–56, which is listed in "Other Publications from NRAES" at the back of this book.

Mist Systems

A mist system will allow you to root a whole range of plants, both woody and soft tissue (figure 5-22). Although cuttings of some plants like geranium and coleus need only a humid environment to root, other plants need a constant film of water on their foliage to prevent them from wilting and dying before new roots form. This condition can be provided with a continuous misting of the foliage, but large amounts of water can cool the cuttings and the rooting medium to a temperature that inhibits rooting. Intermittent misting, on the other hand, uses very little water and is less chilling.

In the greenhouse, cuttings are usually rooted in flats of propagating mix on a bench. It is especially important that the flats have drainage to allow excess water to run off. Within the flat, the root zone should be kept at a steady temperature of 70–75°F. This is best accomplished with some sort of bottom heat system. (Heating systems are discussed further in chapter 6.)

Most cuttings root best at a daytime air temperature of 70–80°F and a night temperature about 10° lower. Higher temperatures tend to increase water loss from the leaves and promote bud development ahead of root development.

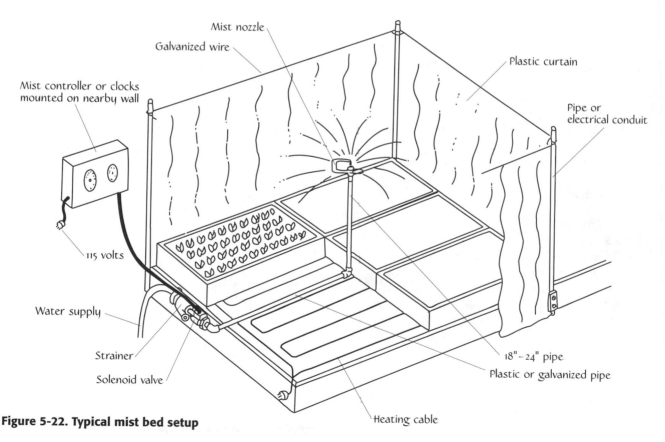

Figure 5-22. Typical mist bed setup

The objective is to keep the leaf surface wet without applying so much water that the root zone is cold, so a fine mist is best. Several deflector-type misting nozzles on the market will operate at 30–50 pounds per square inch (psi) water pressure, which is the level usually found in the home. The mist is formed by a thin jet of water striking a flat surface. For bench and bed widths of 3–5 feet, use a nozzle that has an output of 5–10 gallons per hour. Where more than one nozzle is needed, space them 3–5 feet apart on the supply pipe to give uniform water coverage.

For the supply line, galvanized pipe is better than PVC or polyethylene plastic pipe, as it does not sag when suspended over the bench. If the nozzles are to be tapped directly into the pipe, use the ¾-inch-diameter size; otherwise, ½-inch pipe is adequate. To prevent dripping after the water shuts off, pitch the line downward slightly from the supply end, and install a check valve on the low end of the pipe. The water supply to the mist line can be permanent or installed using garden hose. To prevent the fine holes in the nozzles from clogging, install a 100- to 150-mesh strainer in the supply line before the nozzles.

An electric solenoid valve is needed to turn the water on and off. The valve should be the type that normally closes with a snap action operation, and it should have the same voltage as the time clock or controller you are planning to use. A 24-volt system is safer than a 115-volt one.

A number of timer control systems have been developed to automate mist systems so that they apply the right amount of water. The Mist-A-Matic control simulates a leaf in the propagating bed. It consists of a piece of stainless steel screen attached to an electric switch that is placed in the bed. When the screen is dry, it activates the switch and the solenoid valve in the water supply line. When it gets wet, it gets heavier and turns the valve off. On sunny days when evaporation is greater, the system cycles on more frequently.

Time clocks can also be used to turn the mist system on and off. A day-night clock makes one cycle every 24 hours. It is easy to set the trippers to activate an interval timer in the morning and turn it off during the late afternoon. For most applications, a cycle time of 6 seconds of mist every 6 minutes is sufficient. A timer that allows you to change the interval to meet varying needs is best.

Several companies have assembled day-night and interval time clocks into a plastic or metal box. These mist controllers are completely wired and ready to plug into an electric outlet. The only connection is the wire needed to activate the solenoid valve. The cost for the assembled unit is about the same as the cost of buying the two time clocks separately.

The bench area containing the mist system should be isolated from adjacent growing areas. Clear film plastic attached to a suspended wire makes a convenient barrier.

The day-night time clock should be set to come on shortly after sunrise and shut off before sunset. On warm nights, the system can be operated all night to keep moisture on the leaf surfaces.

Although it would seem that the high relative humidity and wet leaf and soil surfaces would provide an excellent environment for disease development, generally speaking, disease is not a problem. The reason for this may be that the mist is constantly washing any disease spores off the plants. It is imperative, though, that clean, healthy plant material be used and that sanitary conditions be maintained in the greenhouse.

Overhead Watering Systems

Overhead watering systems consist of a filtered water supply, valves, a control system, supply pipe, and nozzles (figure 5-23). They can be set up in the greenhouse on a bench or outside in a growing bed.

Water is applied to the plants from overhead nozzles that create a circular pattern. The nozzles are spaced along the supply pipe at regular intervals. The pipe can be placed on the bench or floor and risers used to support the nozzles above the plants. An alternate method is to hang the pipe from the greenhouse frame above the plants. A minimum water pressure of 20 pounds per square inch (psi) is needed to get good distribution.

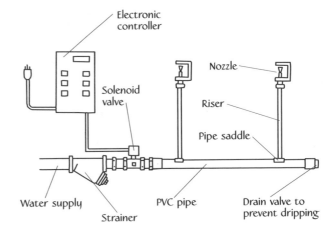

Figure 5-23. Automated irrigation system

Nozzles are available in many gallon-per-minute (gpm) outputs and in pattern diameters ranging from 3 feet to 80 feet. Nozzles also come with either full-circle or part-circle patterns. Part-circle patterns are used along the side or at the end of a bench.

The first consideration when designing a system is to determine the water supply available. A ½-inch pipe will supply about 5 gpm, a ¾-inch pipe about 8 gpm, and a 1-inch pipe about 12 gpm at 30 psi water pressure. You can also check this by measuring the water collected in a pail for 15 seconds. Pour the collected water into a gallon bottle to determine the amount collected. Multiply this amount by four to get gallons per minute. For example, if you collect 2 gallons in 15 seconds, the water supply is 8 gpm (2 gallons x 4 = 8 gpm).

Next select a nozzle that has a coverage about 10% larger than the bench width or area to be irrigated. Most nozzle types are available in several outputs (in gallons per minute). Output is changed by varying the nozzle hole size.

A nozzle spacing of at least 50% of the spray diameter will give fairly uniform coverage (figure 5-24). For example, if the spray diameter is 6 feet, the nozzles should be placed 3 feet apart along the pipe. To calculate the number of nozzles that can be fed from your water supply, divide the gallons per minute by the output of the nozzle. For example, if your hose bibb yields 8 gpm and the nozzle output is 1 gpm, you can supply up to eight nozzles on the line. If you need to cover more area, you can either select a nozzle with less output and operate the system longer or make two zones that are operated independently.

Galvanized iron pipe is better for mounting nozzles that will be suspended above the plants. If the pipe will be supported on the bench or ground, PVC pipe can be used. A short piece of garden hose will connect the nozzle boom to the hose bibb. A filter should be placed in the supply line to catch any particulate matter that could block the small nozzle openings. A 100-mesh screen is commonly used.

For manual control, the hose bibb will provide the shutoff. For automatic control, a solenoid valve and controller are needed.

Trickle Watering Systems

Trickle systems are used when you do not want to wet the foliage. Water is supplied at a low pressure (8–20 psi) over a longer period of time. With this system, you can realize a savings of up to 80% in water quantity, because only the root zone area is watered.

Several trickle systems are available. Drip tubes, also know as leader or spaghetti tubes, are widely used for pot watering. This system consists of small-diameter plastic capillary tubes connected to a polyethylene supply pipe (figure 5-25). Drop-in

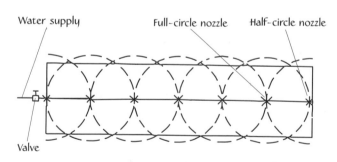

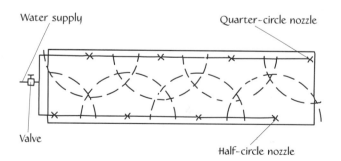

Figure 5-24. Layouts for automatic watering systems

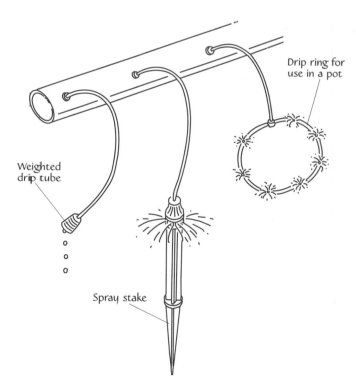

Figure 5-25. Drip-tube irrigation systems

weights hold the tubes in the pots. Some weights are available with a shutoff so that water flow to an individual pot can be stopped when the pot is removed. The diameter and length of the tube determine its water flow rate. Tubes are available with 0.036- to 0.076-inch diameters and 12- to 72-inch lengths.

Low-flow porous or perforated tapes are designed for watering benches, beds, and capillary mats (figure 5-26). Water oozes from seams, tiny holes, or emitters at a very low flow rate. Uniform distribution is achieved over long lengths by using double chambers or pressure-compensating emitters. Output can be continuous along the tape, or emitters can be spaced at intervals of 4 inches, 8 inches, 12 inches, and so on. Flow rates of 0.2–2.0 gpm per 100 feet are common. Water filtration with a 150- to 200-mesh screen is needed to keep the water outlets from clogging. Drip irrigation systems can be a good method for accurate soil moisture control in many greenhouse crops. In addition to saving water, they reduce the potential for groundwater pollution.

Capillary Mats

An alternative to spaghetti tubes for watering potted plants is the capillary mat (figure 5-27). With this system, water from the mat reaches the roots by capillary action through holes in the bottom of the pot. The system needs to be set up properly to get good results:

- The bench should be level to prevent water from draining to one point.

- A layer of black polyethylene plastic should be placed on top of the bench to prevent dripping and to spread the water uniformly.

- A layer of capillary mat material should be placed on top of the plastic. Mats are usually made from a fabric composed of natural and synthetic fibers. Some mats come with the plastic attached to the bottom. Some have perforated plastic attached to the top to reduce evaporation and algae growth.

- The mat should not extend over the edge of the bench; otherwise, water will run onto the floor.

- A drip hose system should be placed on top of the mat to distribute the water. Lines should be 12–16 inches apart.

- A solenoid valve and timer should be used to keep the mat wet. Before placing the pots, wet the mat thoroughly.

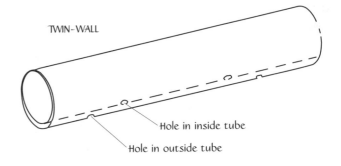

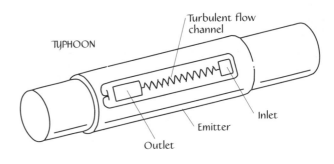

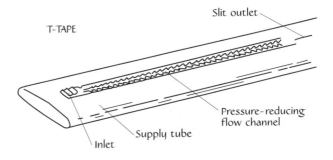

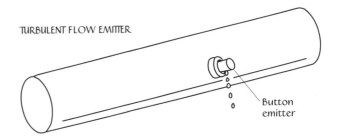

Figure 5-26. Low-flow tape and emitter watering systems

- The pots should have a hole in the bottom so that contact is made between the mat and the soil.

- Initially, the soil in the container may need to be soaked from overhead.

- The mat should be kept wet at all times.

- If algae develops, the mat should be turned over.

The capillary mat system provides even moisture, which contributes to uniform crop growth. It allows you to use different-size pots and to easily vary spacing. Leaf spotting from overhead watering is eliminated.

Hydroponics and Soilless Culture Systems

Hydroponics involves growing plants in a medium other than soil using essential plant elements dissolved in water. True hydroponics, as defined by Dr. W. F. Gericke of California in the 1930s, is a system where plants are supported above a container of nutrient solution. Some of the roots are submerged in the solution; others are exposed to the air. Since that time, many variations and hybrid systems have been developed.

A common fallacy is that you can grow better plants using hydroponics. This is generally not true. If optimum conditions are given to plants grown in soil, yield and quality will be the same.

There are some advantages and disadvantages to hydroponic systems that need to be considered.

Advantages of Hydroponics

1. Greater plant density — With some types of hydroponic systems, plants can be spaced as they grow. For example, lettuce plants grown in troughs are initially transplanted at a 3-inch spacing. When the leaves start to touch, the troughs are moved to a 4-inch spacing, then 5-inch, and then 6-inch. During this time, every other plant may be moved to another empty trough. A final spacing of 6 inches by 6 inches is achieved at that time. Yields are several times greater than those achieved with a fixed-spacing system. There are some systems under development that mechanically space the plants every day.

2. Reduced water consumption — Some hydroponic systems recycle the nutrient solution by pumping it from a tank to the crop area. The solution then returns to the tank by gravity. Less water is needed, and the chance of polluting the groundwater is all but eliminated.

3. Reduced incidence of disease and insects — Hydroponic greenhouses tend to be cleaner than greenhouses that use soil. However, if a waterborne disease is introduced, it can be transmitted to all the plants very rapidly.

Disadvantages of Hydroponics

1. Increased initial investment — It costs more to set up a hydroponic or soilless system because of the added materials and equipment. Soilless mixes are relatively expensive. Other expenses include pumps, tanks, controls, and a support system.

2. Higher energy costs — Operation of the pumps, lights, and controls increases the electric bill.

3. Greater technical skill needed — Mixing and maintaining the nutrient solution with the proper balance requires an understanding of chemistry. To overcome this, some growers change the nutrient solution once a week.

Crops Suitable for Hydroponics

Almost any crop can be grown hydroponically, but different support systems may be needed for different crops. Leaf lettuce, tomatoes, cucumbers, peppers, watercress, and some herbs are some common commercially grown crops.

Types of Hydroponics Systems

Many of the systems discussed below are illustrated in figure 5-28 on page 66.

1. Sand/stone culture — This technique can be used to grow almost any kind of plant. It consists of plastic-lined troughs or beds that slope to a drain. Sand, peastone, or trap rock is the support medium. Seedlings are transplanted directly into the medium and watered several times a day with the nutrient solution.

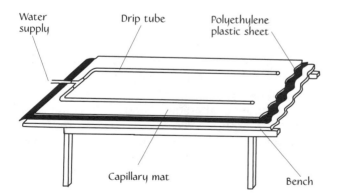

Figure 5-27. Capillary mat irrigation system

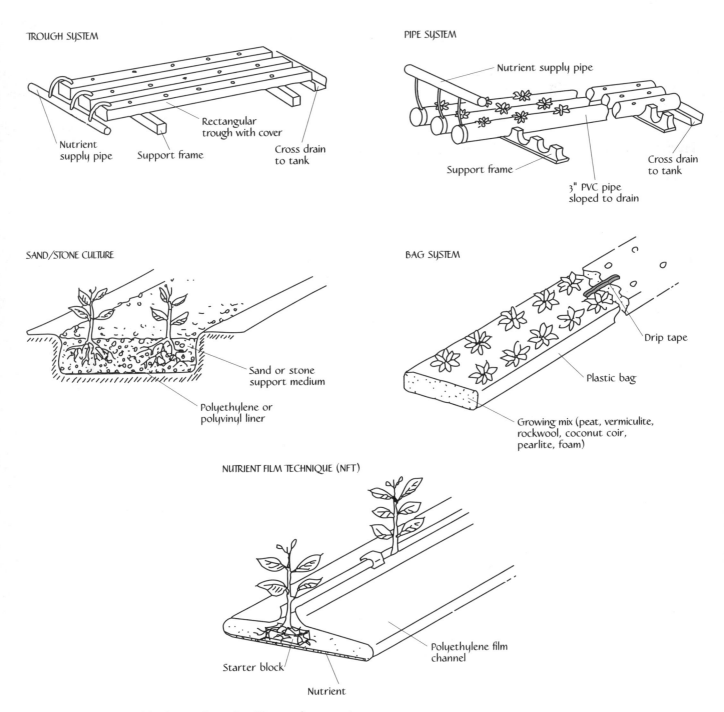

Figure 5-28. Typical hydroponic and soilless culture systems

2. Troughs or pipes — Open or closed troughs are commonly used for lettuce, spinach, and herbs. The troughs may contain just the nutrient solution, or they may be filled with peat moss, vermiculite, or perlite. The troughs slope about 1%, so nutrient solution that is dribbled in at the high end drains to a sump at the low end. The liquid may flow continuously or intermittently.

Troughs are about 3 inches wide by 2 inches high and made of PVC plastic. A cover is usually available to keep light away from the nutrient solution. Seedlings are inserted through holes in the cover into the nutrient solution. An alternate system uses standard PVC drain pipe with a 2-inch or 3-inch diameter. Hole spacing and size vary depending on the crop. For example, lettuce requires a ¾-inch-diameter hole spaced 6 inches on center. A galvanized steel frame supports the troughs or pipes and allows for adjustable spacing.

3. Nutrient film technique (NFT) — Developed by Dr. Allen Cooper in England, NFT uses channels formed out of thin, black film plastic. The channels are placed on a floor or bench that slopes to one end of the greenhouse. Nutrient solution is supplied from plastic tubing at one end of the channel and drains into a sump at the other end. Seedlings in pots, polyethylene bags, or grow blocks are placed in the channel. This system has been used mainly with tall crops such as tomatoes and cucumbers, but it can be adapted to most plants.

4. Pond system — With this system, a plastic-lined pond 8–12 inches deep is formed in the floor of the greenhouse and filled with nutrient solution. Low-profile plants such as lettuce, spinach, and strawberries are transplanted from a nursery area into holes in polystyrene rafts about 2 feet square. The rafts float on the nutrient solution. Spacing is achieved by removing some of the plants from the raft and moving them to an empty raft.

5. Ebb-and-flood — With this system, periodically flooded trays are used to grow lettuce, spinach, herbs, and flowering potted plants. Trays are made from molded plastic, waterproof plywood, or aluminum. They are mounted on a steel tubing frame with a slight slope to a drain. Nutrient solution from a tank on the floor is pumped up to flood the tray to a depth of about 1 inch for 10 minutes and then drained back into the tank. This may be done several times a day, depending on the weather and the size of the plants.

6. Bags — This modified hydroponic system is easy to set up. Plastic bags filled with peat-vermiculite mix, rockwool, bark, or foam are placed on the floor end-to-end. A drip tube system is placed through the top of the bags for irrigation and feeding. Seedlings are placed into the bags through holes cut in the top. An overhead wire support system is needed for crops such as tomatoes and cucumbers. The bags are good for several crops if no disease develops.

7. Aeroponics — With aeroponics, plants are supported through a plastic cover over a closed tank. Nutrients are intermittently supplied to the roots in a fine mist or fog.

All the above systems require tanks, pumps, piping, and controls. For small systems, plastic or fiberglass tanks work well. They are available in many sizes.

A small submersible pump placed in the bottom of the tank is all that is needed to move the solution. Select one made for chemical solutions, as fertilizer salts will corrode a pump made for use with water.

PVC or polyethylene piping is good for handling nutrient solutions. Pipe with a ½-inch or ¾-inch diameter is adequate for small systems.

A time clock or timer can provide the control needed. It should be able to provide the necessary interval.

For additional information on soilless culture, see the references section at the back of this book or contact the Hydroponics Society of America (contact information is included in the references section).

Fertilizing Systems

If you grow plants in soilless growing mixes, you have to provide all the essential nutrients. This is done in three ways: 1) adding slow-release granular fertilizer when the soilless mix is made, 2) mixing liquid fertilizer in water and then feeding the plants every week or two, or 3) mixing a weak fertilizer solution and feeding the plants every time you water.

Preparing liquid fertilizer can be a chore if you have a lot of plants. It means mixing watering can after watering can of solution. An alternative is to purchase a fertilizer injector to feed the plants automatically.

The key to these injectors is the proportioner, a simple device that introduces concentrated fertilizer into the hose or pipeline that supplies the greenhouse with water. The simplest of these devices, and the most suitable for small home greenhouses, uses the Venturi principle, which was first observed and identified by eighteenth-century Italian physicist G. B. Venturi. The Venturi principle works by creating a pressure difference between the container holding the fertilizer solution and the water line. As water passes through a constricted area of the injector, its velocity increases, creating a vacuum. A small tube connected to the injector allows the fertilizer to be siphoned into the hose, where it mixes with the water before reaching the plants (figure 5-29, page 68).

Selecting a Proportioner

Injectors should be made of brass, stainless steel, or plastic to resist corrosive fertilizers. The Hyponex Siphon Mixer (and others of the same type) is a good

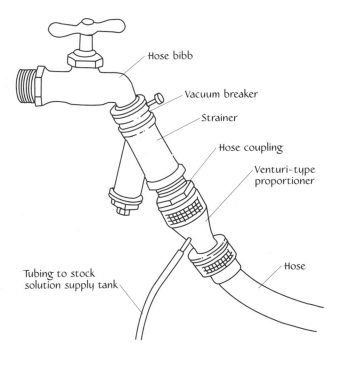

Hose bibb

Vacuum breaker

Strainer

Hose coupling

Venturi-type proportioner

Tubing to stock solution supply tank

Hose

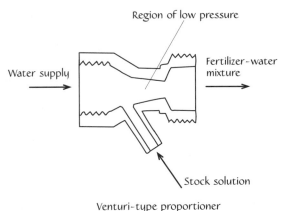

Region of low pressure

Water supply

Fertilizer-water mixture

Stock solution

Venturi-type proportioner

Figure 5-29. Fertilizer proportioner installation

choice. Designed to fasten to a hose for easy installation and use, it is available at many garden centers and greenhouse suppliers. It currently costs around $10. Nearly all such mixers come with a dilution ratio of 1:15, meaning that you will mix 1 gallon of fertilizer concentrate with 15 gallons of water.

Water pressure fluctuations, common in homes supplied by wells with pumps, can cause the feed rate to fluctuate, and the hose length and diameter can alter specified ratios. Tests conducted at the University of Kentucky found ratio fluctuations as wide as from 1:10 to 1:17. Although this seems like a lot of variation, nursery operators continue to grow excellent plants using siphon proportioners. So you need not worry about your plants getting too much or too little food.

If you are nonetheless concerned, some clever inventions will, for a price, solve the water pressure fluctuation problem. The M-P Mixer Proportioner uses a plastic bag within a tank to hold the fertilizer solution. Water from the supply line surrounds the bag and forces the solution through a metering valve into the flowing water. Variations in water pressure therefore directly affect and adjust the feed rate. The smallest unit, a ½-gallon size, has a 1:50 fixed ratio and currently sells for about $50. A larger unit is available with a variable-proportion metering valve.

The Merit Commander Proportioner uses a water-operated piston pump (figure 5-30). No internal source of power is needed; water from the supply line forces a piston back and forth in a cylinder. This draws the fertilizer concentrate from a pail or supply tank. It adds 1 fluid ounce of concentrate to each gallon of water flowing through it for a 1:128 ratio. It can handle 2–400 gallons per hour. The Commander currently sells for about $200.

When selecting a proportioner, consider its use. If you will be replacing a watering can in which you mix several tablespoons of fertilizer, a siphoning-type proportioner is the answer; the slight variations should not affect plant growth. If you have a larger greenhouse or want to liquid-feed your garden or lawn, a proportioner with a greater dilution ratio may be in order.

Proportioner Installation and Use

The types of injectors described above come with clearly written installation manuals. Hyponex and hose-end types conveniently connect to the water supply with a garden hose. If the proportioner is permanently installed, you should install a water-bypass line around the unit to make unfertilized water available. Even with a faucet/hose arrangement, the addition of a "Y" coupling at the hose bibb will allow access to clear water.

More important is the installation of a vacuum breaker. Many states now require that backflow be prevented where there is a chance of contaminating drinking water. The vacuum breaker is a combination check valve and air-relief valve that shuts off the water supply should low pressure develop. Vacuum breakers are readily available at plumbing-supply houses. Some proportioners, such as the Hyponex, include an internal check valve.

Another simple device you should install is a strainer to filter out small particles of dirt that could block the small opening in the proportioner.

Use a plastic or rubber pail to hold the stock solution of fertilizer. Also use plastic pipes where needed; most metals corrode rapidly from contact with fertilizers, so pails or pipes will develop leaks.

Fertilizer injectors let you feed plants continuously, every time you water. Most growers feed plants intermittently, topdressing with fertilizer or diluting fertilizer in the watering can once every several weeks. Advantages of continuous feeding include higher-quality crops, because a more constant supply of nutrients is available and there is less chance of overfertilization, which often results in injury to plants. Constant fertilization requires less thought and fuss; there is no need to remember to feed plants as long as you remember to water them.

Continuous feeding is not always the answer. Nutrients are not evenly available in nature, and there really is no reason they should be in the greenhouse. Some plants require long periods of dormancy (months during which water, nutrients, and even sunlight must be sharply reduced for optimum performance in the plant's season of bloom).

Adjusting Proportions

Accurate preparation of the stock solution is crucial. You have to take into account the approximate amount of water you want to give, the amount and strength of fertilizer required, and the ratio of the proportioner. The simple arithmetic shown below will help.

1. Determine the approximate amount of water to be applied for bench crops or potted plants. Proper watering provides 10% more water than necessary to ensure thorough fertilizer distribution and enough leaching to prevent the buildup of soluble salts. For bench crops, use this formula:

$$\text{Number of gallons} = \frac{\text{(bench square feet)} \times \text{(soil depth in inches)}}{15}$$

For example, a greenhouse with two 3-foot-by-12-foot benches containing 6 inches of soil requires:

$$\text{Number of gallons} = \frac{(2 \times 3 \text{ feet} \times 12 \text{ feet}) \times 6 \text{ inches}}{15} = 28.8 \text{ gallons}$$

For potted plants, use the following guideline: thirty-five 4-inch pots, eighteen 6-inch pots, or four 8-inch pots can be watered with 1 gallon.

A normal application for most gardens and lawns is 1 inch of water per week. This can be converted to a rate of 60 gallons per 100 square feet. For example, if your garden covers 400 square feet, you should use about 240 gallons of water.

2. To calculate the amount of stock solution (the diluted fertilizer before it enters the water

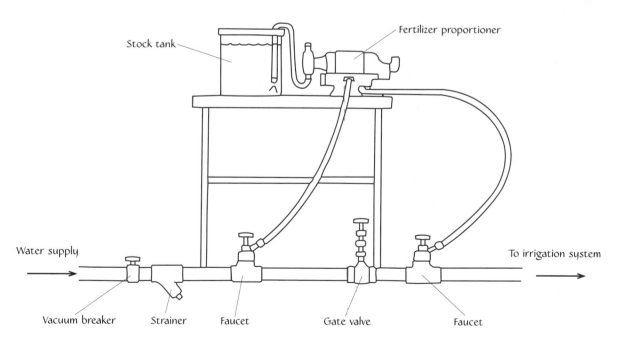

Figure 5-30. Fertilizer proportioner with a water-operated piston pump

supply), divide the total gallons of water needed by the ratio of the proportioner. In the above greenhouse example, which requires about 29 gallons of water, you should prepare 2 gallons of stock solution if you are using a Venturi proportioner with a 1:15 ratio.

$$\text{Amount of stock solution} = \frac{\text{water to be applied (gallons)}}{\text{proportioner ratio}}$$

$$\text{Amount of stock solution} = \frac{29 \text{ gallons}}{15} = 2 \text{ gallons}$$

Since water-soluble fertilizers are not perishable, you may want to prepare a much larger batch of stock solution and tap into it each time you water.

3. The amount of fertilizer to add to each gallon of stock-solution water depends on the dilution ratio. Many formulations of water-soluble fertilizers are available, and garden centers or department stores usually carry several. Refer to the container or to a trusted gardening book to determine the best formulation for the plants you grow. If you grow a variety of plants, compromise by using one of the balanced fertilizers.

If the recommended rate is 1 teaspoon per gallon and you are using a 1:15 siphon mixer, then add 15 teaspoons to a gallon of water for the correct stock solution. For most general-purpose, balanced fertilizers (those with 10–20% nitrogen), the recommended ratio is 10 ounces of fertilizer per 100 gallons of water if you fertilize the plants each time you water (continuous feed) and 2½ pounds per 100 gallons if you fertilize the plants every other week (intermittent feed).

Table 5-1 shows the amount of fertilizer to add to each gallon of stock solution using these rates. In the above example with the 1:15 ratio, after pouring 2 gallons of water into a pail, you would mix in 3 ounces of fertilizer for a continuous-feed program and 12 ounces if you were going to fertilize once every two to four weeks. Once you have made the calculations, record them for future reference.

4. Now you are ready to feed your plants. Connect the hose to the proportioner and turn on the valve. When the water shows a color change from the dye in the fertilizer, you can start watering the plants.

5. When you have finished watering, run some clean water through the injector to remove any traces of fertilizer. It will now be ready for the next use.

Table 5-1. Preparation of fertilizer stock solutions

| Proportioner ratio | Fertilizer to mix with 1 gallon water | |
	Continuous feed (ounces)	Intermittent feed (ounces)
1:15	1.5	6
1:50	5	20
1:128	12.5	51

The Greenhouse Environment: Heating, Cooling, and Plant Lighting

Controlling the environment within the greenhouse in both winter and summer is an important part of growing high-quality plants. After all, this is why you built the greenhouse in the first place. A system that will provide the optimum environment under all outside conditions is what you should strive for. Temperature, humidity, and air quality need to be considered.

This chapter covers the basics of heating, energy conservation, and cooling to help you understand why systems are designed the way they are. Many types of systems will be reviewed, from the simple to the complex.

Energy conservation measures can be installed to lower heating costs in winter and cooling costs in summer. With the rising costs of fuel and electricity, this is becoming increasingly important.

The humidity level in the greenhouse is important. A high level may be needed for propagation and for tropical plants. A low level is needed to keep diseases under control.

All of these factors have to be integrated to achieve the optimum environment. This is the job of the control system.

Heating the Greenhouse

Like all buildings, greenhouses lose heat by conduction, convection, and radiation. Usually all three are taking place at the same time.

Heat travels through solid material such as glass or metal from a warm area to a cooler area by *conduction*. The greater the temperature difference between inside and outside, the more rapid the heat movement. Generally, the heavier or denser a material is, the greater the heat flow will be per unit of time. Unless it is protected by a thermal barrier, a metal frame will lose heat faster than a wood frame. Porous material, such as insulation board, or material that consists of air space between two solid layers, such as thermopane glass, will reduce heat flow.

Convection is the removal of heat by air currents. When you blow on the back of your hand, it feels cooler, as heat is being removed. In a greenhouse, wind blowing over the surface will increase the heat loss.

Greenhouses gain and lose heat by *radiation*. The short radiation waves from the sun pass through the glazing material and strike objects such as the plants, benches, or the floor. They are then reradiated as long waves that are trapped by the glazing. This is the "greenhouse effect."

One other method of heat loss is *infiltration*. This is air exchange between the inside and outside of the greenhouse through holes or cracks in the shell of the structure. No greenhouse is completely tight. Even in film-plastic-covered structures, there are possible leaks around the doors, vents, and base. In older glass houses with lap glass, this form of loss can add a significant heat load at times. The heat requirement doubles when the wind speed goes from 0 to 15 miles per hour.

Sizing the Heater

With all of these forms of heat loss, how do you calculate what size heater is needed? A reasonably close estimate can be obtained from a chart such as the one shown in table 6-1. To get the heater size for your greenhouse, multiply the length by the width to obtain the floor area in square feet. Then multiply this number by the value from the table.

For example, if you live in zone B and are building a double-glazed, 8-foot-by-12-foot lean-to greenhouse, it will require a heater having a capacity of 15,360 Btu/hour output (8 feet x 12 feet x 160 Btu/square foot= 15,360 Btu/hour).

The above calculation is based on maintaining the greenhouse at 60°F on the coldest night. These values are valid for greenhouses up to 150 square feet. For a larger greenhouse, the values can be reduced by 10–20% because of a smaller surface-area-to-ground-area ratio. If you purchase a prefab greenhouse, the manufacturer or supplier may do the calculations or give you a value for your location.

More accurate heat loss values can be calculated from the basic formula that is used for all buildings, including greenhouses:

> Heat loss (HL) = Surface area of the greenhouse or part thereof (SA) times the heat loss factor for the roof or wall material (U) times the difference between the desired nighttime temperature and the winter design temperature where your live (TD)

Therefore,

HL = SA x U x TD

As you can see, if you increase any one of these, the size of the heater must be larger.

Heat loss is a measure of the quantity of heat needed to maintain the desired temperature for one hour. This is how heaters are rated. In the English system, heat loss is calculated in Btu/hour. You will need to purchase a heater that will supply enough heat to keep the greenhouse at the desired temperature on the coldest nights.

The value for the surface area can be calculated by adding the surface areas (width times length in feet) of the different sections of walls and roof. Areas having different materials, such as concrete

Table 6-1. Estimated heat requirements, in Btu/square foot of floor area

	Zone			
	A	**B**	**C**	**D**
Lean-to greenhouse				
Single glazing	290	250	210	175
Double glazing	190	160	130	100
Freestanding greenhouse				
Single glazing	320	280	240	180
Double glazing	200	175	150	110

Note: The above table assumes a 60°F inside night temperature and the following average minimum temperatures:

Zone A: −20°F	Zone C: 0
Zone B: −10	Zone D: +15

Individual locations may have temperatures lower than this. In borderline locations, select the colder zone.

To get the heater size for your greenhouse, multiply the length by the width to obtain the floor area in square feet. Then multiply this number by the value from the table.

kneewalls or different glazings, should be totaled separately. The wall separating an attached greenhouse from the home usually is not included, as the temperature in the home and in the greenhouse is about the same.

The heat loss factor depends on the insulation properties of the glazing. The more insulative the glazing, the lower the value. Table 6-2 gives values for some of the most common materials. As you can see, adding an insulation barrier to a wall will greatly reduce the heat loss.

The desired nighttime temperature inside the greenhouse will depend on the crops grown. Cool-season crops such as snapdragons, lettuce, and cabbage can be grown at 50°F. Other crops may require temperatures as high as 65° or 70°F. When sizing a heating system, it is best to assume that the crops may change and design for at least 60°F.

The winter outside design temperature is based on where you live. It is not the coldest temperature recorded but an average of the coldest days of the year. Figure 6-1 (page 74) shows values for the United States.

The examples below may help if you have to do your own calculations. The examples also show the effect of surface area on heat loss.

Table 6-2. Overall heat transfer coefficients

Greenhouse glazing or wall material	U-value (Btu/hour-°F-square foot)
Single layer glass	1.2
Single layer plastic film	1.25
Single layer fiberglass reinforced plastic (FRP)	1.2
Single layer polycarbonate	1.2
Single layer glass plus internal thermal blanket	0.5
Double layer plastic film	0.8
Double layer acrylic or polycarbonate structured sheet	0.6
Double layer plastic film plus thermal blanket	0.4
Standard concrete blocks, 8 inches	0.5
Poured concrete, 6 feet	0.75
Softwood lumber, 1 inch thick	1.10
Concrete block, 8 inches plus 2 inches foamed urethane board	0.07
Concrete block, 8 inches plus 2 inches foamed polystyrene board	0.10
Poured concrete, 6 inches plus 2 inches foamed urethane board	0.07
Wood-framed wall with 1½-inch-thick urethane board	0.12
Perimeter, uninsulated	0.8 Btu/hour-linear foot
Perimeter, insulated: 2-inch foam board, 24 inches deep	0.4

Source: Adapted from Aldrich and Bartok, *Greenhouse Engineering,* NRAES–33, 1994.
Note: The lower the U-value, the more insulative the glazing.

EXAMPLE 1: 10-foot-by-12-foot freestanding greenhouse with polycarbonate structured sheet glazing.

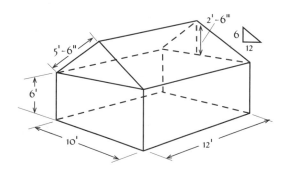

Assume:
U-value = 0.6 Btu/hour-°F-square foot
TD = 60°F

Surface Area:

(*Note:* Area of a triangle = ½ x base x height)

Sides: 2 x 6 feet x 12 feet = 144 square feet
Ends: 2 x 6 feet x 10 feet = 120 square feet
Roof: 2 x 5.5 feet x 12 feet = 132 square feet
Roof peaks: 2 x ½ x 10 feet x 2.5 feet = 25 square feet
    TOTAL: 421 square feet

Heat Loss (HL) = 421 square feet x 0.6 Btu/hour-°F-square
        foot x 60°F = 15,156 Btu/hour

EXAMPLE 2: 10-foot-by-12-foot lean-to greenhouse with polycarbonate structured sheet glazing.

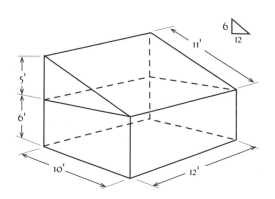

Assume:
U-value = 0.6 Btu/hour-°F-square foot
TD = 60°F

Surface Area:

(*Note:* Area of a triangle = ½ x base x height)

Sidewall: 6 feet x 12 feet = 72 square feet
Endwalls: 2 x 6 feet x 10 feet = 120 square feet
Endwall peaks: 2 x ½ x 10 feet x 5 feet = 50 square feet
Roof: 11 feet x 12 feet = 132 square feet
    TOTAL: 374 square feet

Heat Loss (HL) = 374 square feet x 0.6 Btu/hour-°F-square
        foot x 60°F = 13,464 Btu/hour

EXAMPLE 3: 10-foot-by-12-foot lean-to greenhouse glazed with polycarbonate structured sheet and with a 3-foot concrete kneewall insulated with 1 inch of polyurethane.

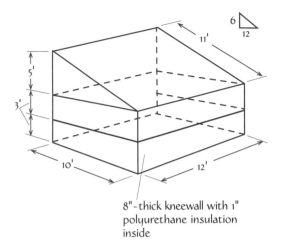

8"-thick kneewall with 1" polyurethane insulation inside

Assume:
U-value = 0.6 Btu/hour-°F-square foot for the glazing
U-value = 0.07 Btu/hour-°F-square foot for the kneewall
TD = 60°F

Surface Area:

(*Note:* Area of a triangle = ½ x base x height)

Glazed portion...
Sidewall: 3 feet x 12 feet = 36 square feet
Endwalls: 2 x 3 feet x 10 feet = 60 square feet
Endwall peaks: 2 x ½ x 10 feet x 5 feet = 50 square feet
Roof: 11 feet x 12 feet = 132 square feet
    TOTAL: 278 square feet

Kneewall portion...
Sidewall: 3 feet x 12 feet = 36 square feet
Endwalls: 2 x 3 feet x 10 feet = 60 square feet
    TOTAL: 96 square feet

Heat loss (HL),
glazed area = 278 square feet x 0.6 Btu/hour-°F-square
                feet x 60°F = 10,008 Btu/hour

Heat loss (HL),
kneewall area = 96 square feet x 0.07 Btu/hour-°F-square
                foot x 60°F = 403 Btu/hour

TOTAL: 10,411 Btu/hour

Choosing a Fuel

Which fuel is best? The right answer depends on price, convenience, and availability. Some fuels have a higher heat value than others, and some heating units have a greater efficiency. A good way to com-

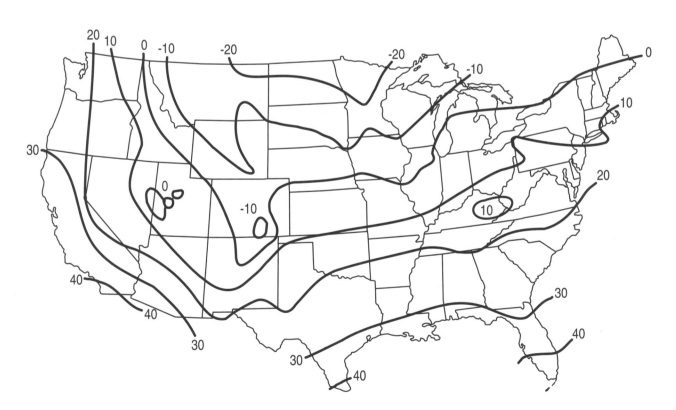

Figure 6-1. Winter design temperature map for estimating heat loss

pare the cost of fuels is on a million-Btu basis. What is the cost of one million Btu's of heat?

By definition, one Btu equals the amount of energy required to raise a pound of water 1°F. It takes 8.3 Btu's to raise 1 gallon 1°F.

The heat value ranking below may change slightly depending on where you live in the United States. For example, natural gas is less expensive in the Southwest near the gas wells, but wood is a good buy in the North where the land is heavily forested.

HIGH: Electricity
MEDIUM: Propane, kerosene, natural gas, fuel oil, wood pellets
LOW: Cord wood (if harvested yourself), passive solar

If you want to get more accurate comparisons in your area, call local fuel suppliers and ask for the current price. Then compare fuels using table 6-3. This chart uses average heating unit efficiencies.

Convenience can also affect your decision. Plugging an electric heater with a thermostat into an outlet probably tops the convenience list. There is no mess and no maintenance, and the unit takes up little space. On the other hand, having to get up during the night to fuel a wood stove is not the type of choice that most people enjoy. So consider convenience when you make your decision.

Cost of Heating the Greenhouse

It is difficult to estimate the cost of heating a greenhouse because of the many variables that have to be considered. Besides the obvious things like the size of the greenhouse, the location in the United States, and the cost of the fuel, there are factors such as whether the structure has single or double glazing, how windy the location is, how efficient the heater is, and what the inside temperature is. Another factor is that fuel usage can vary considerably from year to year, depending on the severity of the winter.

The following formulas will help you get a reasonably accurate estimate to help in making decisions relative to the size of the greenhouse or type of heater.

$$HC \text{ (electricity)} = 0.0056 \times SA \times DD \times FC$$
$$HC \text{ (propane)} = 0.00028 \times SA \times DD \times FC$$
$$HC \text{ (natural gas)} = 0.00026 \times SA \times DD \times FC$$
$$HC \text{ (fuel oil)} = 0.00018 \times SA \times DD \times FC$$

Where:

HC = Yearly heating cost in dollars

SA = Surface area of the greenhouse (square feet)

DD = Heating degree-days for your location

FC = Cost of fuel:

　　Electricity — $/kilowatt-hour

　　Propane — $/gallon

　　Natural gas — $/therm = 100,000 Btu

　　Fuel oil — $/gallon

The value for DD can be taken from table 6-4 on page 76 or from nearby weather station data. Use of a 55°-day base rather than the normal 65°-day base assumes that the additional 5° to provide a 60° night temperature will be made up from solar gain and heat from electrical equipment in the greenhouse.

The above yearly heating cost formulas assume:

1. Fuel efficiency = 75% for propane, natural gas, and fuel oil and 100% for electricity.

2. Nighttime greenhouse temperature = 60°F.

Table 6-3. Fuel cost comparison

Fuel	Assumed heating unit efficiency	Formula
Kerosene or #2 fuel oil	75%	$/MBtu = $/gal x 9.5
Natural gas	75	$/MBtu = $/therm x 13.3
Propane	75	$/MBtu = $/gal x 14.0
Electricity	100	$/MBtu = $/kwhr x 293
Mixed hardwood, 20% moisture content	50	$/MBtu = $/cord x 0.75
Wood pellets	75	$/MBtu = $/ton x 0.81

Note: The constants in the formulas take into account the heat value of the fuel and the efficiency of the heating unit. Example: If propane costs $1.50 a gallon, one million Btu's (MBtu) of heat will cost $1.50 x 14.0 = $21.00.

Table 6-4. Degree-days (55°F base)

State	City	Degree-days	State	City	Degree-days
Alabama	Birmingham	853	Michigan (cont.)	Saginaw	4552
	Mobile	245		Sault Ste. Marie	6575
	Montgomery	504	Minnesota	Duluth	6774
Arizona	Phoenix	229		Minneapolis	5417
	Yuma	37		Moorhead	6572
Arkansas	Fort Smith	1478		St. Paul	5497
	Little Rock	1188	Mississippi	Vicksburg	468
California	Eureka	1328	Missouri	Columbia	2939
	Fresno	718		Hannibal	3231
	Los Angeles	17		Kansas City	2980
	Red Bluff	822		St. Louis	2745
	Sacramento	803		Springfield	2423
	San Diego	26	Montana	Havre	5874
	San Francisco	384		Helena	5071
	San Luis Obispo	230		Kalispel	5131
Colorado	Denver	3440	Nebraska	Lincoln	3850
	Grand Junction	3433		North Platte	4152
	Pueblo	3261		Omaha	3982
Connecticut	Meriden	3734	Nevada	Winnemucca	3468
	New Haven	3237	New Hampshire	Concord	4640
D.C.	Washington	2487	New Jersey	Atlantic City	2904
Florida	Pensacola	127	New Mexico	Sante Fe	3106
Georgia	Atlanta	1165	New York	Albany	4302
	Augusta	661		Binghamton	4296
	Macon	711		Buffalo	4316
	Savannah	231		Ithaca	4023
Idaho	Boise	2814		New York	3089
	Lewiston	2688		Rochester	4231
	Pocatello	4140	North Carolina	Charlotte	1388
Illinois	Cairo	2119		Raleigh	1080
	Chicago	3743		Wilmington	729
	Springfield	3289	North Dakota	Bismarck	6468
Indiana	Evansville	2335		Williston	6399
	Indianapolis	2829	Ohio	Cincinnati	3003
Iowa	Charles City	5293		Cleveland	3795
	Davenport	4142		Columbus	3255
	Des Moines	4180		Dayton	3147
	Dubuque	4468		Toledo	3757
	Sioux City	4732	Oklahoma	Oklahoma City	1835
Kansas	Concordia	2690	Oregon	Baker	4307
	Dodge City	2962		Portland	1911
	Topeka	1811	Pennsylvania	Erie	3837
	Wichita	2587		Harrisburg	3236
Kentucky	Lexington	2557		Philadelphia	2695
	Louisville	2294		Scranton	3755
Louisiana	New Orleans	30		Pittsburgh	3028
	Shreveport	565	Rhode Island	Block Island	3388
Maine	Eastport	5236	South Carolina	Charleston	336
	Portland	4572		Columbia	759
Maryland	Baltimore	2491		Greenville	1502
Massachusetts	Boston	3603	South Dakota	Huron	5678
	Nantucket	3419		Pierre	5234
Michigan	Detroit	4089		Rapid City	4628
	Grand Haven	3435		Yankton	6045
	Grand Rapids	4177	Tennessee	Chattanooga	915
	Lansing	4444		Knoxville	1741
	Marquette	5842		Memphis	1294
	Port Huron	4275		Nashville	1678

continued on next page

Table 6-4. Degree-days (55°F base) — *continued*

State	City	Degree-days	State	City	Degree-days
Texas	Abilene	915	Washington	Seattle	2185
	Amarillo	2220		Spokane	3672
	El Paso	919		Tacoma	2365
	Fort Worth	754		Walla Walla	2565
	Galveston	34	West Virginia	Elkins	3327
	Houston	110		Parkersburg	2784
	San Antonio	305	Wisconsin	Green Bay	5331
Utah	Modena	3981		La Crosse	3992
	Salt Lake City	3202		Madison	4850
Vermont	Burlington	4984		Milwaukee	4617
	Northfield	7121	Wyoming	Cheyenne	4700
Virginia	Lynchburg	1928		Lander	5450
	Norfolk	1496			
	Richmond	1895			

Source: Adapted from American Society of Heating, Refrigerating, and Air Conditioning Engineers, Inc.; *Heating, Ventilating, Air Conditioning Guide;* 1956.

3. Double greenhouse glazing. Multiply the value calculated from the above formulas by 1.5 to get the heat cost for a greenhouse that has single glazing.

4. For a windy location, add 10%.

Here is an example of the calculations:

What is the yearly heating cost for the greenhouse shown in example 1 on page 73 if it is heated with propane and located in Chicago, Illinois?

Assumptions:

SA = 421 square feet

DD = 3,743 (from table 6-4)

FC = Propane at $1.20/gallon

HC = 0.00028 x SA x DD x FC

HC = 0.00028 x 421 square feet x 3,743 x $1.20

HC = $529 for the heating season

Heating Units

Many types of heating units can be used in home greenhouses. Some transfer heat by hot water, others heat the air directly. If you are building an attached greenhouse, you may want to explore the possibility of connecting to the home heating system.

The following sections discuss the advantages and disadvantages of some of the most common units.

Gas Heaters

Through-the-wall gas heaters are low-cost, floor-mounted units. They are available in several sizes that fit the needs of a small home greenhouse (figure 6-2). Flue gases are vented from the back of the unit through an insulated pipe to the outside. Combustion air is brought in through the same vent. A pilot light operates continually, and the thermostat on the outside of the cabinet turns the gas valve on when heat is needed. A safety shutoff valve is also included. Some heaters have an integral air circulation blower; in others, the blower is optional. Some heaters without blowers will operate without electricity. These units are good when the greenhouse is

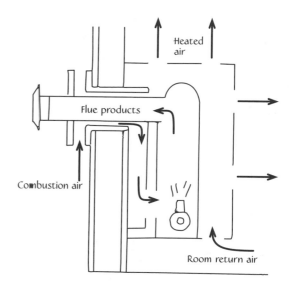

Figure 6-2. Cross-section of a through-wall gas heater

located away from a power supply. They are available in either natural gas or propane.

Unit heaters are economical, small heaters that are suspended overhead from the frame (figure 6-3). This type of mounting can save valuable growing space. An efficiency of 80% or more can be achieved through design of the heat exchanger and integral low-energy input fan. The fan also circulates the heat within the greenhouse, helping to maintain a uniform temperature. A pilot light maintains the flame and a low-voltage thermostat controls the automatic gas valve. Flue gases are exhausted by a vent pipe through the endwalls. Combustion makeup air must be supplied. Units are available that will burn either natural gas or propane that is supplied from ½-inch copper tubing from a tank or underground service.

A domestic water heater can be set up to provide hot water for space heating and plant watering (figure 6-4). These tank-type units are available with heat outputs ranging from 25,000 to 40,000 Btu/hour in both natural gas and propane.

As with any heating system, safety is a main concern. All heaters and heating systems must be installed to meet the codes. A building permit is required in most communities. The instruction manual that comes with the unit will give the installation requirements and operating instructions. Because most heaters and heating systems require electrical, gas, or fuel oil connections, installation is best done by a licensed professional.

A thermostat on the tank allows you to adjust the water temperature over a range of 90–170°F. Foam

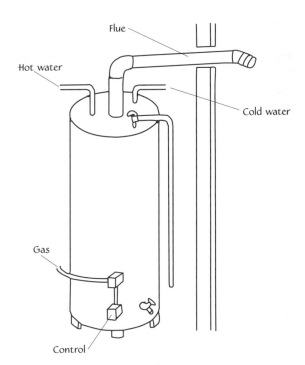

Figure 6-4. Gas-fired hot water heater

insulation inside the jacket retains the heat. An additional insulation jacket will improve efficiency. Heat distribution can be through radiators supplied by a thermostatically controlled circulating pump. Tempered water for irrigation requires a mixing valve to lower the tank water to about 90°F. Most units use a standing pilot light. More expensive units are available with an electronic ignition. Flue gases are vented to the outside through double-walled vent pipe. Install a cap at the end to prevent backdrafts.

When the greenhouse size exceeds 300–400 square feet of floor area, a conventional furnace or boiler can be used (figure 6-5). The smallest units have a minimum output of about 50,000 Btu/hour. As with any heating system, safety is a main concern. All heaters and heating systems must be installed to meet the codes. A building permit is required in most communities.

In both furnaces and boilers, the fuel—either natural gas or propane—is burned in a firebox. The heat generated is transferred by conduction to the heat exchanger.

In a furnace, air is the transfer medium. A blower or fan moves air past the heat exchange surfaces and transfers it to the greenhouse. Cool air that settles along the floor moves back to the furnace to be reheated. Advantages to using a furnace for greenhouse heating include:

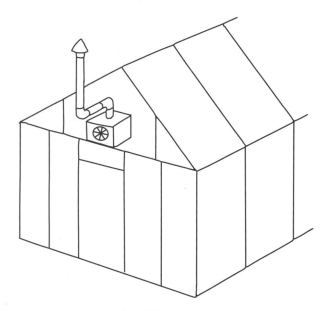

Figure 6-3. Gas-fired unit heater

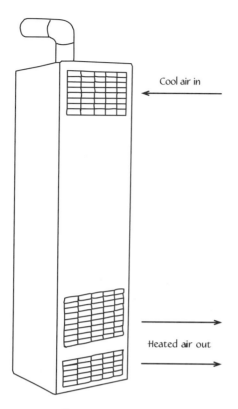

Figure 6-5. Counter-flow gas wall furnace

1. Air gets warmed rapidly. (However, once the furnace shuts off, the greenhouse starts to cool down.)

2. There is no water to drain, so furnaces are a good choice where the greenhouse is not operated during cold weather.

3. The system cost is lower, as heat distribution is by low-cost circulating fans or cylindrical plastic tubes with vent holes (polyduct).

In a boiler, water is the heat transfer medium. The heat exchanger, pipes, and radiators are always full of water. Provisions are needed to add water if a small leak occurs and to allow for the expansion of the water when it is heated. Advantages of a boiler system include:

1. A more uniform greenhouse temperature is possible, as the water in the radiators and piping gives off heat after the burner is shut off.

2. Water temperature can be modulated for spring and fall operation, which can save energy.

3. If the greenhouse contains multiple sections, different temperatures can be maintained using separate circulating pumps and thermostats.

4. Finned radiators can be used to give even distribution of the heat.

Nonvented heaters should not be used to heat greenhouses. The flue gases given off contain a number of pollutants, including sulfur dioxide and ethylene.

Both natural gas and propane can contain small amounts of sulfur. During the combustion process, the sulfur and hydrogen combine to form a weak sulfuric acid. If this condenses on the plant leaf surface, burn spots may occur. You will notice these as white spots on the leaves. Tomato and white petunia seedlings can be used as indicator plants for early detection of sulfur injury.

Concentrations of ethylene above 0.1 part per million can have a detrimental effect on plant growth. Effects include stem bending, premature leaf and petal drop, terminal bud abortion, and prevention of flower development. Damaging levels of ethylene can also come from a gasoline engine that is operated in or near a greenhouse. If the gas contains very little sulfur and the burner is properly adjusted, a nonvented heater may not cause plant injury (figure 6-6).

Electric Heaters

Although operating an electric heater is more expensive than gas, there are some situations where electric heaters can be used to advantage. For example, a greenhouse operated only during the spring to grow transplants for your garden may need only a little heat on the colder nights. Another example is a greenhouse located in a southern climate that has only a few nights of cold weather.

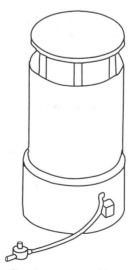

Figure 6-6. Gas-fired nonvented heater

Utility heaters are small, portable heaters that have an output of 10,000–20,000 Btu/hour and can be plugged into a 240-volt outlet (figure 6-7). A thermostat turns the heating element on or off, and an integral fan distributes the heat within the greenhouse. Some units are available with several levels of heat output. Utility heaters are frequently used in the headhouse/work area to provide supplemental heat.

Larger units can be mounted to the overhead frame. They require a permanent electric supply. Utility heaters are easy to install and require very little maintenance other than an occasional cleaning of the heating surface.

Baseboard heaters are installed around the perimeter of the greenhouse, attached to the wall near the floor (figure 6-8). They come in different lengths with different heat outputs. Units with low outputs (less than 200 watts/foot of length) are best for under benches to reduce drying of the plants. Baseboard heaters require a permanent electric circuit. They are best controlled by a thermostat located at plant level near the center of the greenhouse.

An infrared heater (figure 6-9) provides heat similar to the sun. Radiant energy is transmitted through the air and turns to heat when it strikes solid objects, such as the plants, benches, or the floor. The air becomes warm from transfer of heat from these objects. Because the rays do not penetrate very far into solid objects, soil temperatures may be cooler with this type of heater than with convection-type heaters.

Research at the University of Connecticut showed a savings of over 25% in electricity costs in an 8-foot-by-12-foot greenhouse heated with radiant electric heat as compared to an identical greenhouse heated with utility hot air heaters.

Infrared heaters are best mounted overhead so that the heat rays can blanket the growing area. The location and height should be selected so that the rays stay within the greenhouse; otherwise, some of the heat will go through the walls and be wasted.

Because infrared heaters produce heat by radiation (similar to the sun), they work best with a low, uniform crop, such as bedding plants or potted plants. They are not as efficient when tall crops such as roses, tomatoes, and cucumber are grown, as the tops of the plants absorb the heat before it can reach the soil level. Under-bench crops and hanging baskets also will not receive uniform heat.

Units are available in many sizes, and they operate on either 120-volt or 240-volt circuits. The thermostat should be protected from receiving direct rays from the heater.

Kerosene and Fuel Oil Heaters

It is recommended that nonvented portable kerosene heaters not be used in a greenhouse. However, some growers have had good success using the 1-K grade of kerosene in a heater designed for household use (figure 6-10). The heater must be cleaned and maintained frequently to keep the heat output clean.

These heaters are available with heat outputs up to about 15,000 Btu/hour. Therefore, more than one may be needed to keep the greenhouse warm on a cold night. They also do not have thermostatic temperature control, so the setting you select has to be right for the anticipated weather.

These heaters are best used as an emergency source of heat should the power be disrupted or your heating system fail. A few models of kerosene heaters can be vented. They will work well in a greenhouse.

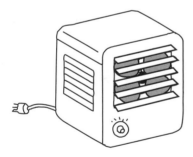

Figure 6-7. Electric utility heater with fan

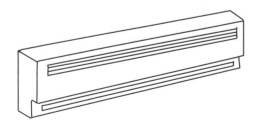

Figure 6-8. Electric baseboard heater

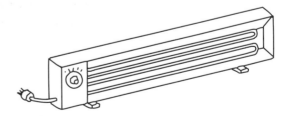

Figure 6-9. Infrared heater

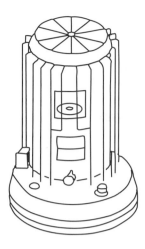

Figure 6-10. Portable kerosene heater

The smallest oil-fired furnaces have about 50,000-Btu/hour output (figure 6-11). They are also fairly bulky and take up a considerable amount of greenhouse space. They are generally used in larger greenhouses over 400 square feet.

Extension of the Home Heating System

Extending the home heating system may be an option if you are building an attached greenhouse or one that will be located near the home. This option requires that the furnace or boiler have adequate capacity to handle the heat needs of the greenhouse on the coldest night.

This option is most commonly done with a hot water boiler system. An additional zone with a circulating pump, piping, radiators, and a thermostat is needed (figure 6-12).

The pump located on the boiler is controlled by the thermostat in the greenhouse. When heat is called for,

the pump circulates the hot water through the piping and radiators. Supply and return pipes are needed and should be insulated to reduce heat loss. A heating contractor should be hired to do this work. Advantages to this option include:

- There is only one heating unit to maintain.
- A separate flue and fuel supply are not needed.
- The cost may be less than that of an independent system in the greenhouse.
- Space is not taken for the heater in the greenhouse.

It is possible to supply heat from a hot air furnace in the home, but this is usually more difficult. Additional ducting, dampers, and controls are required.

Heating with Wood

If you have access to a good low-cost supply of wood, you may want to consider a wood stove as your main source of heat or as a supplemental source

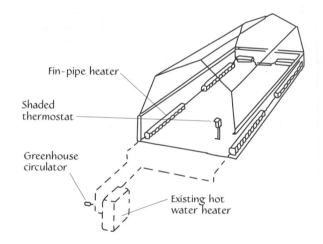

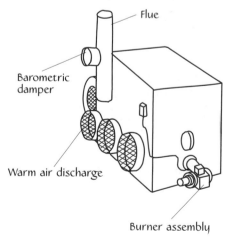

Figure 6-11. Oil-fired furnace

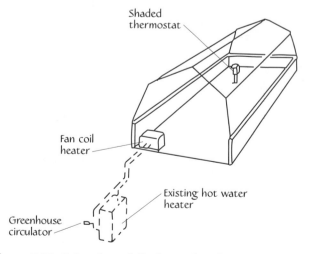

Figure 6-12. Extension of the home heating system

(figure 6-13). A wood stove has to be installed safely with adequate clearance around it. It also requires more labor to feed the wood, clean the ashes, and do the occasional sweeping of the chimney.

Wood stoves come in several sizes. The stove you select should have a large enough firebox so that it will maintain the fire throughout the night. It should be able to take chunks of wood that are at least 24 inches in length.

Another disadvantage to a wood stove is that it is more difficult to regulate heat output. In a manually operated stove, you have to adjust the damper to control the air getting to the fire and therefore the rate of burn. Thermostatically controlled stoves are better, but they have a minimum rate of burn to keep the fire going so there is always some heat output. A wood stove is not like an oil or electric heater that is off when heat is not needed.

If you have the space, a wood stove installation works well if you can operate it during the day and evening when you are around and if you have an automatic unit such as a gas or electric heater that can take over when the wood burns out. This setup also gives you a backup heating system for times when the power goes off.

Wood pellet stoves are like gas and electric heaters in that they are thermostatically controlled (figure 6-14). They also have a fuel bin that is large enough to supply the fire all night.

Unlike wood stoves that requires a chimney, most pellet burners are just vented to the outside with a flue pipe. This reduces the installation cost and maintenance considerably.

Disadvantages to pellet systems are the initial cost of the heater ($2,000–3,000) and the cost of the pellets ($150 per ton or more). At $150 per ton, pellets are equal in cost to natural gas at $0.91 per therm and propane at $0.87 per gallon. Wood pellets are delivered in bags (40–50 pounds) and have a high heat value because they are very dry.

Solar Heating

Although all greenhouses are solar collectors, a greenhouse designed to utilize solar energy as the main source of heat is designed differently than a conventional one. Through design, energy conservation measures, and energy storage, a greenhouse can collect and store a substantial part of the heating needs.

Active solar heating systems that utilize external solar collectors, blowers, and pumps are rarely used in greenhouses, because they are too costly for the amount of heat gained. Passive systems are common. They capture and store the solar energy that comes through the glazed area.

Orientation of the greenhouse is important to collect maximum sunlight. The major glazed area should face within 20° from true south (figure 6-15).

The slope of the glazing also affects the amount of energy collected. Maximum gain occurs when the sun is perpendicular to the glazing. A rule of thumb

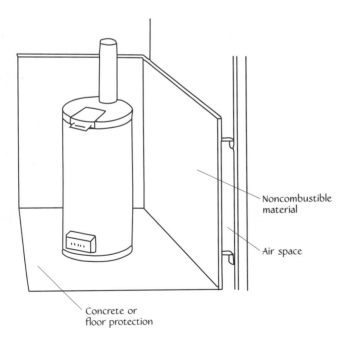

Noncombustible material

Air space

Concrete or floor protection

Figure 6-13. Wood or coal stove

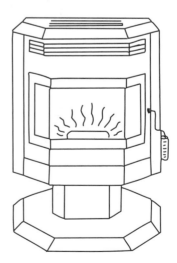

Figure 6-14. Pellet stove

is to add 15° to your latitude to get the desired slope. A steeper angle is desirable for greater winter collection or where there is a high percentage of days with sunny weather. Use a shallower slope for spring and fall use or in areas with cloudy weather (figure 6-16).

In March in a northern climate, with a well-positioned and well-insulated greenhouse, you can expect to collect enough heat on a bright sunny day to supply the heat needs for two additional days. In the winter, the shorter days and more cloudy weather reduce the collection potential.

The amount of heat that is available for collection also depends on how many plants are in the greenhouse. In a greenhouse full of plants, about 50% of the solar energy is used to evaporate water from the leaf and soil surfaces.

Several materials work well for storing the excess heat (table 6-5 on page 84). The simplest and one of the best materials is water in jugs or barrels. Barrels can be placed along the back wall or under the benches. On a volume basis, water has about three times the storage capacity of rock or concrete.

Rocks in boxes or in the floor are also commonly used. They should be ½–1½ inches in diameter for best results.

Glauber's salt and calcium chloride hexahydrate are two materials that have a large heat storage capacity. These materials change from the solid phase to the liquid phase at about 85°F and store heat in the phase change. They are contained in plastic or stainless steel tubes that are placed along the back wall of the greenhouse.

Except for the south-facing glazing, most of the wall and roof area in a solar greenhouse is insulated. In an attached greenhouse, the back wall is usually the wall of the house or accessory building. It may be possible to utilize excess heat in this area.

To reduce heat loss from the glazed area at night, use an insulating blanket. These are rolled up or drawn out of the way during the day. Supplemental heat should be installed for extended periods of cloudy weather.

Additional design information for solar greenhouses can be found in *The Solar Greenhouse Book* by McCullagh and *The Food and Heat Producing Solar-Greenhouse* by Yanda and Fisher. See the references section for more information.

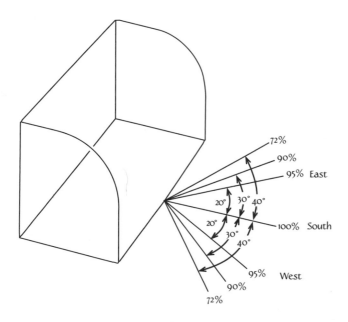

Figure 6-15. Reduction in solar gain as the face of the greenhouse is located east or west of true south

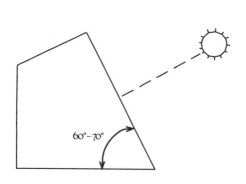

Slope of glazing to get maximum solar gain in winter

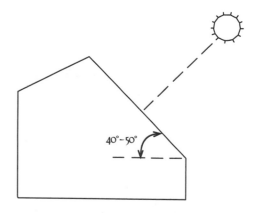

Slope of glazing to get maximum solar gain in spring or fall

Figure 6-16. Slope of glazing to get maximum solar gain

Table 6-5. Solar heat storage

Water/air temperature	Btu's stored		
	30-gallon barrel	**55-gallon barrel**	
60°F	2,500	4,590	
70	5,000	9,170	
80	7,500	13,760	
90	10,000	18,340	

30- OR 55-GALLON BARRELS

Insulation

	1-gallon jug	**5-gallon jug**	
60	83	417	
70	167	834	
80	250	1,251	
90	334	1,668	

1- OR 5-GALLON JUGS

	Rocks in crate	
60	220/cubic foot	
70	440	
80	660	
90	880	

ROCKS IN CRATE UNDER BENCH

	Stone in floor	
60	240/cubic foot	
70	480	
80	720	
90	960	

⅜"–½" diameter

Insulation

STONE IN FLOOR

	Concrete/concrete block	**Brick**
60	224/cubic foot	271
70	448	542
80	672	813
90	896	1,084

Insulation

CONCRETE OR BRICK IN WALL

Source: Bartok et al, *Solar Greenhouses for the Home*, NRAES–2, 1984 (out of print).

Note: The above assumes a minimum greenhouse temperature of 50°F. Uniform water/air temperature through containers is difficult to achieve.

Root Zone Heating

Research has shown that root zone temperature is more critical than leaf temperature in achieving good plant growth. Optimum temperatures in the root zone can also reduce the time needed to germinate seed and root cuttings.

It has also been shown that when the temperature in the root zone drops below 45°F, most plants stop growing. When you water plants with cold tap water, it may take several hours until the root zone warms up enough to reestablish good plant growth. This is where bottom heat can pay off, as the heat sensor that controls the heating system is located in the soil, not in the air above the plants.

Bottom heat can also save energy if it is installed on most of the growing area, as it will provide all the heat needed by the greenhouse during the spring and fall in cooler climates and year-round in warmer climates. For most plants, if the root zone is kept at the optimum temperature, the air temperature can remain 5–15°F cooler without affecting plant growth. This saves energy, as the heat loss from the green-house surface is less. A number of systems have been developed to provide heat to the root zone.

For heating small areas, germinating a few flats, or rooting some cuttings, a propagation mat is a good choice (figure 6-17). Mats are available in several sizes and are carried by most greenhouse suppliers. Operation consists of rolling the mat out on the bench and plugging it into the thermostat. The capillary tube sensor connected to the control unit is placed in the soil, and the dial on the thermostat is set to the desired temperature. Although it is not the least expensive method of providing bottom heat, a mat is easy to use.

One of the many uses for electric heating cables is for bench heating (figure 6-18). These cables consist of a loop of resistance wire that heats up when electricity passes through it. Plastic-covered cables are insulated to give mechanical toughness and resistance to heat, moisture, and chemicals. Cables are available in many lengths and with several different heat outputs per foot.

One method of installation is to place a 1-inch aluminum foil–covered insulation board on top of the bench. Then place the heating cable on top of the insulation. To determine the amount of cable needed, multiply the square footage of bench area to be heated by 8 watts per square foot. For example, a 3-foot-by-6-foot bench will need 144 watts (3 feet x 6 feet x 8 watts/square foot = 144 watts). Select a length that most closely corresponds to the wattage needed, and space it evenly over the bench area. Locate the plug where it will be convenient to attach it to the thermostat. Place ½-inch mesh wire hard-ware cloth over the cables. Flats or pots can be set on the hardware cloth. As with the propagation mat, the thermostat sensor should be placed into the soil in one flat or pot to sense soil temperature. Be careful not to overload the electrical circuit. A 15-amp circuit will carry up to 1,500 watts of cable, and a 20-amp circuit will carry as much as 2,000 watts.

The Agritape system, available from many green-house suppliers, consists of thin, closely spaced electrical resistance wires sealed between two layers

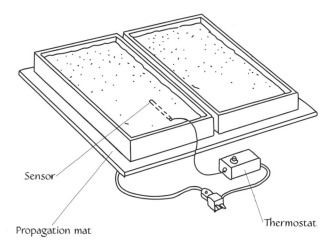

Figure 6-17. A propagation heat mat can provide the ideal temperature for seed germination

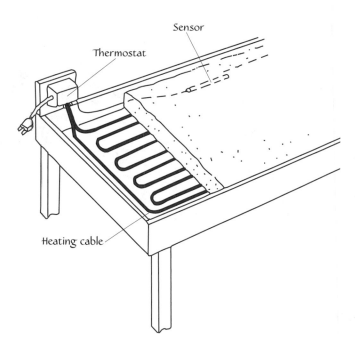

Figure 6-18. Electric heating cables are available in many lengths

of mylar plastic (figure 6-19). Agritape is easy to install. It can be placed on any type of bench or on a table in the basement if you are doing your propagation there. As with heating cables, an inch of insulation board placed under the Agritape reduces heat loss to the bottom of the bench. After rolling out the heater, it must be covered with a piece of aluminum screening that is connected to an electrical system ground or a ground rod driven into the soil. This will prevent you from receiving an electrical shock should the tape become punctured with a hand tool or sharp edge of a flat. Next, plug the tape into the control unit and bury the thermostat bulb in a flat or pot. Set the dial for the desired root zone temperature, and watch the plants grow.

Warm water systems are practical in larger home greenhouses of 300 square feet or more. A typical system contains tubing, a circulating pump, a source of hot water, and a control system (figure 6-20). It can be installed in the floor, on benches, or in soil beds. Warm water (90–120°F) is circulated through the pipes, providing an even heat to the root zone area.

Small-diameter, rubber tubing is spaced evenly across the growing area. One end of each tube is connected to a warm water supply header, and the other end is connected to a return header. Because the rubber tubing is very flexible, it conforms to the surface on which it is placed. Pre-assembled, ready-to-roll-out units that include the pipe and header can be ordered from a greenhouse supplier or one of several root zone system manufacturers.

Polyethylene or PVC pipe with a ½-inch inside diameter also works well, but it is not as flexible and requires more fittings and installation time.
To get even distribution of the heat, the pipe or tubing should be covered with moist soil or sand. For benches where the pipes are placed 4–8 inches apart, 3–4 inches of cover is needed. In a soil bed or floor installation, the pipes may be spaced up to 12 inches apart and buried 8 inches deep.

A small circulating pump similar to that used in solar hot water heating systems circulates the water through the pipes in the growing area. A thermostat connected to a sensing bulb in the soil turns the pump on when heat is needed. The heated water can be supplied from a gas or electric hot water heater.

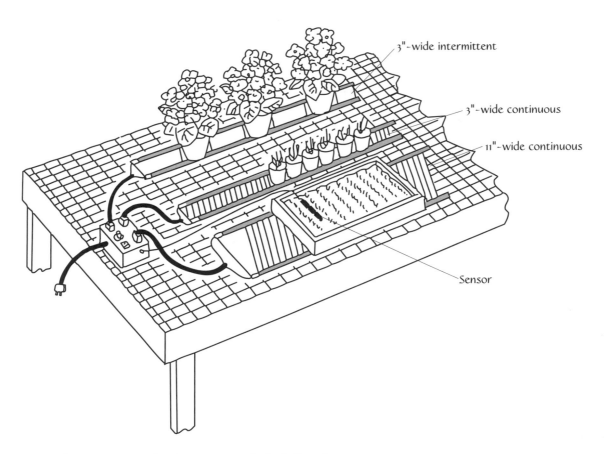

Figure 6-19. Agritape root zone heaters are easy to install and use

Agritape root zone heaters are manufactured by Ken-Bar; see "Greenhouse and Equipment Suppliers" on page 131.

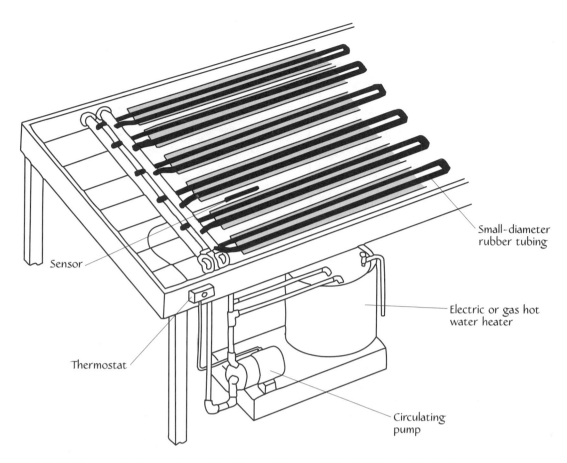

Figure 6-20. A typical warm water root zone heating system contains tubing, a circulating pump, a source of hot water, and a control system

Energy Conservation

If you had lived during the late 1800s when the United States faced a shortage of fuel wood, you probably would have covered your greenhouse with straw mats at night to save heat—a practice still followed in China and other Far Eastern countries. However, modern technology and space-age materials have made energy conservation easier and more effective than using straw mats.

In total, a single-layer glass greenhouse will lose from ten to fifteen times more heat than an equivalent area of a well-insulated home. In northern climates, this can amount to 2.5 gallons of fuel oil, 3.5 therms of natural gas, 4 gallons of propane, or 75 kilowatt-hours of electricity per year for each square foot of floor area when the greenhouse is heated to about 60°F at night.

There are several ways to minimize the amount of heat lost through glazing. All of them will reduce your fuel bill significantly compared with a single layer of glass, polyethylene, or fiberglass (table 6-6).

Interior Liners

One of the simplest and most effective methods is to line the inside of the greenhouse with plastic film for the winter months. Clear 6-mil polyethylene is easy to work with and can be reused for several years before it deteriorates significantly. It is available in construction grade from most lumberyards and in a stronger, more durable greenhouse grade from greenhouse suppliers. One disadvantage is that it will reduce the amount of light that reaches the plants by 10–15%.

Table 6-6. Approximate heat loss reduction

Double-layer polyethylene	35%
Polyethylene over or under glass	35
Double glass	40
Acrylic or polycarbonate — structured sheets	40
Thermal blanket — polyethylene film	45
Thermal blanket — aluminized fabric	50
Polyurethane insulation on sidewall	90

Note: These do not include savings due to tightening up the greenhouse to reduce infiltration.

If your greenhouse has wooden bars, cut the plastic to fit a section and staple it underneath the bars. Better yet, staple lengths of twine over the plastic to lessen the chance of the plastic pulling through the staples. Provide a couple of inches of overlap to seal the joints. As an alternative method, support the plastic on clothesline strung across the greenhouse above head height. Provisions will have to be made for ventilation if your greenhouse has a ridge vent system. The vent section can be left unlined, or a small, thermostatically controlled fan can be installed to provide necessary ventilation during the winter.

In greenhouses that have metal bars, you must use another method of attaching the plastic. The clips used to support ventilation tubing or thermal blankets work well (figure 6-21). They are available from greenhouse suppliers.

One caution should be exercised with any interior insulation system. When you reduce heat loss through the roof, a heavy load of snow can build up. In narrow home greenhouses, which have steep roofs, this is usually not a problem. But in older or wider houses, provisions should be made to allow heat to reach the glass when it snows.

Exterior Covers

If your greenhouse has a lot of hanging plants or other obstructions overhead, an interior liner may not be practical. One option is to install an inflated double layer of poly covering over the greenhouse during the winter. The two layers are separated by slight air pressure from a squirrel-cage blower about the same size as a blower in a hair dryer (see figure 4-10, page 46). The blower operates continuously to keep the two layers separated. This method of insulation will work for a home greenhouse.

This method requires sheets of greenhouse-grade plastic large enough to cover the roof and sidewalls. The plastic can be attached by means of either wood furring strips or one of the aluminum extrusions available from a greenhouse supplier (see figure 4-9, page 45).

The following procedure can be used:

- Wash the outside glass to ensure maximum light transmission.

- Cover or remove all sharp edges that could puncture the plastic. Duct tape and foam padding or adhesive-backed weather stripping works well for this purpose.

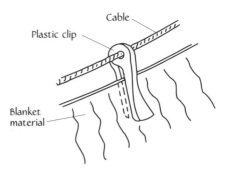

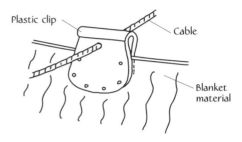

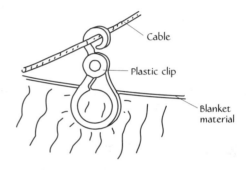

Figure 6-21. Methods for supporting poly liners or blanket materials on cables or clothesline

- Attach the wood or aluminum securing devices to the foundation wall and sidewalls. If roof vents are to remain in operation, attach securing device just below each vent. Use through bolts or long screws.

- Remove a section of glass where the duct connection will be made to the inner layer of plastic.

- Select a calm day to install the plastic.

- Fasten the plastic film with the securing devices. Pull the plastic taut. Wrinkles will disappear after inflation.

- The blower should have an output of less than 100 cubic feet per minute and a cut-off pressure of less than ½ inch static pressure. Blowers are available from greenhouse or electrical supply houses.

- Mount the blower near the point where the duct will be connected to the plastic. Flexible vacuum hose or dryer duct works well for the connection. Connect the intake to draw in outside air, as it is drier.

- Once the connection is made, plug the blower in and start inflation. Place a metal plate over the intake of the blower to adjust the pressure in the liner until it feels about as taut as a medium-hard balloon.

- The blower should operate continuously. It will use about 10 cents worth of electricity per day.

Sealing Laps

For many years, growers with older glass greenhouses claimed that the cracks between panes of glass were necessary so air could get in. But recent experience has shown that fine crops can be grown in tight polyethylene-covered houses. For a few dollars' worth of clear silicon sealer (available in tubes at hardware stores), laps can be sealed. This will save 5–30% of the yearly fuel bill.

As you inspect your greenhouse in the fall, look for broken, cracked, or slipped panes of glass, and check to see whether the laps are full of dirt or algae. Repair the glass first, then wash the laps. If necessary, you can rent a high-pressure washer for this job. When the glazing dries, squirt sealer between the laps with a caulking gun. You can do this from either the outside or the inside. If you work from outside and have to get up on the greenhouse roof, be careful to distribute your weight over a large area to avoid overloading the frame.

Thermal Blankets

An alternative to tightening and insulating the exterior glazing is installing an interior thermal blanket. A blanket is generally a fabric or plastic that is supported or suspended above the plants at night and retracted during the day to allow maximum light to enter. A comparison of different blanket materials is shown in table 6-7.

The key to the effectiveness of a blanket system is not so much the material used as how faithfully you open and close the blanket and how carefully the edges are sealed to prevent heated air from escaping from underneath. To determine whether a blanket system can be used in your greenhouse, consider the following:

Table 6-7. Comparison of greenhouse blanket materials

Material	Approximate cost ($/square foot)	Average life (years)	Energy savings [a] (%)
Black or clear polyethylene film	0.10	5	30–40
Woven polyester	0.30	5	50
Aluminized polyethylene film	0.35	4	40–50
Foam-backed fiberglass drapery material	1.00	6	40–50
Polyethylene bubble insulation, foil-faced	1.25	5	35–40

Source: Adapted from Aldrich, The Pennsylvania State University

[a] Compared to single-glazed greenhouse when the blanket is closed.

- The blanket needs clear space in which to open or close. Obstructions such as vent controls, lights, automatic watering systems, and hanging plants may have to be moved.

- The heat source should be inside the blanketed area.

- The blanket should not interfere with the plants as it is being extended or retracted. Growing benches or beds should be 6–9 inches from the wall.

- The blanket should be tear- and mildew-resistant as well as easy to repair.

- The material should not be so bulky that it creates a lot of shade in the stored position.

- The system should be easy to operate and require only a few minutes of time, morning and night.

Several types of support systems are available—some homemade, others commercial. One simple, inexpensive system uses 14-gauge galvanized wire and screw eyes. A clothesline and five pulleys can be used to raise and lower the black polyethylene blanket. This system works well for sloping roofs or vertical walls (figure 6-22, page 90).

Another simple system uses a ¾-inch galvanized conduit suspended horizontally from eave to eave in greenhouses with 7-foot or higher sidewalls. Plastic closet rollers or shower-curtain slides support the blanket (figure 6-23, page 90).

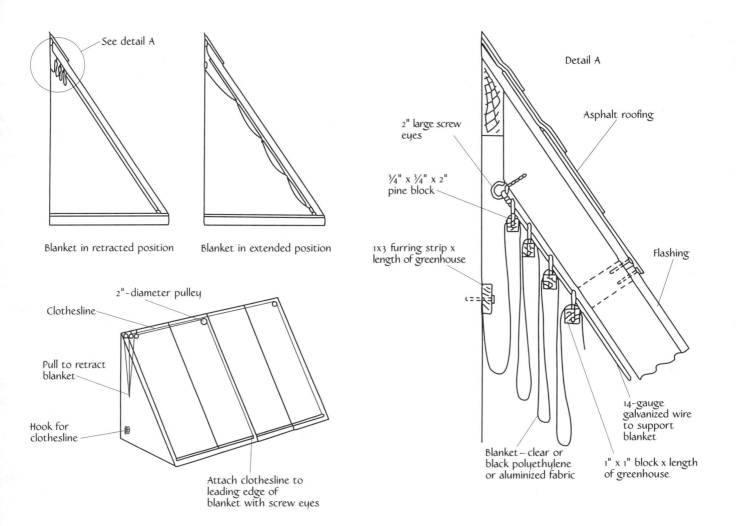

Detail A

See detail A

2" large screw eyes

¾" x ¾" x 2" pine block

Asphalt roofing

1x3 furring strip x length of greenhouse

Flashing

Blanket in retracted position

Blanket in extended position

2"-diameter pulley

Clothesline

Pull to retract blanket

Hook for clothesline

Attach clothesline to leading edge of blanket with screw eyes

14-gauge galvanized wire to support blanket

Blanket—clear or black polyethylene or aluminized fabric

1" x 1" block x length of greenhouse

Figure 6-22. Low-cost blanket support for a sloped roof or wall

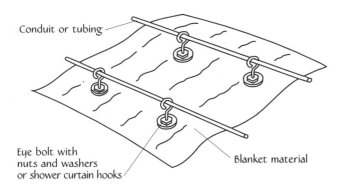

Conduit or tubing

Eye bolt with nuts and washers or shower curtain hooks

Blanket material

Figure 6-23. Method of supporting blanket material on conduit or tubing

Some kit greenhouse manufacturers have blanket systems available. The blanket may be supported by hangers that slide in a slot in the frame members (figure 6-24). These systems are usually manually operated. A few manufacturers have motorized roll-up systems that store near the greenhouse peak.

After selecting the hardware system, you will need to choose a blanket material. The best materials are lightweight and strong and fold into a relatively small volume for storage. Nonporous materials retain more heat but can increase humidity in the crop zone. Some porous materials can be used as a thermal blanket in the winter and as a shading material to reduce light intensity in the summer (figure 6-25).

Installation of a blanket system takes some planning and at least a day's time, even for a small greenhouse. Basic hand tools are all you need, although an electric drill will speed up the job. The following procedure describes the installation of a track system. Other systems are slightly different.

• Design the installation so that the blanket will store in a convenient location. In attached greenhouses, this is usually in the ridge against the house (figure 6-26). In freestanding models, it is often better to store the blanket against one

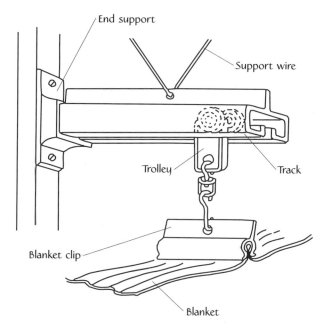

Figure 6-24. Track-supported system for hanging blanket material

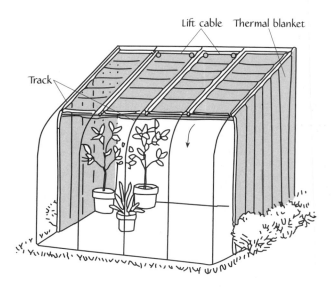

Figure 6-26. Thermal blanket system for an attached greenhouse; side blanket is attached to top blanket

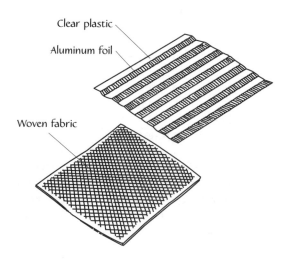

Figure 6-25. Woven blanket materials

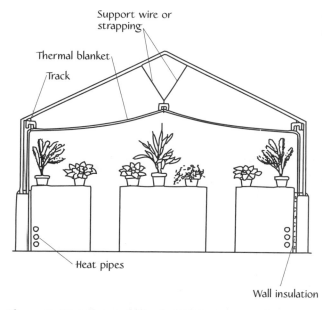

Figure 6-27. A thermal blanket that stores against one endwall works well for freestanding greenhouses

endwall (figure 6-27). Track sections should be spaced 4–6 feet apart. Provide space for the blanket to clear plants, benches, and doors.

- Attach the track to the greenhouse frame, or support it with wires or strapping. The track can be bent slightly to follow the roof's contour. Track sections should remain parallel and level with each other. Remember to insert trolleys before closing the ends.

- If you are making the blanket yourself, allow extra material for seams, slight sagging, and a seal at the side of the greenhouse. The leading edge should have a stiffener (conduit or furring strip) sewn in or be otherwise attached to provide uniform movement.

- Position grommets, tabs, or hooks carefully so that the blanket will hang and close evenly. Remember that the spacing of the supports should be twice the distance you want the fold to hang (3-foot spacing of support = 18-inch fold).

- Make provisions for sealing the sides (figure 6-28, page 92).

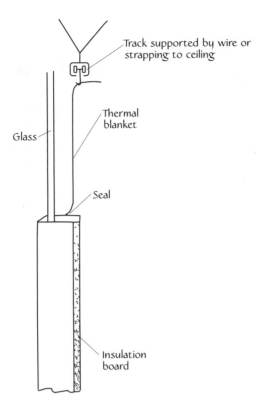

Track supported by wire or strapping to ceiling

Glass

Thermal blanket

Seal

Insulation board

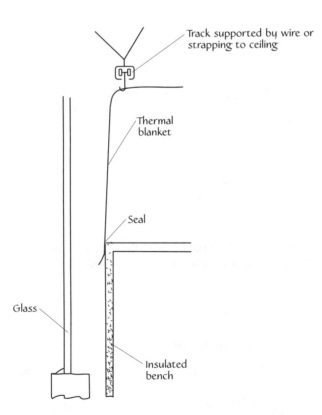

Track supported by wire or strapping to ceiling

Thermal blanket

Seal

Glass

Insulated bench

Figure 6-28. Edge seals keep heat inside the thermal blanket

- For ease of operation, install a cable/pulley system to open and close the blanket. A blanket in a horizontal track can be manually operated.

- To extend the life of the blanket, store it away from sunlight during the summer.

Permanent Insulation

To eliminate some of the problems of maneuvering blankets along sidewalls, it may be more practical to install permanent insulation. The polyethylene-bubble material used as cushioning in packages is available in rolls from greenhouse suppliers. At a cost of about 20 cents per square foot, it will give the same effect as an interior liner or inflated outer layer. Caution: Do not use this material on the roof of the greenhouse, as it will keep snow from melting.

Install the material by stapling pieces to the frame. An alternate method is to cut pieces of material to fit between the bars, wet the glass, and then allow surface tension to hold the material in place. Suction cups are also available.

If you have visited your local florist recently, you may have noticed some polystyrene or polyurethane insulation board along the greenhouse sidewall behind the benches. In research conducted at the University of Connecticut, the exterior wall temperature behind heat pipes was found to be 40° cooler when 1 inch of polystyrene was placed between the wall and the pipes. Many growers now use insulation in areas where light is not needed for plant growth. In home greenhouses, insulation board can be used on foundation walls, on glazing below benches, behind heat pipes, and on the north walls, up to eave height. This material is available from most lumberyards in 2-foot-by-4-foot and 4-foot-by-8-foot sheets, in thicknesses of ½ inch, 1 inch, and 2 inches. Use the thicker material, except in areas where there is limited space, such as behind heat pipes. You might also consider a foil-faced board that provides a higher insulating value and greater protection from things that bump it. Whatever the material, make sure it has a low flammability.

If you cannot fit insulation board in, buy a roll of the aluminum-faced kraft paper used as a vapor barrier in house construction, and slide pieces of it behind the heat pipes. The cost of this material — about 3 cents per square foot — can be recovered very quickly from the energy saved.

Tests have also shown that placing 2 inches of insulation board along the foundation wall to a depth of 2 feet below ground will reduce the perimeter heat loss. A difference of 8–12° in soil temperature has been observed between an insulated and an uninsulated wall section during the middle of winter (see figures 3-10, page 26; 3-11, page 27; and 3-14, page 29 for location and techniques).

Bags of leaves collected in the fall or bales of hay or straw placed against the foundation exterior will give about the same result. These can then be used for mulch in the garden in the spring.

Heating system efficiency should be checked periodically. For suggestions on items to check, refer to appendix A, "Maintaining the Greenhouse: A Checklist," on page 129.

Management Practices to Reduce Energy Usage

Several other management practices can reduce the amount of energy used in a home greenhouse. One of the most important practices is matching plants with their minimum acceptable temperature. Reducing the night temperature by 5° can result in a 10–20% reduction in the heating bill in northern climates.

Many ornamental plants tolerate low light and cool temperatures. During the coldest months, grow plants that tolerate 45°F or less, such as calceolarias, cinerarias, begonias, bromeliads, geraniums, tulips, daffodils, and some orchids. Foliage and succulent plants that tolerate low temperatures include philodendron, podocarpus, agave, araucaria, fatsia, citrus, lithops, and many cacti. If your preference is for vegetables, select leaf lettuce, spinach, Swiss chard, cabbage, broccoli, and edible-pod peas.

When growing crops that tolerate colder temperatures, you may need to modify cultural techniques. Use a light, well-drained soil. Water and fertilize according to plant growth, which is directly related to the light and temperature received by the plants. Good air circulation is also important to reduce fungal diseases.

Cooling the Greenhouse

Ventilation is an important part of producing quality plants. High temperatures reduce flower size, weaken stems, delay flowering, and cause bud abortion. Ventilation also reduces greenhouse moisture levels and increases carbon dioxide levels.

Greenhouses are good collectors of heat, especially during the summer when the days are long and the sun's angle is high. Heat loss by conduction and radiation through the glazing is slow; most of the heat has to be removed by the ventilation system. An understanding of the basics and common systems will help you decide what is best.

Heat Exclusion

Shading will reduce the amount of the sun's rays that enter the greenhouse and therefore reduce the internal temperature and the light level. Most flowering crops grown in the greenhouse require full sunlight for maximum growth. Light levels vary, however, from as low as 500 foot-candles (ft-c) on a sunny midwinter day to more than 10,000 ft-c during the summer. Even though leaves become light-saturated at 2,000–3,000 ft-c, most flowering plants can tolerate much higher light levels without adverse effects.

On the other hand, most foliage or "green" plants require much lower light levels and can be injured by full summer sunlight. Good growth on dracaenas, peperomias, and sanseverias occurs at about 2,000 ft-c; philodendrons and syngoniums require 1,500 ft-c; and dieffenbachias do well at 1,000 ft-c.

In sunlight, leaf temperatures may be as much as 30–40°F higher than the air temperature. As the leaf temperature increases, transpiration increases, and if dehydration takes place, burning can occur. Shading the greenhouse or the plants can help lower the temperature.

Two basic methods of greenhouse shading are used, internal and external. In an internal system, the shade is placed inside the greenhouse above the plants. Cheesecloth, tobacco netting, or polypropylene shade fabric can be supported on wire or on a pipe framework that is attached to the bench or the overhead frame. This can be rolled or bunched up on cloudy days to increase the light level (figure 6-29 on page 94).

The external system, where the shade is outside the greenhouse, is better in that the sun's rays are reflected before they enter the structure and turn to heat. Also, the shade material does not get in the way as it sometimes does with the internal system.

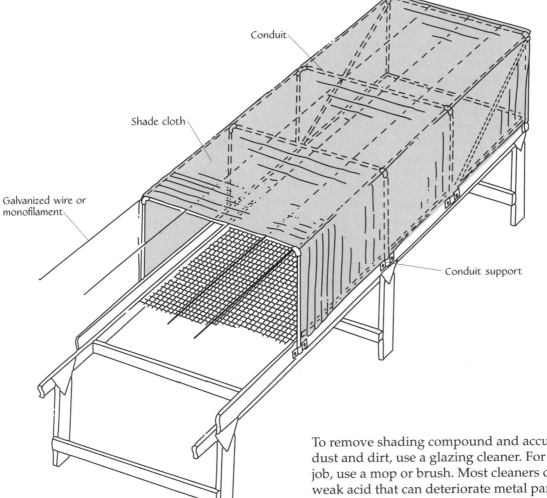

Conduit

Shade cloth

Galvanized wire or
monofilament

Conduit support

Figure 6-29. Shade cloth installation over individual bench

Shading Compounds

Shading compounds are materials that are brushed, rolled, or sprayed onto the glazing. They should be applied during warm, dry weather to get good adhesion. Frequently, a light coat is applied in late spring and then one or more additional applications are made during the summer. As fall sets in, the shade compound will start to wear off from the rain, and the first frost loosens most of the remainder. With some compounds, the shading density can be adjusted by varying the amount of water that is mixed with the compound. Other compounds are sensitive to moisture; they let in more light when they are wet (for example, when it is raining) than when they are dry.

To remove shading compound and accumulations of dust and dirt, use a glazing cleaner. For a thorough job, use a mop or brush. Most cleaners contain a weak acid that can deteriorate metal parts of the greenhouse, so be sure to thoroughly rinse off the cleaner with clean water. The glazing should be as clean as possible before winter to get maximum sunlight into the greenhouse.

If your greenhouse is covered with film plastic, you can make a low-cost shading by mixing ten parts of water with one part of white latex paint. The mixture can be applied using a long-handled paint roller or a knapsack sprayer. Application equipment should be thoroughly cleaned when you are done. This mixture will not come off, so it should only be used on plastic that is to be replaced before the coming winter.

Shade Fabrics

Shade fabrics are woven or knitted materials such as polypropylene, saran, polyethylene, and polyester. They are lightweight, easy to apply, and available in several degrees of shading (figure 6-30). Because they are manufactured in only a few widths, they have to be custom-fabricated to fit the greenhouse. This consists of cutting the material, sewing or taping the pieces together, reinforcing the edges, and inserting grommets. You have to specify the dimensions of the greenhouse area to be covered. The material is attached to the exterior of the greenhouse with rope or tie-downs that are anchored to screws or hooks placed into the frame.

When selecting a shade fabric, select the type of material carefully. Polypropylene is strong, tough, and highly resistant to flexing, abrasion, and chemical attack. It will shrink about 1% when placed on the greenhouse. Saran is fireproof and shrinks about 3%, so it has to be installed with a slight sag. Lock-stitched, knitted polyethylene netting will not fray or rip-run when cut. Its ultraviolet resistance extends its life. Polyester material is fire- and mildew-resistant and easily washable. It should only be used inside the greenhouse.

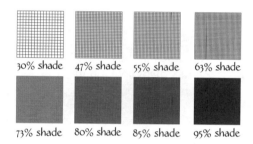

30% shade   47% shade   55% shade   63% shade

73% shade   80% shade   85% shade   95% shade

Mesh fabric shade

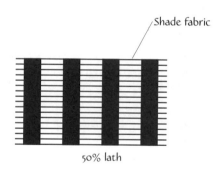

Shade fabric

50% lath

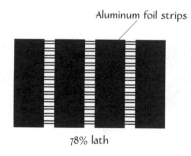

Aluminum foil strips

78% lath

Shade fabric with aluminum foil strips

Figure 6-30. Shade fabric is available with different levels of shading

All of the above materials are available in several degrees of shading. Table 6-8 lists the percentage of shade normally used for different crops under average summer conditions. Because plants adapt well to wide ranges of light, these values should be used only as a guide. For a hobbyist growing a variety of houseplants, a shade fabric in the 40–60% range will work well. To keep a sunspace cooler during the summer, install a fabric of 60–70% shade over the roof area.

The cost of shade fabric increases with the amount of material used and therefore the degree of shade. You can expect to pay forty to sixty cents per square foot for a piece to cover a hobby-size greenhouse. This includes the cost of material, edging, and grommets.

A more traditional shade system available from some glass greenhouse manufacturers is the external roller blind (figure 6-31). Fastened to the ridge of the greenhouse, it can easily be rolled up or down. Blinds can be made of wooden slats, bamboo, or aluminum. Systems for rolling up shade fabric are also available. Because of the hardware, this system is more expensive than other shading methods but has more versatility and a longer life.

Table 6-8. Chart for the selection of shade fabric

Suggested degree of shade	Type of plants
25–35%	Geraniums, chrysanthemums, snapdragons
45–50	Bedding plants, lilies, cladiums
50–55	Azaleas, begonias, gloxinias, African violets, poinsettias
55–60	Orchids, pachysandra, ivy, bromeliads, ficus
60–65	Rhododendron, dieffenbachia
70–75	Fern, philodendron, dracaena
75–80	Palms

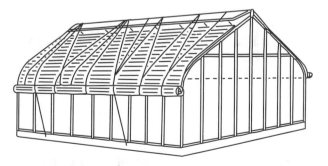

Figure 6-31. Wood or aluminum slat roll-up external shade

Natural Ventilation Systems

Natural ventilation systems operate on the principle that heat is removed by pressure created by temperature and wind gradients. On sunny days, the air within a greenhouse becomes lighter as it is heated and rises to escape out the ridge (top) vents. This hot air is replaced by cooler air coming in through side vents, through laps in the glass, or, in the case of some greenhouses, by air exchange through the same or an adjacent ridge vent (figure 6-32).

Wind-induced ventilation can be a significant factor in how much cooling is obtained. The greatest effect is seen when the sidewall is perpendicular to the wind direction. Research has shown that at wind speeds of more than 1 mile per hour, there is more cooling from wind than from temperature gradients. That is why on calm, hot days, very high temperatures can occur in a greenhouse. To get good cooling, it is important that both ridge and sidewall vents be kept operational and in use. Roll-up sides, now popular on some plastic-film-covered greenhouses, are most effective in a location where good wind currents occur.

For vents to be effective, the total vent area should be 20–30% of the floor area. Ridge vents should be capable of adjusting to a 60° angle with the roof to provide a large opening. Remember that if exhaust fans are used, uniform cooling will occur only if vents are adjusted to a narrow slot opening. Otherwise, the air for the fan will short-circuit from the nearest vent.

Vents are hinged on one side and open with levers or arms (figure 6-33). They can be opened by hand or powered by a crank and gear box, motorized drive,

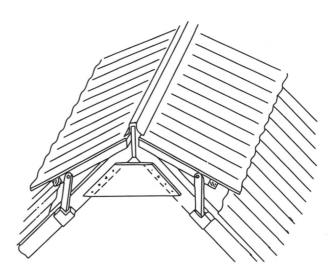

Figure 6-33. Hinged vents can be opened by hand or powered with a thermostatically controlled vent motor

or solenoid motors. Powered systems are controlled with a thermostat and can be opened to several positions. They may also have a high wind setting that closes the vents when a storm approaches.

Nonelectrical (solar-powered) units are also available (figure 6-34). These open from the expansion of a mineral wax enclosed in a cylinder. The warmer the temperature, the more the wax expands. This pushes a piston that connects by arms to the greenhouse vent. A strong spring pulls the vent closed when the temperature cools and the wax contracts. The force exerted ranges from 15 to 35 pounds, depending on the model. This limits the size of vent that this system can open.

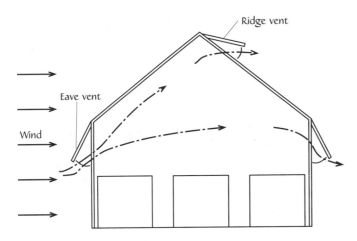

Figure 6-32. Wind has a significant influence on the ventilation rate; open eave and leeward vents to get uniform cooling

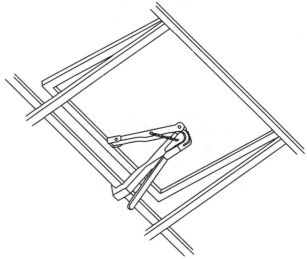

Figure 6-34. Nonelectric, solar-powered vent opener (lifting force = 15–35 pounds)

Fan Systems

Exhaust fans combined with intake louvers provide better temperature control than vent systems. The most common system uses fans to create a negative pressure (vacuum) that exhausts the heated air out of the greenhouse. Cooler outside air enters through louvers or vents in the opposite endwall (figure 6-35).

When sizing equipment for the exhaust system, it is important to consider the fan capacity and intake louver or vent area. Fan capacity is the volume of air that the fan blows in 1 minute. It is measured in cubic feet per minute (cfm).

For most areas of the country, fan capacity should be based on 12 cubic feet per minute (cfm) per square foot of floor area. For example, a 10-foot-by-12-foot greenhouse should have a fan with a capacity of 1,440 cfm (10 feet x 12 feet x 12 cfm/square foot).

Fan capacity should be measured at ⅛ inch water static pressure (sp) to overcome the friction losses of moving the air through the louvers. If air is drawn through evaporative pads or insect screening, fans operating at ¼ inch sp may be needed. The output of a fan at different static pressures can be found in the manufacturer's technical data (or see table 6-9).

Table 6-9. Typical fan performance

Blade diameter (inches)	Free air (cfm)	CFM performance [a]	
		0.05" sp (cfm)	0.125" sp (cfm)
10	880	820	740
12	1,390	1,330	1,260
14	2,100	2,000	1,850
16	2,760	2,680	2,510
18	3,620	3,500	3,280

[a] Fan output in cubic feet per minute (cfm) at different static pressures. Output can vary depending on the design and manufacturer. sp = static pressure

Because ventilation needs vary from season to season, it is best to provide for several rates of ventilation. This can be done by using a two-speed or variable-speed fan. A two-stage thermostat or a temperature controller is needed to operate these fans. Locate the sensor at plant height in the middle of the plant area away from exterior walls. Shade the thermostat or sensor from direct sunlight (figure 6-36 on page 98).

Where possible, locate the fan so it works with the prevailing summer wind. A reduction in output of 10% or more occurs if a fan exhausts into the wind.

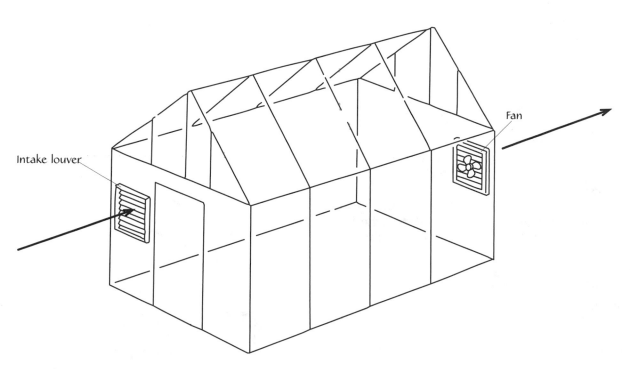

Place fan and intake louver at bench height and on opposite endwalls. On greenhouses over 12 feet wide, two intake louvers will give more even cooling. Fan location is not critical.

Figure 6-35. Fan ventilation

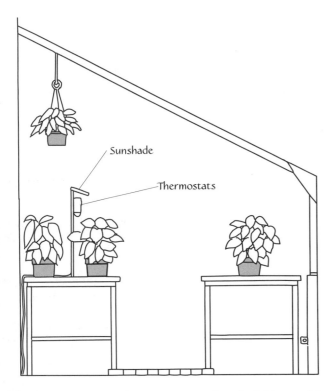

Figure 6-36. Locate thermostats at plant height; provide shade over thermostats

To provide adequate air, the intake louver area should be at least 1¼ times the fan area. Louvers should be operated by motorized dampers that are connected to the control that operates the fans.

Locate fans and intake louvers so the air flows over and through the plant canopy, rather than under the benches or in the ridge of the greenhouse. The bottom of the fans or louvers should be located about 3 feet above the floor.

A door on the same end of the greenhouse as the intake louver can be left open during warm weather when the fan is operating. This will enhance ventilation. A door on the same end as the fan should never be left open, as the air will short-circuit from the door to the fan, reducing the cooling in the rest of the greenhouse.

Most small fans are direct-drive, where the fan blade is mounted directly to the motor. These tend to be noisy because of the high speed. If you work in the greenhouse for hours at a time when the fan is operating, this noise can become very annoying. Selecting a fan with two speeds, variable speed, or a belt-driven motor will reduce the noise level.

Evaporative Cooling

If you operate your greenhouse during the summer, the temperature inside the greenhouse could exceed the outside temperature by 10–20°F with natural ventilation and by 10°F with a well-designed fan ventilation system. This puts stress on plants, reducing their quality and growth.

Evaporative cooling, which uses the heat in the air to evaporate water from leaves and other wetted surfaces, can be used to cool the greenhouse to as much as 10–20°F below the outside temperature. It takes 1 Btu of heat to raise the temperature of 1 pound of water 1°F, but it takes 1,060 Btu's of heat to change the same amount of water to a vapor.

With an evaporative cooling system, humid air containing all of the heat that it picked up is exhausted out of the greenhouse, and drier, cooler air is brought in. Evaporative cooling works best when the humidity in the outside air is low. These conditions are most common in the dry Southwest, but even in the more humid northern sections of the United States, significant evaporative cooling can occur most days in the summer.

Figure 6-37 shows the effect of the relative humidity of the outside air on the temperature of the air that leaves the evaporative cooling system. For example, at a 90°F outside temperature, the air would be

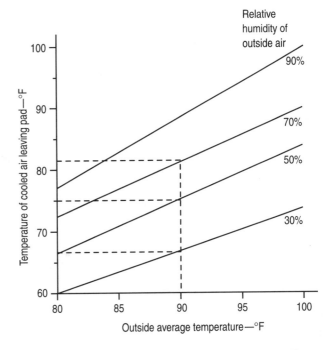

Figure 6-37. Effect of relative humidity of outside air on evaporative cooling

cooled to 67°F if the relative humidity is 30% but only to 82°F if the relative humidity is 70%. Outside air with a lower relative humidity will result in greater greenhouse cooling.

Several methods can be used to add moisture to the air. The simplest but least effective is just hosing down the floor. Evaporation from the floor is slow, and the floor must be hosed down frequently to get significant cooling.

An atomizing humidifier works, as it produces fog-size droplets (figure 6-38). It should have an output of 1–2 gallons of water per hour per 100 square feet of floor area. A good place to locate it would be near the intake louver or vent.

An evaporative cooler, also called a swamp cooler, is the most common way of cooling a home greenhouse (figure 6-39). The unit is mounted on a concrete pad adjacent to the greenhouse. It consists of a metal enclosure that contains a blower and either cellulose pads and a water pump or a polyester belt that rotates in a pan of water. The dry outside air drawn in through the pads or belt picks up moisture before it enters the greenhouse. After the cool air is heated inside the greenhouse, it is exhausted through the louvers or vents, taking the heat with it.

This unit can replace the exhaust fan, as cool outside air is forced into the greenhouse and the warm air is exhausted out the louvers or vents. It can be controlled to operate with or without the addition of the water. It is a good idea, especially in hard water areas, to add a wetting agent to the water to obtain more uniform wetting of the pads. Use a commercial product, or use liquid household detergent at the rate or 2 tablespoons per 100 gallons of water.

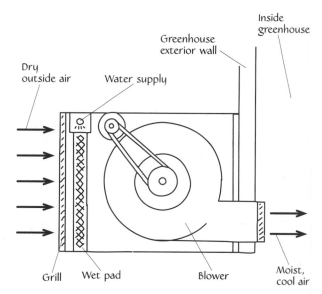

Greenhouse vents should be open when the cooler is operating to let heat out.

Figure 6-39. Evaporative cooler (swamp cooler)

Algae growth in the pads can become a problem that will reduce the effectiveness of the system and result in accelerated deterioration of the pads. Adding an algaecide to the water supply will help control this problem. Drying the pads out at night is another alternative.

Larger home greenhouses (those greater than 1,000 square feet) and many commercial greenhouses use a fan-and-pad evaporative cooling system (figure 6-40). In this system, cellulose pads with a water supply

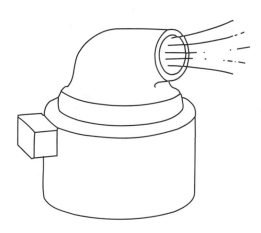

Figure 6-38. An electric humidifier will increase the moisture level and cool the greenhouse

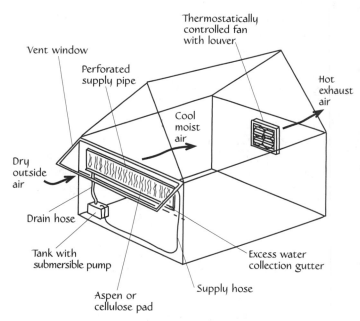

Figure 6-40. Fan-and-pad evaporative cooling system (best for larger greenhouses)

During bright, sunny days in the winter, ventilation may be needed to keep temperatures at an acceptable level for good plant growth. Ventilation also removes excessive humidity and replaces stale air.

If you have a greenhouse with vents, the easiest way to provide winter ventilation is to crack the vents open about an inch. This allows heat to escape and cooler air to enter.

If your greenhouse has fans for ventilation, set the thermostat at the desired temperature and operate the fans on the lowest speed. A piece of plywood or plastic can be attached around the intake louver to deflect the incoming cold air up toward the peak to moderate the air temperature a little before it reaches the plants. Otherwise, you could freeze the plants next to the vent if the outside temperature is below freezing.

pipe above and a gutter below are attached to the endwall opposite the fans. A tank and pump supply the water. The air drawn through the wet pads is saturated and cools the house. Approximately 1 square foot of pad area is needed for 20 square feet of floor area.

Air conditioners are not normally used to cool greenhouses because of the large capacity needed and the high operating cost. Evaporative coolers are about four to five times more efficient.

Controlling Humidity

Many problems in a greenhouse can be attributed to the moisture level of the air. Excess moisture can cause leaf spotting from drips, increase the incidence of fungal disease, and result in poor growth patterns. Very dry air can reduce the rooting of cuttings and cause leaves to wilt.

Humidity generally means relative humidity. This is the amount of moisture in the air expressed as a percentage of the maximum that the air can hold at a given temperature and pressure. The warmer the air, the more moisture it can hold. Generally, with every 20°F rise in temperature, the moisture-holding capacity doubles.

During the summer, some sections of the United States experience very hot, sticky weather (approaching 100% relative humidity). When a cold front passes through, the moisture is condensed out as rain, and the air dries out. Similar conditions occur frequently in a greenhouse, where the moisture is removed naturally by condensation on cool surfaces such as the greenhouse glazing or leaf surfaces. Moisture can also be removed by exhausting the air and replacing it with drier outside air.

The optimum moisture level for plant growth varies by plant. Review the native habitat of the plants you plan to grow. For example, cacti are found in hot, dry climates with a relative humidity less than 30%. On the other hand, orchids require the high humidity of the rainforest.

Humidity is closely associated with the respiration of plants and the manufacture of food within the plant. At high humidity levels, leaf stomata open wider and stay open longer. Where plants are grown in very dry conditions, transpiration from the leaves will be greater than moisture intake by the roots. The growth and vigor of the plants will be reduced.

There is also a direct relation between humidity and the growth factors of light and temperature. During dull winter days, an excess of humidity is not desirable, as moisture that remains on leaf surfaces encourages the growth of fungus diseases. On bright summer days when fans are operating and on cold winter days when the heater is operating, it might be beneficial to add moisture.

Measuring Humidity

The sling psychrometer (figure 6-41) is one of the fastest and most accurate methods of determining relative humidity. This device uses two thermometers, one with a wick and one without. The thermometers are attached to a holder that can be swung like a fan. Wetting the wick with water and rotating the thermometers for about a minute gives the wet-bulb and dry-bulb temperatures. After subtracting the wet-bulb temperature from the dry-bulb temperature, the humidity can be determined from a chart such as the one shown in table 6-10. Sling psychrometers are available from greenhouse suppliers and scientific equipment stores. A more expensive device uses a battery-operated fan to blow air over the wick.

Other devices, such as a hygrometer ($500) or a recording hygrothermograph ($600–$700), usually contain human hair as the sensing element. Expansion and contraction of the hair moves a pointer on a

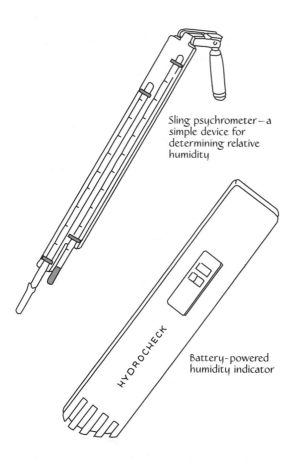

Sling psychrometer—a simple device for determining relative humidity

HYDROCHECK

Battery-powered humidity indicator

Figure 6-41. Instruments for measuring humidity

dial that indicates the percentage of humidity. Accuracy varies at the top and bottom of the scale and depends on whether the device is located in a dusty area.

Increasing Humidity

The simplest way to add moisture to a greenhouse is to wet the floor and walk areas with a hose. In the summer months, the effectiveness of this method is limited, as high outside temperatures and air exchange by the ventilation system remove the water rapidly. To be effective, watering may have to be done once an hour on warmer days.

Several types of electric humidifiers are available. In the most common ones, the water level is maintained by a float valve. A revolving impeller attached to a small motor atomizes the water into a fine mist that is distributed throughout the greenhouse. An output of about 1 pint per hour per 100 square feet of floor area is needed for most greenhouses. A humidifier can be controlled manually with an on-off switch or automatically by installing a humidistat. The equipment cost for an automated system for a hobby-size greenhouse is about $200.

The humidity in a greenhouse can also be raised using an irrigation system with mist or fog nozzles. This is the type of setup that you could also use to propagate cuttings. Nozzles with a low output of 1–2 gallons per hour are desirable to get the fine droplet

Table 6-10. Relative humidity chart for interpreting sling psychrometer readings

Dry bulb temperature	Difference (°F) between dry bulb and wet bulb temperature									
	2	4	6	8	10	12	14	16	18	20
	Relative humidity (%)									
50	87	75	62	51	39	29	18	9		
52	87	75	64	52	42	32	21	12	6	
54	88	76	65	53	43	33	23	14	8	
56	88	77	66	55	45	35	26	16	10	
58	88	78	67	56	47	37	28	18	12	4
60	89	78	68	58	48	39	30	21	14	5
62	89	79	69	59	50	41	32	24	17	8
64	90	79	70	60	51	43	34	26	19	11
66	90	80	71	61	53	44	36	29	22	14
68	90	80	71	62	54	46	38	31	24	16
70	90	81	72	64	55	48	40	33	27	19
72	91	82	73	65	57	49	42	34	28	21
74	91	82	74	65	58	50	43	36	30	23
76	91	82	74	66	59	51	44	38	32	25
78	91	83	75	67	60	53	46	39	33	27
80	91	83	75	68	61	54	47	41	34	29

size. The system is controlled by a humidistat or interval timer set to activate an electric solenoid valve in the water line. A strainer in the supply line and in each nozzle is needed to prevent the tiny holes in the nozzles from becoming plugged. Water high in calcium can also cause problems.

Decreasing Humidity

Most greenhouse crops are grown at higher temperatures during the day than at night. As the temperature decreases in the late afternoon, the humidity level increases. Normally, ventilation is the most effective way to decrease humidity. In the winter, when the outside air is dry, it can be brought into the greenhouse to replace the moist inside air. During the spring and fall, however, the moisture content of the outside air is quite high, and ventilation is much less effective.

Turning on the heater can have a positive effect on the humidity level, as heat increases the moisture-holding capacity of the air. Open the vents or turn on the exhaust fan to remove moisture and to bring in drier outside air. The cost of the heat used is less than one cent each time the greenhouse volume is changed, which may have to be done several times to dry out a saturated greenhouse.

Continuous air movement in the greenhouse lowers the humidity in the plant canopy by providing air exchange at the leaf surfaces. This reduces the incidence of disease, as the plants remain drier.

Moisture removal through condensation occurs naturally at certain times of the year. When moist air comes in contact with a cool surface such as the glazing, the water that is in a vapor state is transformed to the liquid state. If the pitch of the roof is steep enough, the water will flow down to the gutter and be removed. If the roof is not steep enough, droplets will form that drip onto the plants. A wetting agent can be sprayed on the inside glazing to keep the water from forming droplets.

Air Circulation

Greenhouse gardeners know the importance of fresh air to the health of their plants. But ventilation should not be the only concern, especially in winter, when heating the greenhouse is the primary concern and frigid outside air is often best kept outside. Air circulation is equally important. Continuously moving air in a greenhouse keeps temperatures more

uniform, reduces humidity on leaf surfaces, and increases carbon dioxide levels near the leaves, all of which stimulate growth.

In a heated greenhouse with stagnant air, temperatures increase about 1°F for each foot above the floor. In a typical home greenhouse, for example, if a thermometer located on a bench reads 60°, the temperature at the floor is probably 56°, and the temperature at the ridge is probably 68–70°. This can be an advantage for a gardener who grows plants with different requirements. But for most greenhouse gardeners, whose plants require approximately the same conditions, stratified air is a disadvantage. Without constant air circulation, a higher thermostat setting may be needed to keep plants in the coolest areas of the greenhouse warm enough. Moving air eliminates temperature stratification no matter how large the greenhouse is and saves money as well.

Reducing humidity on and near leaf surfaces is perhaps the best horticultural argument for constant air circulation. Plant transpiration increases relative humidity around leaves. Additional moisture from the air condenses on leaves that are cooler than the surrounding air (which often happens at night). Relative humidity levels can reach nearly 100% first thing in the morning in a greenhouse where the air had not been circulating all night. Such high humidity is just what pathogenic bacteria and fungi need to become established and flourish. Common humidity-related diseases are leaf spot, petal blight, *Botrytis* blight, and powdery mildew. By mixing the moist air near the plants with drier air, continuous air movement can prevent these problems.

A third benefit of air circulation is an increased level of carbon dioxide. Most of the carbon dioxide needed by plants for photosynthesis comes from the air. Although air normally contains about 360 ppm (parts per million) carbon dioxide, levels as low as 100 ppm have been recorded in a greenhouse full of plants. And in a greenhouse with stagnant air, carbon dioxide levels at leaf surfaces can be considerably lower than the air outside the plant canopy. Air moving across leaves facilitates diffusion of carbon dioxide into plants and increases the rate of photosynthesis.

Several air-circulating systems can be used in home greenhouses. If your greenhouse is heated with a forced-air heater or a furnace with a blower, consider switching the blower so it will continue to operate when the furnace is off. If your unit does not have such a switch, an electrician can add one. But only in small greenhouses (less than 300 square feet) should furnace blowers be made to do such double duty. In larger houses, the location of circulation fans is important, and the furnace blower is not likely to be in the best spot.

Years of research at the University of Connecticut horticulture greenhouse has shown that a horizontal-air-flow (HAF) pattern is best for plants and most economical, both for large commercial ranges and home greenhouses. With this system, a simple circulating fan pushes air down one side of the greenhouse and back up the other (figure 6-42). Air is heavier than you think; the air in a typical 200-square-foot home greenhouse weighs almost 150 pounds. Once it is moving, air coasts along like a car rolling on a level road. Only a small fan is needed to kick the air along at about 50 cubic feet per minute, which is fast enough to ensure that the air is also mixed from top to bottom as it circulates horizontally. Research at the University of Kentucky suggests that greenhouse air should circulate at a rate between 40 and 100 feet per minute. A slower rate is not adequate to control humidity or increase carbon dioxide diffusion, while a faster rate desiccates some plants and causes foliage to bend and sway too much.

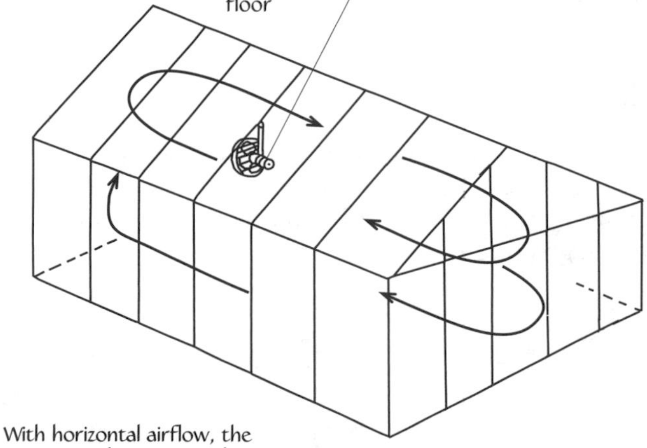

Table 6-11 gives correct fan sizes for various greenhouses. These combinations provide circulation rates of about 50–100 feet per minute. In houses longer than 50 feet, two fans may be needed. Although nearly any type of fan or blower can be used, the so-called circulating fan is the most efficient for this system. Fans should be suspended from the ceiling 7–8 feet above the floor and located one-quarter of the way across the width of the greenhouse. In most installations, an on/off switch is all that is needed. But if your greenhouse is ventilated by an exhaust fan, install a relay that turns the circulating fan off when the exhaust fan comes on. The exhaust fan will provide plenty of circulation when it is running.

Circulating fans come in a variety of sizes (from 8 to 16 inches) and cost from $20 to $100. Operating cost is also reasonable—from ten to twenty-two cents a day based on a rate of ten cents per kilowatt hour. Circulating fans are available at electrical-supply stores and should have a wire guard over the blades for safety.

A ceiling fan can provide gentle air movement in greenhouses larger than 400 square feet but smaller than 800 square feet and with a ceiling height of at least 10 feet. Ceiling fans should be mounted near the center of the greenhouse with their large, slowly rotating blades at least 8 feet above the floor (figure 6-43 on page 104). For a small house with a high enough peak, a fan with a three-speed switch would be adequate. Operating cost is about ten to eighteen cents a day. Such fans are readily available at department stores and electrical-supply houses.

Environmental Control

Devices used to heat and cool the greenhouse have to be turned on and off. This is the job of the sensor, which should be located in the plant zone area. The sensor compares the actual conditions in the green-

Horizontal airflow fan—locate a quarter of the way across the greenhouse and 7'-8' above the floor

With horizontal airflow, the air moves down one side of the greenhouse and back up the other. Mixing occurs from top to bottom.

Figure 6-42. Horizontal airflow in a greenhouse

Table 6-11. Fan sizes for air circulation

Greenhouse floor area (square feet)	Fan diameter (inches)	Air movement (cubic feet per minute)	Daily cost (@ $0.10/ kilowatt hour)
100	6	400	$0.04
200	8	600	0.06
300	10	800	0.10
400	12	1,200	0.12
500	14	1,600	0.15

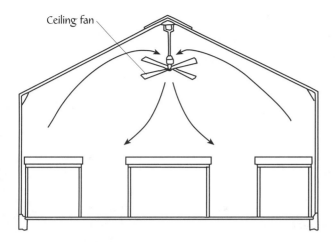

Figure 6-43. The ceiling fan forces air from the ridge down to the floor

house to a set point—the temperature at which the crop needs to be grown. If the temperature is too cold, the sensor activates the heater; if it is too warm, the sensor turns on the fan or opens the vent.

Thermostats

The standard mechanical thermostat used in greenhouses contains a coil filled with a fluid that expands when it is heated (figure 6-44). This activates a switch that turns the appliance on or off, depending on how the electrical connections are made. Most mechanical thermostats have a differential of 4–6°F between when the switch opens and closes.

The development of transistors and circuit boards has led to the development of electronic thermostats. Although a little more expensive, they are more accurate, having a differential of +/-1°F. They have other benefits as well, including remote sensing, a digital display, and day-night operations.

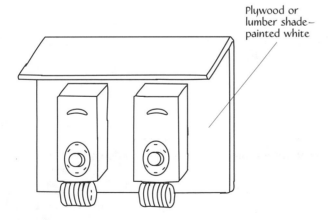

Figure 6-44. Thermostats should be shaded from the sun to prevent false readings

Controllers

A controller uses a solid-state integrated circuit to monitor environmental conditions in the greenhouse and create output signals that activate different pieces of equipment (figure 6-45). It has several advantages over the thermostat.

- The programmed instructions prevent system overlap—for example, the heating system and fan operating at the same time—which can occur with thermostats.

- Installation time is less, as relays, switches, and controls are prewired.

- All components are located in one waterproof enclosure, reducing moisture and dust problems and maintenance.

- Temperature sensing and control are more accurate. The simplest controllers integrate three cooling stages, a set point, and two heating stages. Figure 6-46 shows typical equipment control.

Most advanced units will control other environmental factors, including lighting, carbon dioxide level, mist and irrigation systems, and energy curtains.

Computers

Advances in computer technology are continually taking place. Costs are decreasing as well. Currently, computer systems are still too expensive for most home greenhouses.

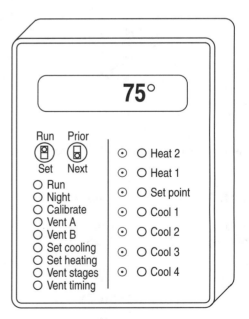

Figure 6-45. Typical step environment controller

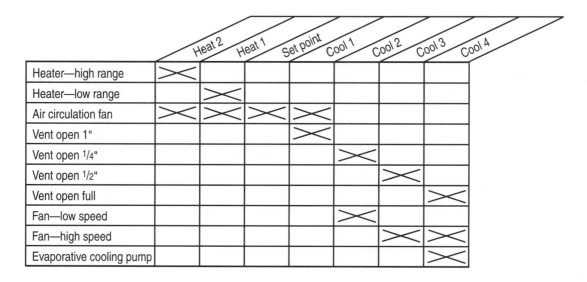

	Heat 2	Heat 1	Set point	Cool 1	Cool 2	Cool 3	Cool 4
Heater—high range	X						
Heater—low range		X					
Air circulation fan	X	X	X	X			
Vent open 1"				X			
Vent open ¼"					X		
Vent open ½"						X	
Vent open full							X
Fan—low speed					X		
Fan—high speed						X	X
Evaporative cooling pump							X

Figure 6-46. Equipment staging for the controller in figure 6-45

Supplemental Lighting

Since light is often the limiting factor in plant growth, especially during the dark seasons, growers frequently consider the use of supplemental lighting. Plant lighting is a very broad topic, as there are many alternatives that can be applied in many ways to influence plant growth.

This section will give a brief overview of the types of light sources, methods of applying light to plants, and light-measuring techniques. More information can be obtained from several books that have been written on the subject.

Lighting Basics

Visible light provides the source of energy for plant growth. Considerable intensity and duration are needed to get good plant growth. That is why plants grow better during the summer when the light is stronger and the days are longer.

Visible light is a composite of wavelengths from violet to red (figure 6-47). Light with wavelengths below 400 nanometers (nm) is called ultraviolet (UV) and can be harmful to plants in large quantities. Glass screens out most UV light and all light below a wavelength of 325 nm.

Far-red light (700–750 nm) occurs at the limit of our visual perception. The ratio of red to far-red is what controls the time of flowering and germination in some plants. This ratio may also have an influence

with blue light on keeping the plant from becoming too short or too tall.

Daylength is also important and is easily controllable with a 24-hour timer that has adjustable on-off settings. Select a timer that has adequate capacity for the size of light you plan to use. For most crops, it is better to spread the light out over a longer period of time at a lower light level. A duration of 16–24 hours per day is common.

Photoperiodism is the response of plants to the day-night cycle. It can affect flowering, tuber and bulb formation, the shape of newly forming leaves, and red pigmentation in bracts of plants such as poinsettia.

Plants are customarily classified as long-night (short-day), short-night (long-day), and day-neutral. The mechanism that permits plants to track time actually measures the dark period (table 6-12, page 106).

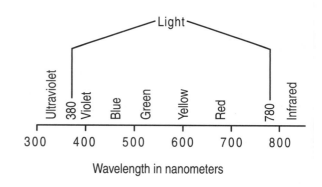

Figure 6-47. The light spectrum

Table 6-12. Photoperiod of some common plants

Short-night (long-day) (6–10 hours darkness)	Long-night (short-day) (11–14 hours darkness)	Day-neutral (12–18 hours darkness)
Annuals	China aster	African violet
Calceolaria	Christmas begonia	Begonia
Carnation	Chrysanthemum	Coleus
Coreopsis	Cineraria	Cucumber
Dahlia	Gardenia	Geranium
Nasturtium	Kalanchoe	Gloxinia
Spinach	Poinsettia	Lettuce
		Rose
		Tomato

Source: Adapted from Aldrich and Bartok, *Greenhouse Engineering,* NRAES–33, 1994.

Long-night plants, such as poinsettias, chrysanthemums, calanchoe, and azalea, will flower only when the length of the night period is a certain number of hours. Tuber formation in dahlia and tuberous begonias is also a long-night response.

Response in short-night plants is initiated when the nights are shorter than a critical number of hours. Short nights influence the height of Easter lily; bud initiation in asters, calceolaria, and cineraria; and plantlet formation on bryophyllum leaves.

Day-neutral plants are not influenced by daylength. Other forces, such as temperature or latitude, may influence reactions in these plants.

Light Sources

While almost any light source can be used for photosynthesis, some are much more efficient (figures 6-48 and 6-49). Knowledge of the light source's construction, efficiency, and electrical characteristics is useful in making the best choice for plant lighting. New lamps and fixtures are always under development by lamp manufacturers. Some are being developed just for plant growth.

Incandescent Bulbs

The standard incandescent bulb is used mainly for daylength control. A very low intensity is needed to extend the daylength or interrupt the night. Most plants will respond to 1–2 foot-candles (ft-c), although a light level of about 10 ft-c should be provided to avoid failure.

For example, a string of 60-watt bulbs spaced 4 feet apart and no more than 5 feet above the plants is adequate for a 4-foot-wide bed or bench. Placing a reflector or aluminum pie plate over the bulbs will reflect most of the light down to the plants. Bulbs with internal reflectors can also be used. Porcelain sockets should be used for safety reasons, and installation should meet the requirements of the National Electric Code.

Quartz-Halogen Bulbs

Quartz-halogen bulbs are more efficient in the use of electricity and produce a whiter light than incandes-

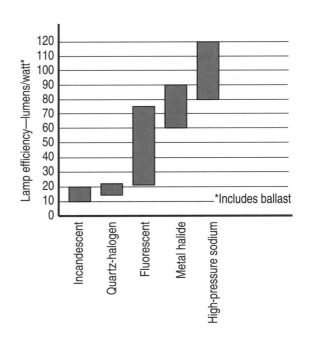

Figure 6-48. Comparison of lamp efficiency

Incandescent

Quartz-halogen

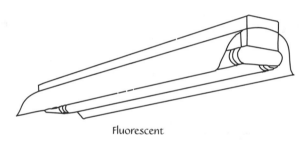

Fluorescent

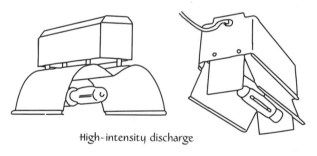

High-intensity discharge

Figure 6-49. Types of lighting common for supplemental greenhouse illumination

Fluorescent Bulbs

Fluorescent lights are commonly used in growth chambers and growth rooms. They are available in several lengths, outputs, and spectral qualities, which makes them adaptable to the needs of most plants and growing situations. Lamp life is 12,000 hours or greater, but output decays drastically over time. The energy efficiency is generally 40–60 lumens/watt. Most fluorescent bulbs are temperature-sensitive and may not start in cold temperatures.

Purchase light fixtures that use energy-saving bulbs and ballasts. A conventional 40-watt bulb can be replaced with one that provides the same amount of light using only 28 watts.

Because fluorescent lamps provide a linear light source rather than a point source like the incandescent, they give off more uniform lighting. Where high light levels are needed, high-output (HO) or very-high-output (VHO) bulbs can be used. Banks of lights can be designed to provide over 2,000 ft-c.

For most horticultural applications, cool white or warm white bulbs will give good plant growth. Bulbs developed specifically for plants will enhance plant appearance.

High-Intensity Discharge (HID) Bulbs

Gas discharge lamps contain a mixture of gases and metals enclosed within a glass tube. As electricity passes between the electrodes at the ends of the tube, the gas/metal mixture heats up and emits light energy. By varying the gases and metals, a different light color can be obtained. HID lights are much more efficient than incandescent bulbs. The main reasons for using HID lighting are high efficiency, long life, and slow-decay output. High-pressure sodium and metal halide, both HID lamps, are able to convert 25% of the supplied electrical energy to visible light.

When appearance of the plants is important, metal halide bulbs should be used, as they produce a white light very close to daylight. High-pressure sodium bulbs, on the other hand, with its unnatural yellowish light, has proven to have no adverse influence on the quality of crop production. The growing results are still excellent, as long as the lamp is a supplement to sunlight.

cent bulbs. Fixtures are available that will give uniform coverage over a wider area. Lamp life is also longer, averaging about 2,000 hours. Efficiency is relatively low compared to other types of lighting.

Choosing a Source

The lumen, the standard measure of light output, is used to compare different lamps. A lumen is the amount of light that is radiated during a period of 1 second as determined by laboratory testing. To get an efficiency rating, divide the lumen output of a lamp by the amount of electrical energy in watts that it takes to make the lamp operate. For some light sources, such as fluorescent, metal halide, and high-pressure sodium, the energy to operate the ballast must also be included. A ballast is used to control the flow of electricity to the gas-filled tube and to prevent premature burn-out.

As shown in table 6-13, efficiency varies from 12 lumens per watt for a 40-watt incandescent bulb to 110 lumens per watt for the high-pressure sodium bulb. To compare this on an operating-cost basis, lighting a growth room or greenhouse with cool white fluorescent bulbs will cost about twice as much as using high-pressure sodium bulbs, assuming that the same level of light is maintained.

You should consider several other factors when making your lighting system choice. Because of their size, fluorescent fixtures create a larger shadow in a greenhouse than HID fixtures that provide an equivalent light level. On the other hand, fluorescents can be placed closer to the plants, as the temperature of the bulb is much cooler.

Sodium vapor and metal halide bulbs are available in several sizes, including 100, 150, 200, and 400 watts. Wide-angle reflectors and lower-output lamps can be placed as low as 2 feet from the plants. For most home greenhouses, one or two fixtures will provide all the necessary light.

HID lights tend to warm up slowly, taking from 3 to 4 minutes to reach full light output. If the power is interrupted, even momentarily, the lamp will have to cool for about a minute before a relight can be initiated. When purchasing HID lights for your greenhouse, consider the following:

1. Select a fixture that provides a rectangular light pattern rather the a circular one. This will make it easier to get good coverage over the bench area. When installing the fixture, adjust the reflector, the height, or both so that the light pattern just covers the bench area and does not spill outside the greenhouse.

2. Use the more efficient high-pressure sodium rather than the metal halide, unless the appearance of the plants is critical.

3. Most fixtures can be purchased with a remote ballast that can be attached to the wall or located under a bench. This will reduce the height and weight of the unit, making it easier to attach to a low ceiling. When mounting the fixture, be sure

Table 6-13. Comparison of light sources

Light source	Typical wattage	Ballast watts	Total watts	Average life (hours)	Lumens/watt, including ballast
Incandescent	40			460	12
	100			to	17
	200			1,000	20
Quartz-halogen	75			2,000	19
	250			2,000	20
Fluorescent	40	8	48	20,000	66
Cool white (CW)	75	16	91	12,000	69
CW—high output	110	16	126	12,000	74
CW—very high output	215	10	225	10,000	67
Gro-Lux	40	6	46	12,000	20
Wide-spectrum	40	6	46	12,000	37
Agro-lite	40	6	46		41
Vita-lite	40	6	46		47
Metal halide	175	40	215	10,000	60
	250	45	295	10,000	68
	400	55	455	15,000	88
High-pressure sodium	150	38	188	24,000	80
	250	50	300	24,000	93
	400	55	455	24,000	110

Source: Adapted from Aldrich and Bartok, *Greenhouse Engineering*, NRAES–33, 1994.

that the weight of it is spread out over a larger area by attaching the mounting bracket or angle iron to a couple of glazing bars.

4. The energy from the lighting units can be used twice: once to illuminate the plants and once more to produce heat that can reduce fuel consumption and heating costs. A 250-watt unit will produce about 900 Btu's per hour, and a 400-watt unit will produce about 1,500 Btu's per hour, or about 10% of the heat needed to keep a 100-square-foot greenhouse warm on a night when the outside temperature falls to freezing.

5. The lights should be operated at night to make best use of the heat generated and to take advantage of off-peak utility rates (if they are available). The light is also more effective for plant growth if it is added after the sun goes down. A time clock can be connected to turn the lights on and off at the desired time.

6. Remember to use the area under the lights as effectively as possible and keep it filled with plants. If you pay ten cents per kilowatt hour for your electricity, it will cost about 2.5 cents per hour to operate a 250-watt fixture and four cents per hour to operate a 400-watt fixture.

Measuring Light

Light can be measured in photometric or quantum units. Photometric units (foot-candles) have been used for many years, and most printed recommendations use these units. Quantum units (micromoles of photons per square meter-second) more accurately represent what the plant sees, and most research is now being reported in these units.

Photometric Units

The illumination of a surface is defined as the amount of light falling on a unit area. It is measured in photometric units (foot-candles, or ft-c). For example, the illumination of a hospital operating room should be at least 1,000 ft-c. In a storage room, illumination can be as low as 5 ft-c. Illumination is the value you commonly see for artificial lighting on plants. For instance, African violets need about 600 ft-c for 12–18 hours per day to produce good growth.

Quantum Units

Quantum units, micromoles of photons per square meter-second (μmol/sq m-s), are used to measure photosynthetically active radiation (PAR). PAR is a better measure of the intensity of light in the 400–700 nm range. This is the light range utilized by plants.

Unit Conversions

Conversion between ft-c and μmol is straightforward, but each light source has its own conversion factor (table 6-14). To convert from photometric to quantum units, divide the foot-candle reading by the conversion factor (k).

For example, if your photometric light meter reads 500 ft-c under a cool white fluorescent fixture, then the quantum value would be 72 μmol/sq m-s (500 ft-c ÷ 6.9 = 72 μmol/sq m-s).

To convert from quantum to photometric units, multiply the light meter reading by the conversion factor (k).

For example, a reading of 100 μmol/sq m-s under a high-pressure sodium fixture would equal 760 ft-c (100 μmol/sq m-s x 7.6 = 760 ft-c).

Table 6-14. Conversion factors — photometric/quantum

Light source	Conversion factor (k)
Sunlight	5.0
Incandescent	4.6
Fluorescent	
Cool white	6.9
Gro-Lux, Plant light, Plant gro	3.2
Wide spectrum	5.0
Metal halide	6.6
High-pressure sodium	7.6

Source: Adapted from research by Thimijan and Heins, U.S. Department of Agriculture and Michigan State University.

Note: To convert from photometric to quantum units, divide the foot-candle (ft-c) reading by the conversion factor (k). To convert from quantum to photometric units, multiply the light meter reading by the conversion factor (k).

Light-Measuring Instruments

Photometers are most sensitive to illumination in the yellow-green range of the spectrum, the area to which our eyes are most sensitive. Commonly referred to as light meters, they are used in photography and lighting work, are low-cost, and are readily available from greenhouse suppliers (figure 6-50). The photovoltaic type uses a selenium cell and contains a receiver that, upon absorption of radiant energy, generates sufficient voltage to operate a small electrical ammeter. It is usually calibrated to give readings in ft-c.

Photometers are available in several models. Things to consider when purchasing one include:

1. Range — If the readings are to be made only on artificial light in a growth room or indoor light chamber, then a maximum reading of 2,000 ft-c is adequate. For measurements in a greenhouse or outdoors, a capacity up to 10,000 ft-c is needed. Most instruments have several ranges to give more accurate readings. A filter or multiplier is frequently used to read the higher levels.

2. Accuracy — Meters having an accuracy of 5% or less are adequate for measurements for hobbyists. Greater accuracy adds significantly to the cost of the instrument.

3. Cost — Good light meters are available in the $50–$100 range.

Quantum meters measure light in the 400- to 700-nanometer (PAR) range (figure 6-51). They are about twice the cost of a photometer.

To get accurate light level measurements, it is important to use the meter properly. Position the sensor parallel to the surface being measured. Move away so you don't create a shadow. Measurements are usually taken at plant level. Take the average of several readings and record the results, including date, time, and crop.

Figure 6-51. Quantum meter (measures in micromoles/square meter-second)

Cost of Supplemental Lighting

The operating cost of supplemental lighting can add significantly to your monthly electric bill. It is important to provide the correct amount of light needed and to get it to the plants.

To calculate the cost of operating a light fixture, multiply the wattage of the fixture by the cost of electricity and the hours that the light is on.

Operating cost = fixture wattage x electricity cost x hours

For fixture wattage, multiply the number of bulbs by the wattage per bulb. To this, add the ballast wattage, if any. For example, a two-tube, 40-watt fluorescent fixture has a wattage of 88 watts (2 x 40 lamp watts + 8 ballast watts = 88 watts).

For electricity cost, take your last electric bill and divide the total cost by the number of kilowatt hours of electricity used. For example, if the total bill is $63 and you used 600 kilowatt hours, then the cost per kilowatt hour is 10.5 cents ($63 ÷ 600 = $0.105/kwhr).

EXAMPLE: The operating cost for a 150-watt sodium vapor light using 8 ballast watts and operating 8 hours per night with a $0.10 per kilowatt-hour electricity cost might be:

Operating cost =

$$\frac{158 \text{ watts x } \$0.10/\text{kilowatt-hour x 8 hours}}{1,000 \text{ watts/kilowatt}} = \$0.12/\text{day}$$

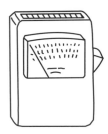

Figure 6-50. Photometer (measures in foot-candles)

CHAPTER 7

Window Greenhouses and Growth Chambers

An alternative to growing plants on a windowsill is to install a window greenhouse or a growth chamber. Both will give better control of the environment around the plants, as they isolate the growing area from the room. They are also less expensive to install than a traditional home greenhouse.

Window Greenhouses

Installing a window greenhouse will allow you to expand the windowsill space and provide better growing conditions for your plants. It will also allow more light to enter the room, bringing the outdoors closer to the living area.

Although window greenhouses can be placed over almost any window in any room, they are most frequently added to a kitchen or bathroom. A window greenhouse adds charm to these areas and blends in well with the decor. The additional light makes a small room such as a bathroom seem larger.

Window greenhouses are a good choice if you have limited time for gardening or do not have the space to put in a full-size greenhouse. It is possible to install one over a window in an apartment or condo unit and then take it with you if you move.

One drawback to a window unit is that the environment is more difficult to control in such a small space, and plant care may demand more of your attention. On a partly cloudy day, temperature swings inside the window may be severe, putting stress on the plants. In some units, this can be compensated for by installing an automatic vent opener or a small thermostatically controlled fan.

Selection

Window greenhouses are made in many styles, sizes, and materials (figure 7-1, page 112). If you are handy with tools, you can build your own or install a kit unit.

The smallest units fit in the lower half of a double-hung window. They are installed similar to a window air conditioner unit. If you can afford to do so, it is better to get a full-size unit that encloses the whole window. This is more cost-effective on a dollar-per-square-foot basis and also provides a larger volume of air for better temperature control. For larger windows, you can combine two or more units to cover the area.

Most kit manufacturers make several styles and sizes. Frame material can be wood or aluminum. Redwood or cypress are long-lasting woods that fit into many home decors. For long life and low maintenance, choose a vinyl-coated wood frame. When sizing a window greenhouse, decide where it will be attached. The window frame is generally the best place to attach the greenhouse if it is smooth and at least 3 inches wide. The next best location may be to fasten it to the house siding outside the window frame. This may give a smooth area and also allows a larger unit with more growing space. Some modification to the siding may be needed if it is clapboards, stone, or

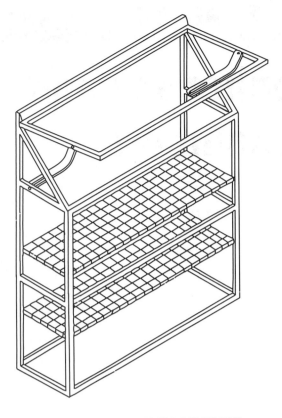

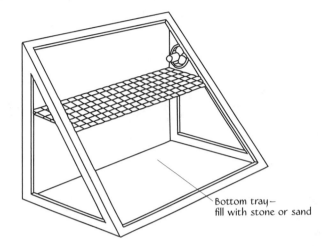

Bottom tray—
fill with stone or sand

WINDOW GREENHOUSE WITH TOP-OPENING VENT

SLANT-FRONT WINDOW GREENHOUSE

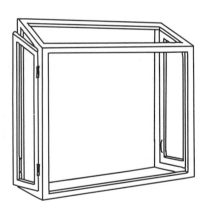

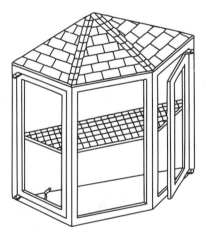

WINDOW GREENHOUSE WITH SIDE-OPENING VENTS

BAY WINDOW GREENHOUSE

Figure 7-1. Types of window greenhouses

brick. Remember that the greenhouse must be fastened securely to the house. Consider this when locating the window.

Other considerations in locating a greenhouse window are the same as those used when locating a greenhouse. It is best if the location gets a minimum of 5–6 hours of sun in the winter. Sites with shade

from adjacent buildings or coniferous trees should be avoided if possible. Also avoid a situation where snow will slide off of the house roof onto the greenhouse.

Glazing choices are usually the same as those for a conventional greenhouse. The most frequently used glazings are glass, acrylic, and polycarbonate. Some manufacturers use conventional window units, either with or without operating hardware. If your yard has a lot of birds, it may be better to select stronger tempered glass rather than double-strength glass, as they tend to fly into glass, especially if they can see through the house to light from another window or see the reflection of light from a mirror.

Double-pane windows should be used in colder climates to reduce heat loss. You could also use interior blinds to give an additional barrier. Low-emissivity glass should be avoided if you want the greatest light transmission. Any windows or vents that open should have screens to keep insects out and good locks for security.

Shelves for plant support can be wire mesh, which gives good air circulation around the plants, or solid material such as glass or plastic, which prevents dripping from one level to another. Most manufacturers supply two or three shelves. Shelves should be adjustable so you can grow a variety of plant sizes. A water containment tray should be placed in the bottom to catch any water that drips. Plastic trays can also be placed on each shelf under the plants.

Environmental Control

Cooling

Vents are the most common method of providing cool, fresh air. Vents should be easy to adjust and operate. Some models have a solar-powered vent opener.

Where better control is desired, a small fan or squirrel cage blower could be installed. It should provide about two volume air changes per minute and be controlled by a thermostat that is shaded and located near the plants.

To reduce the intensity of the sun and heat buildup, attach a piece of shade cloth to the outside of the greenhouse for the summer. Plastic shade film that adheres to the inside of the glazing is available from some manufacturers.

Moisture Control

An easy way to provide additional moisture for plants that require high humidity is to place water in the tray at the bottom. Sand, peastone, or perlite in the tray will give additional surface area and humidity. Some homeowners use a small cool-vapor humidifier.

Heating

In most areas of the United States, adequate heat can be supplied from the room. Most heating systems have registers or radiators underneath the window.

An easy way to provide additional heat if it is needed is to place an electric heating cable, similar to those used for germination, in the tray in the bottom of the window greenhouse. Size it to 10–12 watts per square foot of base area. For example, a greenhouse with a 1-foot-by-3-foot base will require 30–36 watts of heat (1 foot x 3 feet x 10 watts/square feet = 30 watts). Place sand over the heat cable to protect it from damage. The cable should be controlled by a thermostat to maintain the desired temperature. A separate electric circuit to the greenhouse is best if heat, lights, or fans will be installed.

Installation

For most installations, it will take less than a day to attach the window greenhouse and get it into operation. Some units come as kits that have to be assembled. Others come preassembled and ready to attach.

One decision that will have to be made is whether to leave the existing window in place or remove it. Leaving it in place allows you to isolate the greenhouse area. This may be a good option if the greenhouse will not be used year-round or if you need to do some pesticide application.

On the other hand, the window is always in the way when you want to tend to the plants. It also blocks the view of the plants. Windows can be removed and replaced by hinged, louvered doors that provide privacy for the night. Some windows, such as sliders, are easy to remove, and you can decide which way you want to operate.

The plants can exert a considerable amount of weight on the greenhouse, so be sure to have a solid attachment. Follow the manufacturer's recommendations. Knee braces placed under the base can help support some of the load. They should be securely fastened to the house wall.

A tight seal is also important to keep out rain and air infiltration. The top should have flashing that fits under the house siding. The sides should be caulked to seal any cracks. If you live in a cold climate, insulate the bottom to reduce heat loss. Foam board such as polyurethane works well.

Operation

Almost any type of plant can be grown in a window greenhouse. However, it is probably better to limit yourself to plants that have similar environmental requirements, as the temperature will be fairly uniform throughout the growing space.

Avoid overcrowding to avoid disease problems. This is generally more of a problem during the winter when ventilation is at a minimum. Also, be careful when bringing in plants from outside gardens or other greenhouses. Make sure you are not bringing in pests along with them, or the pests may spread to the other plants rather quickly.

From time to time, remove everything from the window and disinfect the growing space. A solution of one part bleach to ten parts water works well. Wash down the glazing, shelves, tray, and any equipment that is installed.

Operating a window greenhouse, especially the vents, can be tricky. Even on a cold winter day, the greenhouse can reach a temperature well over 100°F if everything is sealed up tight. Therefore, if you are not home to manage the greenhouse, keep a vent cracked or open the window into the home to avoid this situation.

Germination and Growth Chambers

Moisture, oxygen, and a favorable temperature are the critical factors in the rapid germination of most seed. Germination begins when absorption through the seed coat increases the moisture level in the seed. Enzyme activity begins, and new tissue starts to form.

Stored food reserves are broken down through respiration, which requires oxygen and energy. Cell division and enlargement cause the seed to expand and crack, and the root begins to extend into the growing medium. The growing tip of the plant then pushes through the surface of the medium, and the seed leaves start to expand. This is followed by emergence of the first true leaves.

Temperature is very important. Each plant species has a temperature range within which seeds will germinate. Optimum germination occurs within a very narrow range, which is usually stated on the seed packet. Most seeds are in the range of 70–75°F.

The need for light during germination varies with the plant species. For some seeds, there is an absolute light requirement. For others, light may inhibit germination. Some seeds are not affected at all and will germinate in either light or dark.

For seeds that require light, intensity and duration may be important. For example, 'Accent Orange' impatiens' germination percentage is highest when seed receive 10 ft-c of light for 6 hours daily or 1,000 ft-c for 1 hour daily. Some seed can receive a prelight treatment and will germinate well. Some seed companies list light requirements on the seed package. Providing the optimum conditions for seed germination can have a significant effect on the germination time.

Germination Cabinet

Although many growers are successful at using an area in the greenhouse for germination, it is usually difficult to get precise control of the environment. A better place would be a germination cabinet.

A simple germination cabinet design is shown in figure 7-2. It is an insulated box that holds up to four flats and is heated with light bulbs that operate continuously. The size of the light bulbs determines the temperature. One or two 15-watt bulbs will probably be all you need.

Growth Chamber

A growth chamber or room has light and heat to grow plants. It can also be used to germinate seeds that require light.

A growth chamber can be as simple as a fluorescent light fixture suspended over the plants or as complex as a room with light racks and an environment control system.

Light-Support Frame

A simple setup for a light-support frame is shown in figure 7-3 on page 116. The rack supports a 4-foot fluorescent light fixture above the plants. The height is adjustable using chains. Daylength is controlled by an inexpensive 24-hour timer. A sheet metal tray in the bottom catches water and can provide moisture to the plant area. Enclosing the rack with plastic will help retain heat and moisture. The rack is portable, so it can be moved if necessary. It could be located in a greenhouse, basement, or spare room.

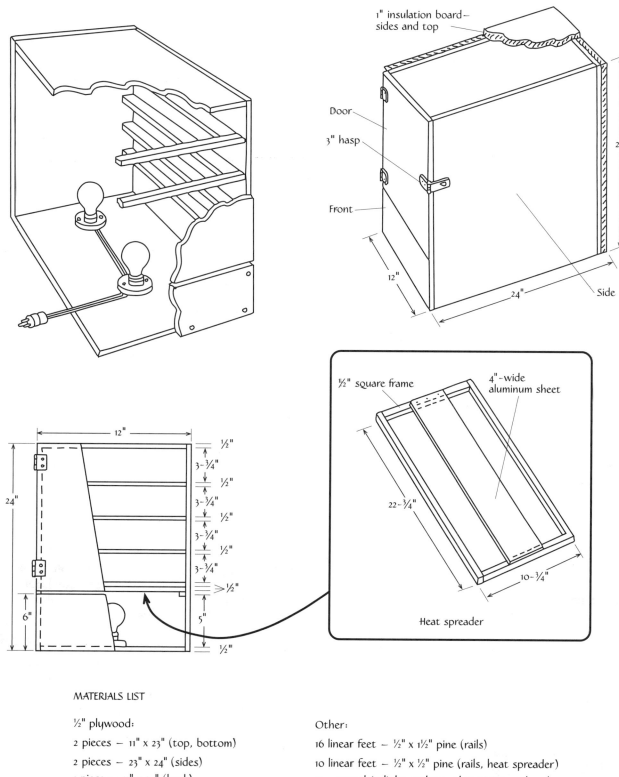

1" insulation board—
sides and top

Door

3" hasp

Front

24"

12"

24"

Side

½" square frame

4"-wide
aluminum sheet

22-¾"

10-¾"

Heat spreader

12"

½"

3-¾"

½"

3-¾"

½"

3-¾"

½"

3-¾"

½"

24"

>½"

5"

6"

½"

MATERIALS LIST

½" plywood:

2 pieces — 11" x 23" (top, bottom)

2 pieces — 23" x 24" (sides)

1 piece — 11" x 24" (back)

1 piece — 12" x 18" (door)

1 piece — 6" x 12" (front)

Other:

16 linear feet — ½" x 1½" pine (rails)

10 linear feet — ½" x ½" pine (rails, heat spreader)

2 — porcelain light sockets, plus wiring and a plug

1 pair — 2½" x 2½" hinge

1 — 3" hasp

1 — 4"-wide x 23"-long aluminum sheet

finish nails, screws, glue

1 piece — 4' x 4' x 1"-thick insulation board

Figure 7-2. Germination cabinet construction

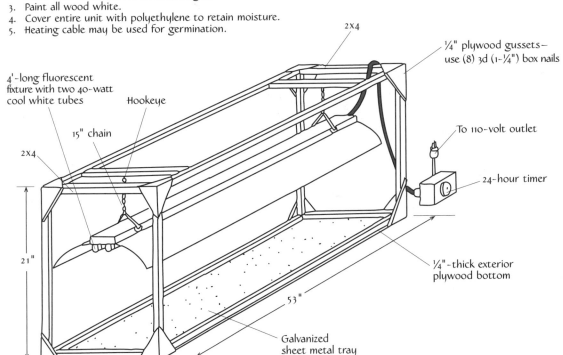

Notes
1. All lumber is 2x2, except as noted.
2. If strip fluorescent fixtures are used, cover with aluminum foil to reflect light.
3. Paint all wood white.
4. Cover entire unit with polyethylene to retain moisture.
5. Heating cable may be used for germination.

2x4

¼" plywood gussets—
use (8) 3d (1-¼") box nails

4'-long fluorescent
fixture with two 40-watt
cool white tubes

Hookeye

15" chain

To 110-volt outlet

2x4

24-hour timer

21"

¼"-thick exterior
plywood bottom

53"

Galvanized
sheet metal tray

14"

Figure 7-3. Light-support frame construction
Adapted from University of Connecticut plan number SP 596.

Cart

If you require more space, a cart is a good choice (figure 7-4). Prefabricated carts are available from greenhouse suppliers and seed catalogs. They contain two or more trays with fluorescent light fixtures.

Rack System

A rack system can be built in the basement or garage (figure 7-5). It is best if the area is isolated from the rest of the building so heat and humidity can be controlled.

Walls can be constructed of 2x4 lumber with a polyethylene vapor barrier on the room side. Add polystyrene or polyurethane insulation board if the building is unheated. Finish wall and floor surfaces with either a white polyester or epoxy chemical-resistant paint, and install a drain in the floor for water removal.

Design the electrical system with adequate capacity for lights, a heater, a fan, and refrigeration equipment. It should be installed to meet the National Electric Code and local codes.

Flats or pots can be supported on fixed or portable shelves. Pressure-treated wood will give good service. Allow for access from one or both sides with an 18- to 24-inch aisle width. When spacing tiers, consider the size of plants to be grown and the height of the light fixtures.

Install fluorescent strip fixtures, 4 feet or 8 feet long, to provide uniform light over the growing area. Cool white bulbs, warm white bulbs, or a combination of the two have been used with success. Install 25 lamp watts per square foot to provide 500–700 ft-c at the leaf surface. Bulbs can be located as close as 6 inches from the plants. A timer or time clock will control daylength.

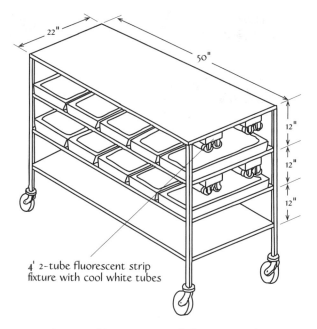

4' 2-tube fluorescent strip fixture with cool white tubes

Use heating cable or agritape with thermostat on bottom shelf. Enclose sides with white poly to retain heat and reflect light.

Figure 7-4. Portable germination/light cart

The heat from the lights should be more than adequate to maintain temperatures between 65° and 85°F. Make provisions for adding heat when the lights are off, or arrange the light scheme so that some lights are on at all times.

Depending on the size of the room and the amount of lighting installed, you may need a ventilation or refrigeration system to remove excessive heat. Each 4-foot fluorescent bulb, including the ballast, gives off 170 Btu's per hour. An 8-foot tube doubles that.

Air circulation within the room is important to maintain a uniform temperature. A small circulating fan with a capacity of about 2 cubic feet per minute per square foot of floor area will work well. Install it to operate continuously or when a temperature difference of more than 3°F occurs between the floor and ceiling.

A high level of moisture keeps the seed and growing medium from drying out. Install a fog or fine-mist nozzle near the floor to add moisture. The nozzle can be controlled by a humidistat.

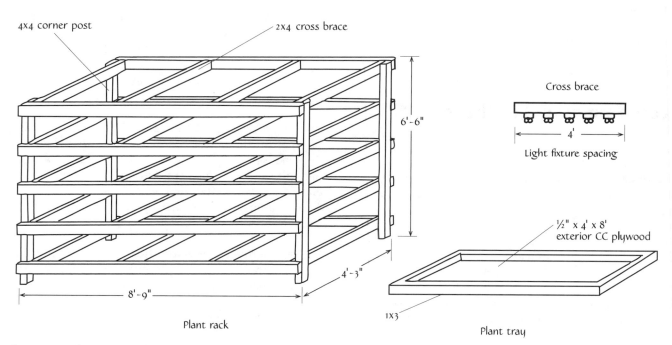

4x4 corner post

2x4 cross brace

6'-6"

Cross brace

4'

Light fixture spacing

½" x 4' x 8' exterior CC plywood

8'-9"

4'-3"

1x3

Plant rack

Plant tray

Figure 7-5. Plant rack system

CHAPTER 8

Garden Structures

Over the years, many structures and methods other than greenhouses have been developed to protect plants. This chapter will discuss several options that can be used in conjunction with a home greenhouse to provide additional low-cost growing space. Even if you don't have a greenhouse, these systems can be fun to work with if you want to beat your neighbor to get the first ripe tomato or if you want to have leafy greens all winter.

Cold Frames and Hotbeds

A cold frame or hotbed makes a great supplement to a greenhouse. It can add low-cost growing space for hardening off annuals in the spring, propagating perennials and herbs, or overwintering plants that need a little extra protection.

If you are just starting to grow plants and don't have a greenhouse, you can use a cold frame or hotbed to grow some early lettuce or start some transplants for your garden. In northern climates, these structures can extend the fall season and provide you with leafy vegetables well into December.

The basic difference between a cold frame and a hotbed is the source of heat. The only heat for a cold frame comes from the sun shining through the cover. At night, the cover slows the loss of heat. The hotbed, on the other hand, was traditionally heated by the decomposition of horse manure. Today, electric heating cables are a cleaner and more efficient alternative. In either case, the basic frame construction is the same.

Constructing the Frame

Building a frame is an excellent weekend project. All you need are a few common hand tools and materials that are readily available at a lumberyard.

Although a hotbed or cold frame can be built to any size, a 3-foot-wide by 6-foot-long structure is convenient for the home gardener. This size is easy to reach into and can be built so it disassembles for easy storage if you do not want to leave it in place during the summer.

Several materials can be used for the frame, including rough or finished lumber, treated or untreated plywood, or concrete blocks. An easy-to-use material that will last a lifetime is pressure-treated plywood, a relatively new product for consumers now available at most lumberyards. When selecting this material, observe several precautions.

1. Be sure that the pressure-treating preservative is not creosote or pentachlorophenol, as the fumes from them are toxic to many types of plants.

2. Plywood treated with chromated copper arsenate (CCA) or ammonical copper arsenite (ACA) should be given a coat of white latex paint to reflect light and to seal in the preservative.

3. After working with these materials, dispose of scraps and sawdust by ordinary trash collection and wash your hands.

Wood such as redwood or cypress will last a long time but is fairly expensive. Untreated lumber such as pine, spruce, or oak will rot in a few years unless it is protected with a preservative such as copper naphthanate.

Glass is the most permanent type of glazing material for a cold frame or hotbed. If you have a couple of storm windows, you can incorporate them into the design. Polyethylene film or acrylic plastic sheets can also be used. Because the low-cost polyethylene film commonly found in hardware and department stores has a life of less than one year when exposed to sunlight, a longer-life greenhouse grade available from greenhouse suppliers is a better choice. One disadvantage to this material is that it comes in rolls of 50 or 100 feet. Acrylic is a more permanent material having a life of 10–15 years. It can be purchased at most home centers. A ⅛-inch thickness will give good service, especially if you live in an area that receives a lot of snow.

Locating the Frame

A gently sloping, well-drained site is the best location for the frame, because rainwater will drain away rather than fill up the bed area. A south-facing, sunny site with wind protection on the north and west is ideal (figure 8-1). An east or west orientation will do but will get less sunlight.

Locating the frame near the house has several advantages. It is close to water and electricity and is easy to reach, which is good because young plants require frequent attention.

Figure 8-1. Locate a cold frame or hotbed where it will receive good sunlight and is protected from wind

Making a Hotbed

The earliest hotbeds were placed over a foot or two of horse or mule manure and bedding. The composting manure heated the frame. Where horse manure is available, this method is still used, but the electric heating cables available today are cleaner, more convenient, and more efficient.

Plastic-covered waterproof heating cables are available from greenhouse suppliers and electric-supply houses. They are flexible and easy to install and will function well for five years or more when used properly.

For the basic 3-foot-by-6-foot frame, a 250- to 300-watt cable is needed. The cable will be 40–60 feet long. Other size hotbeds require 10–15 watts per square foot of area; the higher value is used for winter production or in colder climates. For example, a 4-foot-by-8-foot size would require about 500 watts (4 feet x 8 feet x 15 watts/square foot = 480 watts). The wattage is usually listed on the package.

There are two ways to install the heating cables, depending on how you grow your plants. If the hotbed is to be used to grow plants in pots or flats, the cable can be placed in the middle of a 2-inch layer of sand and then covered with a wire mesh with holes no greater than 1 inch (figure 8-2 on page 120). This protects the cable from damage. Fence wire or hardware mesh, available at hardware stores or garden centers, is a good choice. The plant containers are placed on the wire.

When crops are grown in soil in the hotbed, the cable must be placed deeper (figure 8-3 on page 120). Dig down about 8 inches, removing the soil and storing it nearby. Level the bottom of the bed and space the cable evenly across the bed. Be sure that the cable does not cross itself. Cover the cable with an inch or two of sand. Add the wire as in the previous method. Now replace the garden soil, removing stones and clumps of sod and adding peat, humus, fertilizer, and lime as needed to a depth of 4–6 inches. Now you are ready to plant.

The heating cable must be properly wired to operate satisfactorily. For a location near the house or garage, use heavy-duty, waterproof extension cord. Installations farther from the power source require underground cable (type UF). Make a 6-inch-deep slit trench and place the cable in it. This will keep the cable out of the way of the lawnmower and away from children. For a heating cable up to 500 watts, a no. 12 wire can be used if the hotbed is located less

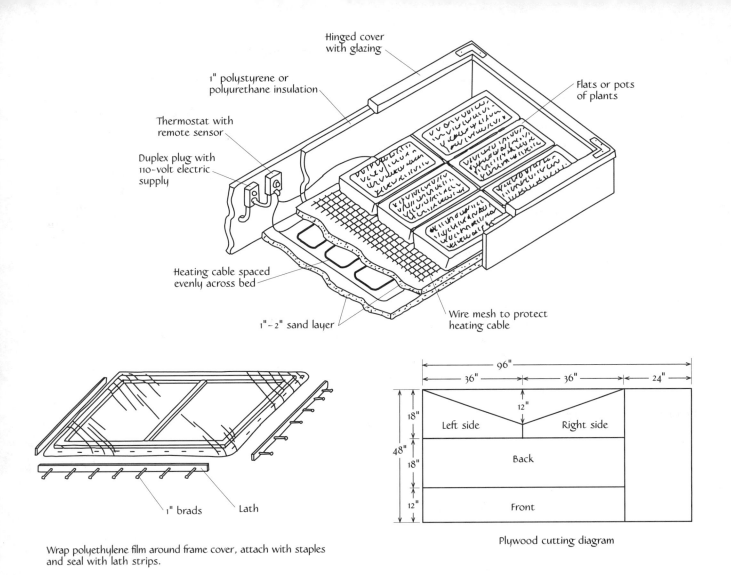

Figure 8-2. Hotbed with electric heating cable for plants grown in flats or pots

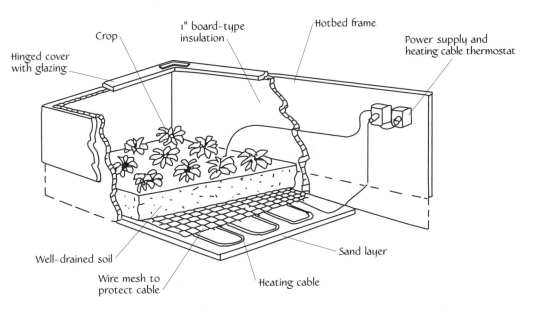

Figure 8-3. Hotbed with heating cable for growing crops in soil

than 120 feet from the power source. Contact an electrician for sizing wire for greater distances.

Heating cables are available either with or without an integral thermostat (figure 8-4). If you will use the hotbed mainly for propagation, the integral thermostat should probably be set at 70°F. If you will grow plants that require a lower temperature, install a separate thermostat with a remote sensor. The thermostat should be housed in a waterproof box to prevent a short circuit.

The control box can be attached to the back of the hotbed and the sensor placed about one-third the distance across the bed in a flat or the soil. The end of the sensor should be buried in the soil. Do not place the sensor directly above a heating cable. Plug the heating cable into the receptacle on the control box.

Set the temperature dial on the control box to the desired soil temperature. Most thermostats have a range of +/−2° between the on and off positions. For example, if you select 70°F as the desired soil temperature, the heating cable will turn on at 68° and off at 72°.

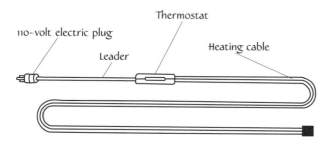

Heating cable with integral thermostat

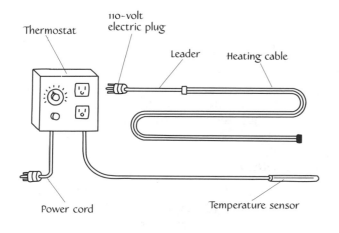

Heating cable with independent thermostat

Figure 8-4. Types of heating cables

Using a Cold Frame or Hotbed

A soil temperature of 70–75°F is ideal for germinating most seed. After the seedlings are up, adjust the temperature to suit the particular plants being grown. Cool-season crops such as lettuce, cabbage, broccoli, and cauliflower do well at a night temperature of 50–60°. Warm-season crops such as tomatoes, peppers, squash, melons, and most annual flowers like a temperature of 55–65°. Day temperatures can run 10–20° warmer.

Ventilation is critical on mild, sunny days. Because of the small volume of air in the frame, the temperature can reach excessive levels (100°F) in a very short time when the sun is out. Most cold frames and hotbeds are ventilated manually by propping up the cover during the day.

Nonelectric (solar-powered) vent controllers are available from garden supply and seed catalogs for about $60 (see figure 6-34 on page 96). They operate on the expansion of a mineral wax in a hydraulic cylinder and work best within a 60–85°F temperature range. Controllers are available that can exert a force up to 35 pounds.

Heat loss, whether you have a cold frame or a hotbed, can be kept to a minimum by making sure that the cover fits tightly on the frame. Use weather-stripping to seal the cracks. Attach 1-inch-thick insulation board to the inside of the frame boards with large-headed roofing nails. Banking soil against the outside will also help. On cold nights, an old blanket or quilt placed over the top will give added insulation (figure 8-5). If the frame is electrically heated, these measures will also save you money.

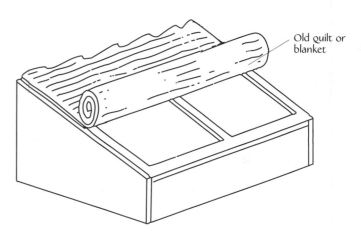

Figure 8-5. Retain heat by covering on cold nights

Construction and Operating Costs

Depending on where you purchase the materials, the cost of the basic frame should be between $40 and $60. A 300-watt heating cable and thermostat, as described above, will cost an additional $125 or so.

Tests at various locations throughout the country indicate that a basic 3-foot-by-6-foot hotbed uses 1–2 kilowatt-hours of electricity a day, which works out to between 10 and 20 cents (at an 8 cent/kilowatt-hour power rate). This is much lower than the cost of operating a light room or small greenhouse.

Plants to Grow in Cold Frames and Hotbeds

What you grow in your cold frame or hotbed will depend on the climate, the season, and your preference for flowers or vegetables. In cold climates, the gardening season is short due to cool temperatures and short days in the spring and fall, which inhibit active plant growth. A frame can be used to extend the season to 10 months or more. Leafy greens such as lettuce, spinach, Swiss chard, and parsley do well in cooler weather and lower light levels.

Wintering over containers of tulips, hyacinths, daffodils, or crocus bulbs and then forcing them in early spring can provide early flowers for your home. Pansies can be seeded in the fall and will be ready for transplanting in early spring.

The most common use of cold frames and hotbeds is for starting annual plants for the garden. With a hotbed, seed can be germinated in flats, and then the seedlings can be transplanted after they develop their first true leaves. With a cold frame, it is best to do germination indoors near a radiator or stove. Once transplanted, seedlings can be moved to a frame for hardening off and holding until the garden is ready. A 3-foot-by-6-foot frame will hold nine standard flats.

During the late summer, crops such as broccoli, pepper, spinach, and lettuce can be planted for early-winter harvest.

Shade Houses

Some plants require subdued light or their leaves will burn. A shade house, or lath house as it is sometimes called, can provide reduced light and also wind protection.

The traditional lath house is a structure covered with wooden lath or slats spaced so that only part of the sunlight gets through. It can be aesthetically pleasing and can be used for relaxation and entertainment in addition to growing plants.

Uses for Shade Houses

Shade houses have many uses that fit in well with a greenhouse. They can add to the growing space at a much lower cost than adding on to the greenhouse.

Propagation

Woody cuttings and some perennials do well under shady conditions. They can be grown in containers or directly in a ground bed. A mist system is needed to keep the cuttings moist.

Finishing

Plants grown in a greenhouse can be conditioned in a shade house. The temperature is cooler, and the plants will be protected from direct sunlight for a period of time before they are placed in the garden.

Shading

Plants that can't tolerate high levels of sun will do well in a shade house. The level of shade can be regulated by changing the material used over the structure. Shade levels can vary from a few percent to 90% or more. See "Shade House Construction" for more information.

Overwintering

Providing wind protection to woody ornamentals, perennials, and herbs is important to keep them from drying out during the winter. Containers can also be covered with an insulation material, such as sawdust, wood chips, or peat moss, to keep the root ball from freezing and thawing. Foliage can be covered with foam sheeting to reduce damage.

Insect Exclusion

Many insects can be excluded by covering the frame with an insect screening. Care should be taken to keep the screening tight without any holes. Because the tiny holes in the screen restrict air movement, a large area of the surface needs to be covered to allow ventilation so that the temperature in the shade house does not become excessive.

Shade House Construction

Almost any structure that can be covered with a glazing material can be covered with a shade material. In northern climates, the structure should be strong enough to support a snow load if the shading is left on all winter. In southern climates, a lighter structure can be built.

A number of materials can provide shade. Woven shade fabrics such as polypropylene saran and polyethylene are available in many levels of shade. Refer to "Shade Fabrics" on page 94 for more information.

Several wood products are commonly used. Furring strips, available at lumberyards, are low-cost and easy to attach to a wood frame. Spacing can be varied to achieve any level of shade. A greater than 50% shade level can be achieved by alternating the lath and an equally wide space.

A treated shade fence made of pressure-treated wood that is resistant to rot and mildew is available from several greenhouse suppliers. Wooden lath is woven with two wires to give an even spacing. It comes in 4-foot or 6-foot widths in rolls 50 feet long. Snow fence, a product used by highway departments to prevent drifting onto the road, is also readily available.

A simple frame to cover a growing bed is shown in figure 8-6. It can be made portable and can be built to any length. A mist line could be added for propagation.

Almost any greenhouse frame can be made into a shade house. Figure 8-7 on page 124 shows a simple A-frame made from 2x4 lumber. Covering can be lath or shade fabric. The endwall can be closed in for the winter.

A simple pipe frame shade area is shown in figure 8-8 on page 124. Standard galvanized water pipe is fastened together with slip-on fittings on the corners. Shade fabric can be custom-fit to cover the structure. In heavy snow areas, the fabric should be removed for the winter.

In areas of heavy rain, the shade house can be covered with film plastic on top to shed water. A slope should be built into the frame, and the covering material should be kept tight to prevent water pockets from forming.

Rowcovers and High Tunnels

The major use of rowcovers and tunnels is to provide enough environmental modification to gain several weeks at both ends of the outdoor growing season. These structures are relatively low-cost and can be built to fit your needs. You can cover just one row or your whole garden.

Rowcovers and tunnels do not require electricity, as they are not heated and ventilation is controlled manually. However, more management is needed to ensure that the temperature doesn't get too low on frosty nights or too high on bright, sunny days.

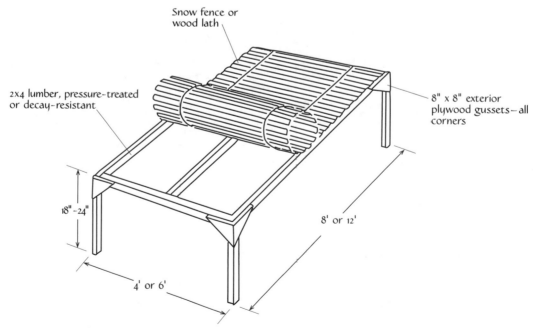

Figure 8-6. Lath-covered frame for shade

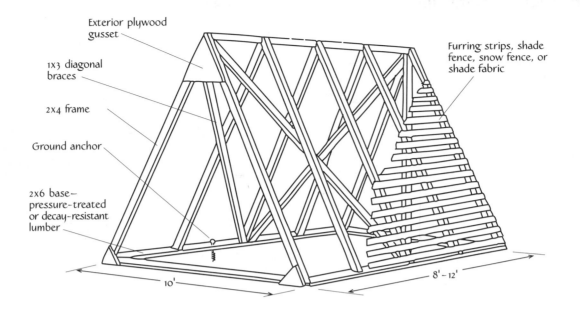

Exterior plywood
gusset

1x3 diagonal
braces

2x4 frame

Ground anchor

2x6 base—
pressure-treated
or decay-resistant
lumber

Furring strips, shade
fence, snow fence, or
shade fabric

10'

8'–12'

Figure 8-7. A-frame shade house

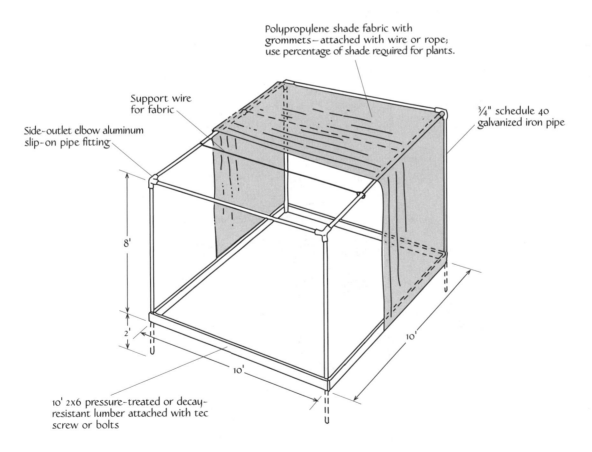

Polypropylene shade fabric with
grommets—attached with wire or rope;
use percentage of shade required for plants.

Support wire
for fabric

Side-outlet elbow aluminum
slip-on pipe fitting

¾" schedule 40
galvanized iron pipe

8'

2'

10'

10'

10'

10' 2x6 pressure-treated or decay-
resistant lumber attached with tec
screw or bolts

Figure 8-8. Shade shelter with a pipe frame

These structures or systems have to be placed where there is fertile, well-drained soil. Mulches may also be needed to keep the moisture level up and to reduce weeds. A thin, black polyethylene mulch plastic is commonly used to absorb heat and eliminate most of the weeds. The types of crops grown need to be carefully selected for the time of year and the type of environment that will be created.

Rowcovers

A rowcover is a flexible, transparent material that is supported by wire hoops or floated over one or more rows of crops in the garden. It is usually put in place when the crop is seeded or transplanted into the ground and remains over the crop for 2–4 weeks during the spring and longer during the fall and winter. A hoop-supported rowcover may also be called a low tunnel.

The main advantage of using a rowcover is to trap the heat of the day to warm the air and soil, thus accelerating growth. It also slows the loss of heat at night but will modify the temperature only about 3–4°F. On a night when the temperature falls below 28°F, plants may still freeze.

Rowcovers provide wind protection, which keeps the plants warmer and reduces moisture loss. They can also keep out some pests, especially those that fly.

Hoop-Supported Rowcovers

Solid, slit, or perforated clear polyethylene (1- to 3-mil) can be used for hoop-supported rowcovers. The solid material is usually placed over hoops that are inserted into the ground along the sides of the row. A typical system uses 65-inch lengths of #9 hardened, galvanized wire, spaced 3–4 feet apart and pushed into the soil until they form hoops about 12–14 inches high at the top (figure 8-9). The hoops are covered with two 3-foot-wide pieces of plastic that are buried along the edge of the row and held together at the top of the hoops with clothespins. Ventilation is easy—just unfasten the clothespins and drop the plastic during warm days. Close it back up again at night.

To overcome the labor involved with opening and closing the plastic, researchers developed a slit plastic that has a double row of 5-inch slits that allow heated air to escape. A perforated plastic with rows of holes is also available. Both of these are not quite as efficient as a solid material but reduce the labor considerably.

A portable rowcover can be made from PVC pipe (figure 8-10 on page 126). The one shown in figure 8-10 can be disassembled and stored when not in use.

Spun-bonded polyester and polypropylene materials are also used for rowcovers. These have about 80%

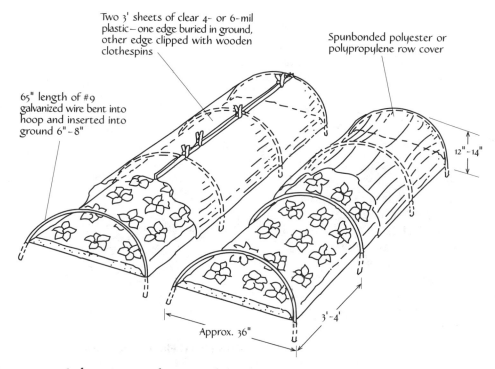

Two 3' sheets of clear 4- or 6-mil plastic—one edge buried in ground, other edge clipped with wooden clothespins

Spunbonded polyester or polypropylene row cover

65" length of #9 galvanized wire bent into hoop and inserted into ground 6"–8"

12"–14"

Approx. 36"

3'–4'

Figure 8-9. Hoop-supported rowcover or low tunnel

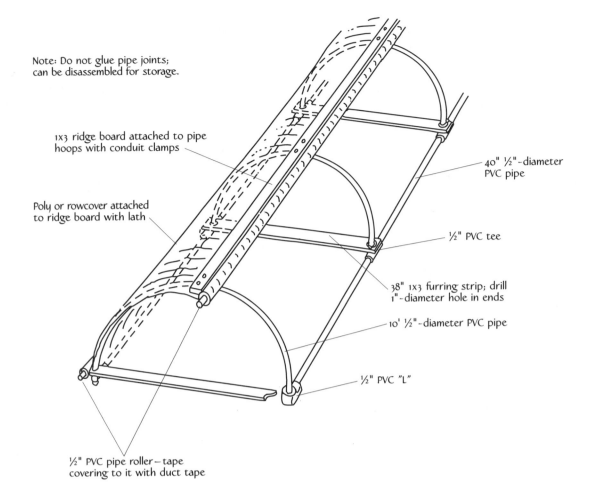

Note: Do not glue pipe joints; can be disassembled for storage.

1x3 ridge board attached to pipe hoops with conduit clamps

Poly or rowcover attached to ridge board with lath

40" ½"-diameter PVC pipe

½" PVC tee

38" 1x3 furring strip; drill 1"-diameter hole in ends

10' ½"-diameter PVC pipe

½" PVC "L"

½" PVC pipe roller—tape covering to it with duct tape

Figure 8-10. Low-cost PVC pipe rowcover

light transmission, are ultraviolet stabilized, and will allow air and water to pass through. These materials can be rolled up and reused for several years. Cost is about 2–3 cents per square foot.

Floating Rowcovers

For floating rowcovers, the cover is placed directly on top of the crop (figure 8-11). The polyester or polypropylene materials come in large sheets that cover several rows at a time. Weighing only 1 pound for 250 square feet, these materials do not damage the plants. They are available at garden centers or greenhouse suppliers. Only the edges of the rowcover have to be secured, so the larger the piece, the less work. Burying the edges in the soil or weighing them down with pieces of lumber, pipe, or rebar are good ways to secure them.

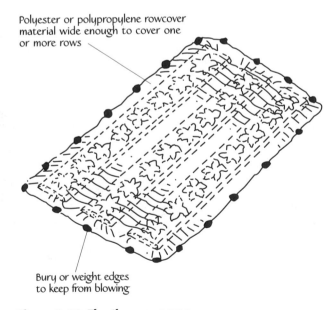

Polyester or polypropylene rowcover material wide enough to cover one or more rows

Bury or weight edges to keep from blowing

Figure 8-11. Floating rowcover

High Tunnels

The high tunnel was developed to grow taller crops such as trellis tomatoes. This is a greenhouse-like structure without heat, mechanical ventilation, or electricity that is tall enough to walk in. It can be built of wood or PVC pipe, but it is usually made from steel tubing bent into a hoop shape. Frequently, it is made so that it can be moved from one section of the garden to another.

These types of structures have been used for many years in Europe, Asia, and the Middle East, where they provide protection for vegetable, fruit, and flower crops. They are fairly new to the United States for vegetables but have been used for about 25 years for overwintering nursery stock in containers.

A typical use in the northern United States is to start a vegetable crop about one month earlier than crops grown outdoors. The growing season can also be extended by 4–6 weeks in the fall. In moderate climates, leafy crops can be grown all winter.

High Tunnel Construction

Most greenhouse manufacturers make a standard-size unit about 15 feet wide that is made from 20-foot lengths of steel tubing (figure 8-12). The bows are normally spaced 4 feet apart. Attachment to the ground is by 3-foot-long stakes driven into the ground about 24 inches. A baseboard and hip board provide stability and anchorage for the plastic. Endwalls are 2x4 lumber covered with plastic. The structure can have a large door to allow entrance by a garden tractor with tillage equipment, or the endwall can be made detachable.

You can build your own high tunnel following the plans in appendix C on page 173. This 10-foot-wide unit is made from ¾-inch conduit and bent into shape using a wooden form. It can be built any length, but a convenient size for the home gardener is 12–20 feet. Ground attachment is by ground stakes, similar to the method used in commercial ones.

Ventilation is provided by roll-up sides (figure 8-13). The plastic is attached with battens only at the hip rail and endwalls. The ends at the baseboard are taped to a length of pipe with a tee handle that allows the sidewall plastic to be rolled up when ventilation is needed. As with the rowcovers, management is critical to keep the temperature in the desired range.

It is best to locate the tunnel where it will get good sunlight, especially early in the season. It should be kept away from the shadows of trees and buildings. The orientation should be so that the roll-up sides intercept summer breezes to get maximum cooling at that time of year.

Water for a small high tunnel can be supplied with watering cans. For larger structures, a hose or piped-in water supply is necessary. The supply can be connected to a drip irrigation system for crops like tomatoes, peppers, or squash that are grown through a plastic mulch. An overhead system could also be set up for leafy and root crops.

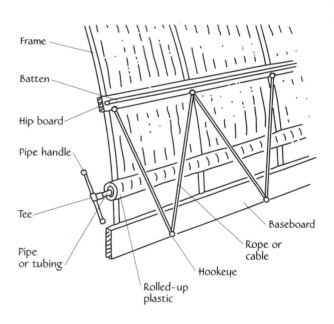

Figure 8-13. Roll-up side construction

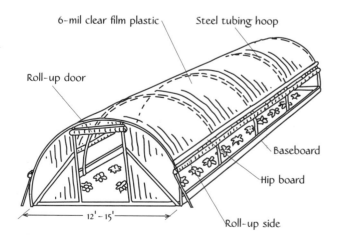

Figure 8-12. High tunnel

Cropping Systems for High Tunnels

Almost any crop can be grown in a high tunnel. It probably makes the most sense to use the structure to grow vegetables that you would like to have early in the summer, such as lettuce, peas, radishes, tomatoes, and squash. Commercially, high tunnels are being used to force strawberries into production before the outdoor ones ripen. Tunnels are ideal for hardening off plants before setting them into the garden.

In cooler northern climates, a tunnel can provide warmer temperatures for growing crops such as peppers, eggplant, and melons during the summer.

You can use the high tunnel in the fall to extend the gardening season by growing vegetables that can be harvested until late December. Seed during August and September so that the crop is approaching maturity before the cooler weather sets in. The yield is limited by available sunlight, which diminishes as the days pass.

With a little straw protection, root crops that are grown during the summer can be dug all winter. High tunnels can provide temperature modification and wind protection to nursery plants, perennials, and herbs during the winter. Extra protection can be provided during the winter by placing rowcovers over the crop. Research on these methods has been done by Eliot Coleman and reported in his book *The Winter-Harvest Manual,* which is listed in the references section on page 191.

Maintaining the Greenhouse: A Checklist

A well-maintained greenhouse operates and performs better. Periodic maintenance keeps equipment operating efficiently and reduces the potential for major expenses.

Home greenhouses are generally trouble-free. Spending a couple of hours from time to time to clean and lubricate the mechanical equipment and occasionally washing and painting the frame is all that is needed. Below is a checklist that includes most maintenance items.

Frame

☐ Adjust door latches and lubricate hinges. Check fasteners for tightness.

☐ Wood — Scrape loose paint, prime and coat with a good grade of white latex paint.

☐ Metal — Loosen paint with a wire brush, prime and coat with a good grade of metal paint.

☐ Metal benches — Clean, brush, and coat with a rust inhibitor before applying a metal paint.

☐ Mildew — Remove mildew before painting.

Mix ⅔ cup household cleaner containing trisodium phosphate, ⅓ cup laundry detergent, 1 quart household bleach, and 3 quarts warm water. Scrub with a medium-soft brush and let stand a few minutes. Rinse with clean water.

Glazing

Permanent glazing and greenhouse-grade film plastic should be cleaned before winter to improve light transmission.

☐ Glass — Wash with clean water and a nonabrasive detergent. Shade compound can be removed with a commercial cleaning compound or a homemade shade remover.

Greenhouse Shade Remover

1 quart hot water

1 pound washing soda (sodium carbonate)

¼ pound Tri-Soda (trisodium phosphate)

Stir until dissolved. Add 1 quart hydrofluoric acid (52%). Pour this into 5 gallons of cold water. Stir. CAUTION: Wear protective gloves and goggles. Rinse thoroughly with clean water.

☐ Polycarbonate, acrylic — Wash panels with mild soap and lukewarm water using a soft cloth or sponge. Do not use a disinfectant, Pinesol, or Lestoil. Remove minor scratches and abrasions by polishing and filling them with a paste wax or plastic polish.

☐ Caulking — Seal water and air leaks with a high-grade silicone sealant.

☐ Replace poly — Greenhouse-grade plastic has a 3- or 4-year warranty. Trying to extend the life beyond that may be putting your plants at risk. Replacement improves light transmission.

Heating System

A first step is to check the accuracy of a good thermometer by placing the bulb in an ice water bath. The reading should be 32°F. After allowing it to reach room temperature, place the thermometer next to the thermostat sensor. The sensor should not be in direct sunlight. Slowly move the setting on the thermostat until the furnace or boiler starts. The reading should be the same temperature as the thermometer reading. If not, determine the temperature difference and mark the thermostat accordingly. Next time a serviceperson comes, have him or her recalibrate it.

☐ Thermostats require very little maintenance. Once or twice a year, the sensing element should be cleaned by wiping or blowing off the dust. The contacts, if exposed, should be cleaned using a piece of cardstock such as a business card or a spray can of contact cleaner, which is available at most electronic shops. At the same time, check wire connections to be sure they are tight and not broken. Disconnect the power before working on any electrical system.

☐ Clean heat exchange surfaces — Wipe or brush radiators and pipes. Check for cracks that could allow fumes into the greenhouse. Avoid the use of chlorinated and fluorinated compounds, as these may be corrosive to the heat exchanger surface.

☐ Service fuel filters, burners, valves, ignition mechanisms, and motors.

☐ Check flue connectors for tightness.

☐ Check the alarm system.

Cooling System

☐ Lubricate vent arms and gears, bearings, fan motors, and louvers.

☐ Clean fan blades, screening, and louvers.

☐ Evaporative coolers — Check for leaks in water piping. Clean the strainer, drain, and sump.

☐ At the end of the season, remove shade cloth, clean it, fold it, and store it in a location out of the sun.

Water System

☐ Clean filters, irrigation system nozzles, and controls.

Lighting

☐ Clean bulbs and fixtures.

☐ Replace bulbs that are burnt out or darkened.

☐ Clean control switch contacts.

General Cleanliness

☐ Remove dirt and plant residue from floors, benches, and beds to reduce disease potential.

Winter Maintenance

☐ If the greenhouse is to be shut down for the winter, drain water lines and the irrigation system. Turn off the water supply and electrical system. Close vents.

☐ Mice like the warmth of the greenhouse as a home for the winter. Place traps or bait to keep them under control.

Greenhouse and Equipment Suppliers

Greenhouse Manufacturers and General Suppliers

Atlas Greenhouse Systems, Inc.
Highway 82 East, P.O. Box 558
Alapaha, GA 31622
Web site: WWW.ATLASGREENHOUSE.COM

Brady Rooms, Inc.
10A New Bond Street
Worcester, MA 01606
Web site: WWW.BRADYROOMS.COM

Carolina Greenhouses
1504 Cunningham Road
Kinston, NC 28501
Web site: WWW.CAROLINAGREENHOUSES.COM

Charley's Greenhouse Supply
17979 State Route 536
Mount Vernon, WA 98273-3269
Web site: WWW.CHARLEYSGREENHOUSE.COM

Conley Greenhouse Manufacturing & Sales
4344 Mission Boulevard
Montclair, CA 91763
Web site: WWW.CONLEYS.COM

Creative Structures, Inc.
281 N. West End Boulevard
Quakertown, PA 18951-0235

Cropking Greenhouses
5050 Greenwich Road
Seville, OH 44273
Web site: WWW.CROPKING.COM

Farm Wholesale Greenhouses
3740 Brooklake Road NE
Salem, OR 97303
Web site: WWW.FARMWHOLESALE.COM

Florian Greenhouse, Inc.
64 Airport Road
West Milford, NJ 07480-4607
Web site: WWW.FLORIAN-GREENHOUSE.COM

Four Seasons Sunrooms
5005 Veterans Memorial Highway
Holbrook, NY 11741
Web site: WWW.FOUR-SEASONS-SUNROOMS.COM

Gardener's Supply Greenhouses
128 Intervale Road
Burlington, VT 05401
Web site: WWW.GARDENERS.COM

Gardenstyles, Inc., The Juliana Greenhouse People
10740 Lyndale Avenue South Suite 9W
Bloomington, MN 55420
Web site: WWW.GARDENSTYLES.COM

Gothic Arch Greenhouses
P.O. Box 1564 (ZN)
Mobile, AL 36633-1564
Web site: WWW.ZEBRA.NET/~GOTHIC/

Grow-It Greenhouses
17 Wood Street
West Haven, CT 06516
Web site: WWW.GROWITGREENHOUSES.COM

Hobby Gardens Greenhouses
P.O. Box 83
Grand Isle, VT 05438
Web site: WWW.HOBBYGARDENS.COM

Hoop House Greenhouse Kits
1358 Bridge Street (Route 28)
South Yarmouth, MA 02664
Web site: WWW.HOOPHOUSE.COM

Hummert International
4500 Earth City Expressway
Earth City, MO 63045
Web site: WWW.HUMMERT.COM

Jacobs Greenhouse
2315 Whirlpool Street, Box 106
Niagara Falls, NY 14305-2413
Web site: WWW.JACOBSGREENHOUSE.COM

Janco Greenhouses
9390 Davis Avenue
Laurel, MD 20723-1993
Web site: WWW.JANCOINC.COM

Mid East Agricultural Service, Inc.
P.O. Box 20123
Greenville, NC 27858
Web site: WWW.MEAS.NET

National Greenhouse Company
Division of Nexus Corporation
10983 Leroy Drive
Northglenn, CO 80233
Web site: WWW.NATIONALGREENHOUSE.COM

North Country Creative Structures
Route 197, RD 1 Box 1060B
Argyle, NY 12809
Web site: WWW.SUNROOMLIVING.COM

Poly-Tex, Inc.
27725 Danville Avenue / P.O. Box 458
Castle Rock, MN 55010
Web site: WWW.POLY-TEX.COM

Private Garden
36 Commercial Drive, Box 600
Hamden, MA 01036
Web site: WWW.PRIVATE-GARDEN.COM

Renaissance Conservatories
132 Ashmore Drive
Leola, PA 17540
Web site: WWW.RENAISSANCE-ONLINE.COM

Santa Barbara Greenhouses
721 Richmond Avenue
Oxnard, CA 93030
Web site: WWW.SBGREENHOUSE.COM

Solar Innovations, Inc.
60 South Prospect Street
Hellam, PA 17406
Web site: WWW.SOLARINNOVATIONS.COM

Stuppy Greenhouse Supply Co.
P.O. Box 12456
North Kansas City, MO 64116
Web site: WWW.STUPPY.COM

Sturdi-Built Greenhouse Manufacturing Company
11304 SW Boones Ferry Road, Department HG
Portland, OR 97219
Web site: WWW.STURDI-BUILT.COM

Sundance Supply
P.O. Box 225
Olga, WA 98279
Web site: WWW.SUNDANCESUPPLY.COM

Sunglo Solar Greenhouses
214 21st Street SE
Auburn, WA 98002
Web site: WWW.SUNGLOGREENHOUSES.COM

SunPorch Structures, Inc.
495 Post Road East
Westport, CT 06880-4400
Web site: WWW.SUNPORCH.COM

Sun Room Designs
Depot and First Street
Youngwood, PA 15697
Web site: WWW.SUNROOMDESIGNS.COM

Sunshine Garden House
P.O. Box 2068
Longview, WA 98632-8190
Web site: WWW.GARDENHOUSE.COM

Sunshine Rooms, Inc.
3333 North Mead
Wichita, KS 67219
Web site: WWW.SUNSHINEROOMS.COM

Texas Greenhouse Company
2524 White Settlement Road
Fort Worth, TX 76107
Web site: WWW.TEXASGREENHOUSE.COM

TRACO Skytech Systems, Inc.
7030 New Berwick Highway
Bloomsburg, PA 17815-8630
Web site: WWW.TRACO.COM

Turner Greenhouses
Highway 17 Bypass
Goldsboro, NC 27533
Web site: WWW.TURNERGREENHOUSES.COM

Under Glass Manufacturing Corporation
2121 Ulster Avenue, P.O. Box 798
Lake Katrine, NY 12449-0541

Greenhouse Replacement Part Suppliers

Ludy Greenhouse Manufacturing Corp.
P.O. Box 141
New Madison, OH 45346
Web site: WWW.LUDY.COM

Rough Brothers, Inc.
5513 Vine Street
Cincinnati, OH 45217
Web site: WWW.ROUGHBROS.COM

Winandy Greenhouse Co., Inc.
2211 Peacock Road
Richmond, IN 47374-3835

Suppliers of Specific Equipment

AFG Industries, Inc.
1400 Lincoln Street
Kingsport, TN 37662
Web site: WWW.AFG.COM
(Solar glass products and specialty glass)

Apogee Instruments
82 Crockett Avenue
Logan, UT 84321
Web site: WWW.APOGEE-INST.COM
(Quantum light meters)

Aquatherm Industries, Inc.
1940 Rutgers University Boulevard
Lakewood, NJ 08701
Web site: WWW.WARMWATER.COM
(Warm water root zone heater/root zone heat mat)

Batrow, Inc.
171 Short Beach Road
Short Beach, CT 06405
Web site: WWW.BATROW.COM
(Single-zone mist and irrigation controllers)

Biotherm Engineering, Inc.
P.O. Box 6007
Petaluma, CA 94953
(Root zone heat mat)

Continental Products Company
1150 East 222 Street
Euclid, OH 44117
Web site: WWW.CONTINENTALPROD.COM
(Adjustable shading compound)

Ken-Bar
25 Walkers Brook Drive
Reading, MA 01867
Web site: WWW.KEN-BAR.COM
(Agritape root zone heaters; see figure 6-19, page 86)

Klerk's Plastic Products Manufacturing, Inc.
546 L&C Distribution Park
Richburg, SC 29729
Web site: WWW.KLERKSUSA.COM
(Interference film plastics)

Phonetics, Inc.
901 Tryens Road
Aston, PA 19014
Web site: WWW.SENSAPHONE.COM
(Programmable security/environmental monitoring
systems with telephone dial-up)

Pro-Grow Supply Corporation
12675 West Auer Avenue
Brookfield, WI 53005
(Waterproof, flexible propagation mat)

SolarSun, Inc.
15 Blueberry Ridge Road
Setauket, NY 11733
Web site: WWW.SOLSUN.COM
(Sprayable greenhouse coatings for the control of
condensation and light)

Southern Burner Company
P.O. Box 885
Chickasha, OK 73023
Web site: WWW.SOUTHERNBURNER.COM
(Greenhouse unit heaters; no electricity required,
available for natural gas or propane)

Structural Plastics Corporation
2750 Lippincott Boulevard
Flint, MI 48507
Web site: WWW.STRUCTURALPLASTICS.COM
(Lightweight reinforced plastic greenhouse benches)

Thermalarm Products, Inc.
P.O. Box 809, Route 153 South
Center Ossipee, NH 03814
Web site: WWW.THERMALARM.COM
(Low-cost alarm system that activates at high or low
temperatures)

Greenhouse Plans

The following plans are included to give you some ideas and construction techniques. They show a number of different materials that are commonly used in greenhouse construction. They were adapted from plans developed by the University of Connecticut, Rutgers University, and Virginia Polytechnic Institute and State University and have been updated to reflect available materials.

Most of the plans can be modified to fit your needs and location. Length can be increased by adding additional frames. Width is more difficult to modify, as snow and wind loading may affect the size of the structural members. An architect or engineer can help with this modification. All plans should be approved by the building department before construction begins.

The plans include dimensions, cutting and erection diagrams, materials lists, construction notes, and ventilation and heating requirements.

Greenhouse Plan	Page
8' x 12' Lean-to greenhouse	135
8' x 16' Curved-eave, lean-to greenhouse	140
8' x 8' Freestanding greenhouse	145
10' x 10' A-frame greenhouse	147
12' x 15' Gothic greenhouse	151
10' x 12' Slant-leg greenhouse	156
14' x 21' Vertical-leg greenhouse	163
10' x 16' Pit greenhouse	169
10' x 12' High tunnel	173
3' x 6' Cold frame	177

8' x 12' LEAN-TO GREENHOUSE

This greenhouse can be attached to a home, garage, or other building. Constructed of 2x4 lumber, it is attached to a wood post foundation. Length can be varied in 2-foot increments to fit the building it is attached to and your growing space needs. The glazing can be low-cost film plastic, corrugated polycarbonate, or structured sheets. Two 3-foot-wide benches will fit along the sidewalls. This plan was adapted from University of Connecticut plan number 248.

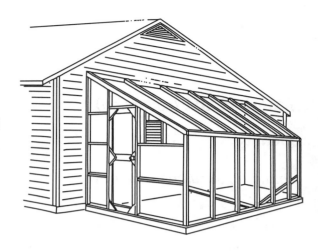

Materials List

Quantity	Item	Location

Frame

☐ 5 pieces	3' 4x4 (pressure-treated)	Foundation posts
☐ 7 pieces	14' 2x4	Rafter and sidewall
☐ 1 piece	12' 2x4	House wall plate
☐ 1 piece	12' 2x4 (pressure-treated)	Base
☐ 2 pieces	8' 2x4 (pressure-treated)	Base
☐ 1 piece	12' ⁵⁄₄x6 (pressure-treated)	Base
☐ 2 pieces	8' ⁵⁄₄x6 (pressure-treated)	Base
☐ 10 pieces	10' 2x3	Endwalls
☐ 1 piece	14' 1x4	Diagonal braces
☐ 1 piece	12' 1x4	Eave

Door

☐ 2 pieces	12' 2x2	Door
☐ —	¼" exterior plywood scraps	Door gussets
☐ 1 pair	3" steel butt hinges	Door
☐ 1	Door latch	Door

Glazing — polycarbonate structured sheet

☐ 3 sheets	4' x 14' x 8mm	Roof and sidewall
☐ 2 sheets	4' x 16' x 8mm	Endwalls
☐ 1 sheet	4' x 8' x 8mm	Door
☐ 70 linear feet	Aluminum double splice	Roof, sidewall, endwall
☐ 170 linear feet	Aluminum single splice	Roof, sidewall, endwall

Materials List *(continued)*

Quantity	Item	Location
Glazing — polycarbonate structured sheet (continued)		
☐ 200	Tec screws #12 x ¾"	Attaching splices
☐ 100	Tec screws #12 x 1"	Attaching sheets
☐ 1 roll	Aluminum foil tape	Sealing top of sheets
☐ 1 roll	Porous tape	Sealing bottom of sheets
Glazing — single layer		
☐ 1 roll	10' x 50' 6-mil polyethylene plastic	
☐ 250 linear feet	1x2 furring strips	Battens
☐ 2 pounds	6d duplex-head nails	Battens
Other		
☐ 1 gallon	White exterior latex paint	All framework
☐ 5 pounds	20d galvanized nails	
☐ 2 pounds	8d galvanized nails	
☐ 2 pounds	6d galvanized nails	

Construction Notes

General

1. Select a level, well-drained site.

2. Select a location that gets good sunlight.

3. Use pressure-treated, decay-resistant lumber that is in contact with the ground.

Frame

1. Use construction-grade lumber.

2. Paint frame with an exterior white paint to reflect light.

3. Door can be placed at either end.

4. Use framing anchors to attach rafters to house or garage.

5. Use flashing between building wall and greenhouse roof.

6. Caulk all cracks.

8' x 12' LEAN-TO GREENHOUSE
(continued)

Construction Notes (continued)

Covering

1. Round and smooth all sharp edges.

2. Polycarbonate will give 20 years of service.

3. For low-cost spring and fall use, a 6-mil layer of polyethylene plastic held in place by 1x2 furring strips is adequate.

4. For year-round use, a double layer of 6-mil polyethylene separated by 2x2 lumber with furring strips over it will work well.

5. The best time to apply plastic is when the temperature is 40–60°F.

Walks

1. A center walk of peastone, brick, or patio blocks laid in sand can be added after the greenhouse is built.

Ventilation

1. A 10"-diameter fan should be used.

2. Locate a 12"-square motorized intake louver in the opposite endwall.

3. Connect the above to a thermostat located in the center of the greenhouse near plant level.

Heat

1. Heat may be supplied from the home heating system or a separate gas or electric heater. The heater output can be obtained from the following table:

Heat requirements — 8' x 12' lean-to greenhouse

		Single-layer glazing (Btu/hour)			Double-layer glazing (Btu/hour)		
			Minimum inside night temperature				
		50°	60°	70°	50°	60°	70°
Minimum	30	9,000	13,800	17,800	6,000	9,150	11,900
outside	20	13,800	17,800	22,350	9,150	11,900	15,350
temperature	10	17,850	22,350	26,800	11,900	15,350	17,800
(°F)	0	22,350	26,800	31,200	15,350	17,800	20,800
	−10	26,800	31,200	35,750	17,800	20,800	23,750

8' x 12' LEAN-TO GREENHOUSE
(continued)

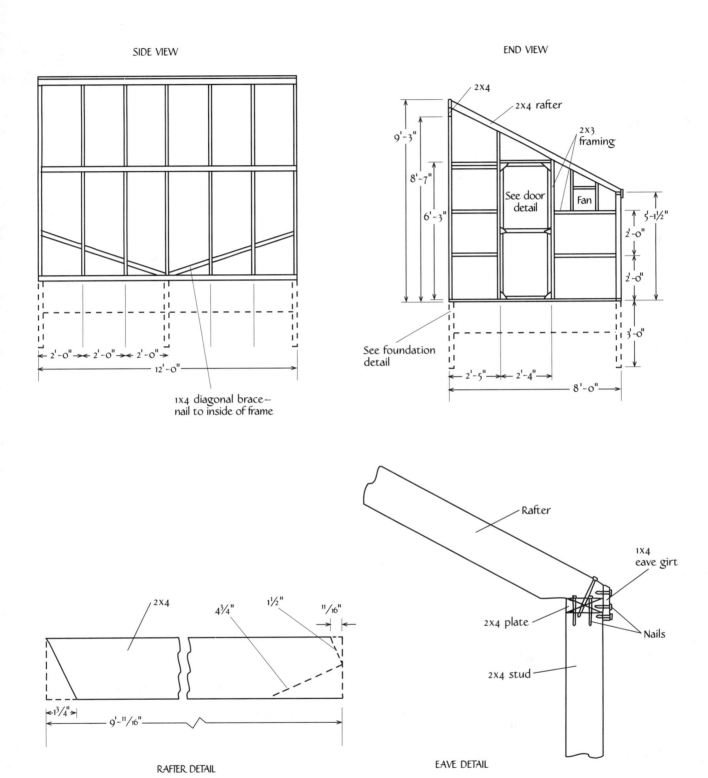

SIDE VIEW

2'-0"   2'-0"   2'-0"

12'-0"

1x4 diagonal brace—
nail to inside of frame

END VIEW

2x4

2x4 rafter

2x3
framing

9'-3"

8'-7"

6'-3"

See door
detail

Fan

5-1½"

2'-0"

2'-0"

3'-0"

See foundation
detail

2'-5"   2'-4"

8'-0"

Rafter

2x4

4¾"

1½"

¹¹/₁₆"

1¾"

9'-¹¹/₁₆"

RAFTER DETAIL

1X4
eave girt

2x4 plate

Nails

2x4 stud

EAVE DETAIL

8' x 12' LEAN-TO GREENHOUSE
(continued)

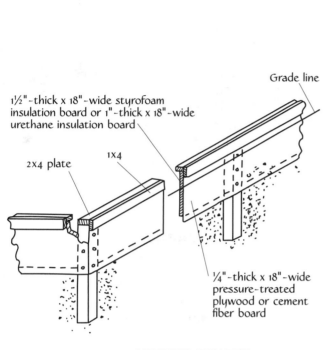

1½"-thick x 18"-wide styrofoam insulation board or 1"-thick x 18"-wide urethane insulation board

Grade line

2x4 plate

1x4

¼"-thick x 18"-wide pressure-treated plywood or cement fiber board

POST FOUNDATION DETAIL

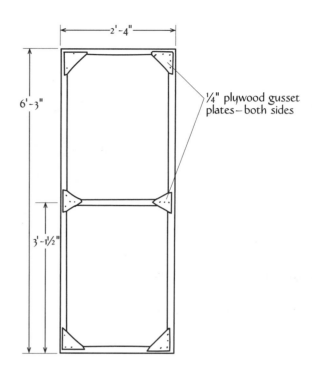

2'-4"

6'-3"

3'-1½"

¼" plywood gusset plates—both sides

DOOR DETAIL

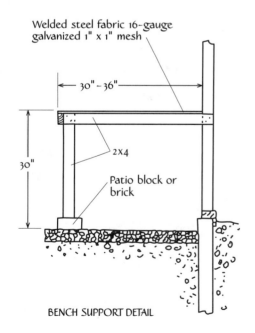

Welded steel fabric 16-gauge galvanized 1" x 1" mesh

30"-36"

30"

2X4

Patio block or brick

BENCH SUPPORT DETAIL

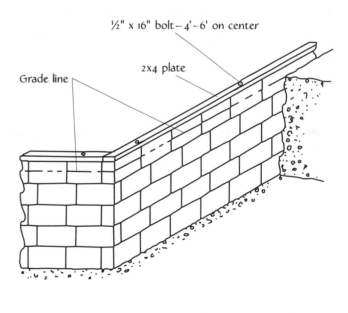

½" x 16" bolt—4'-6' on center

2x4 plate

Grade line

CONCRETE BLOCK FOUNDATION (ALTERNATE METHOD)

8' x 16' CURVED-EAVE, LEAN-TO GREENHOUSE

This is an 8-foot-by-16-foot lean-to greenhouse that can be attached to a home, garage, or outbuilding. The frame is steel tubing bent to shape and supported by concrete piers. Eight-millimeter structural-sheet polycarbonate works well as a glazing, as it will bend over the curved eave to give a smooth appearance and eliminate the eave joint. The greenhouse can be fitted with benches or growing beds. It is also strong enough to support hanging baskets or greenhouse tomatoes.

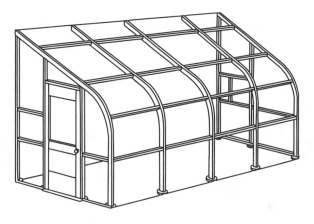

Materials List

Quantity	Item	Location
16-gauge galvanized steel tubing:		
☐ 5 pieces	1" x 2" x 14½'	Rafter
☐ 4 pieces	1¼" x 1¼" x 8'	Endwall posts
☐ 2 pieces	1¼" x 1¼" x 9'	Endwall posts
☐ 16 pieces	1" x 1" x 4'	Roof purlin
☐ 8 pieces	1" x 1" x 3'	Side purlin
8mm clear polycarbonate structured sheets:		
☐ 4 pieces	4' x 14'	Roof
☐ 2 pieces	4' x 10'	Endwalls
☐ 2 pieces	4' x 8'	Endwalls
Aluminum extrusions for attaching the polycarbonate:		
☐ 3 pieces	14' — double splice	Roof/sides
☐ 1 piece	8' — double splice	Endwall
☐ 4 pieces	14' — single splice	Roof/sides
☐ 4 pieces	10' — single splice	Endwall
☐ 1 piece	16' — single splice	Roof

8′ x 16′ CURVED-EAVE, LEAN-TO GREENHOUSE
(continued)

Materials List (continued)

Quantity	Item	Location
☐ 52 pieces	1″ x 1″ x ¼″ aluminum angle	Brackets
☐ 13 pieces	1½″ x 1½″ x ¼″ aluminum angle	Brackets
☐ 5 pieces	Concrete anchor for ⅜″ lag bolt	
☐ Depends on depth of piers	Sand-cement mix	
☐ 6 pieces	6″-diameter cardboard tubes	Piers
☐ 1 roll	Aluminum foil tape	Sealing top of sheets
☐ 1 roll	Porous tape	Sealing bottom of sheets
☐ 1 piece	4′ x 8′ x 1″ polystyrene insulation board (not beadboard)	Foundation perimeter
☐ 200 pieces	No. 10 x ¾″ tec screw	Mounting angle brackets
☐ 2 pieces	½″ x 3′ x 3′ plywood	Form for concrete under door
☐ 2 tubes	Clear silicone caulk	Roof joints
☐ 1	2′6″ x 6′8″ aluminum door	

Construction Notes

Frame

1. Tubing can be purchased from a greenhouse manufacturer, steel company, or machine shop.

2. A machine shop or greenhouse manufacturer can bend the curved eaves.

3. Spacing of the rafters may have to be varied depending on the splice manufacturer. Check this before placing piers.

4. Make sure the frame is securely fastened to the building and to the piers.

5. Paint the frame with white acrylic latex paint.

Covering

1. Place aluminum foil tape over the top edges of polycarbonate sheets to seal.

2. After cutting the sheets to size, place porous tape over the bottoms of sheets.

3. Attach single-splice extrusion to the ridge.

8' x 16' CURVED-EAVE, LEAN-TO GREENHOUSE
(continued)

Construction Notes (continued)

Covering (continued)

4. Attach one extrusion to the top of end roof frame. Do not bend over ridge. Slide polycarbonate sheet into place. Slide double splice onto other side of sheet. Attach with tec screws. Continue with other sheets across the greenhouse roof. Bend assembly over eaves and attach with tec screws.

5. Cut to fit endwall pieces and attach one at a time.

6. After all the glazing is in place, caulk joints to waterproof.

Door

1. The door can be placed on either end.

2. A new or used aluminum storm door makes installation easy. Use a window for the winter and a screen for the summer.

Ventilation

1. A shutter-mounted fan (approximately 16" diameter) with a capacity of 1,500 cubic feet per minute at 0.1" static pressure will provide summer ventilation needs. With a two-speed motor and two-stage thermostat, two stages of cooling can be achieved. A 16" or 18" motorized louver should be located in the endwall opposite the fan. The thermostat should be near the middle of the greenhouse.

Heat

1. An electric, propane, or natural gas heater can provide heat in the winter. Size can be determined from the table. The heater should have a fan for distribution.

Heat requirements — 8' x 16' curved-eave, lean-to greenhouse

		Double-layer glazing (Btu/hour)		
		Minimum inside temperature		
		50°	60°	70°
Minimum	30	4,500	6,750	9,000
outside	20	6,750	9,000	11,250
temperature	10	9,000	11,250	13,500
(°F)	0	11,250	13,500	15,750
	−10	13,500	15,750	18,000

8′ x 16′ CURVED-EAVE, LEAN-TO GREENHOUSE
(continued)

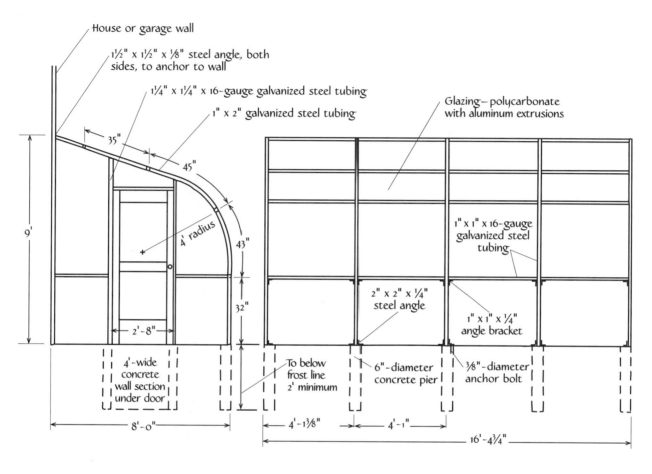

House or garage wall

1½″ x 1½″ x ⅛″ steel angle, both sides, to anchor to wall

1¼″ x 1¼″ x 16-gauge galvanized steel tubing

1″ x 2″ galvanized steel tubing

Glazing—polycarbonate with aluminum extrusions

35″

45″

9′

4′ radius

43″

32″

2′-8″

1″ x 1″ x 16-gauge galvanized steel tubing

2″ x 2″ x ¼″ steel angle

1″ x 1″ x ¼″ angle bracket

4′-wide concrete wall section under door

To below frost line 2′ minimum

6″-diameter concrete pier

⅜″-diameter anchor bolt

8′-0″

4′-1⅜″

4′-1″

16′-4¾″

END VIEW

SIDE VIEW

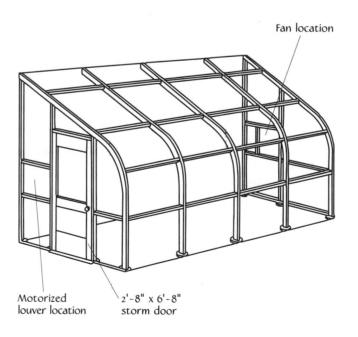

Fan location

Motorized louver location

2′-8″ x 6′-8″ storm door

8' x 16' CURVED-EAVE, LEAN-TO GREENHOUSE
(continued)

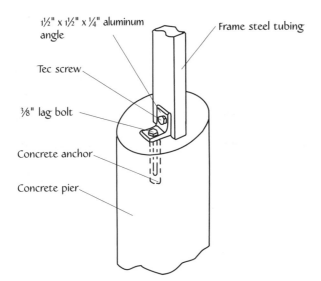

1½" x 1½" x ¼" aluminum angle

Tec screw

⅜" lag bolt

Concrete anchor

Concrete pier

Frame steel tubing

FRAME CONNECTION TO PIER

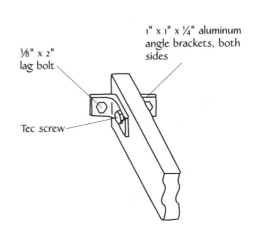

1" x 1" x ¼" aluminum angle brackets, both sides

⅜" x 2" lag bolt

Tec screw

FRAME CONNECTION TO BUILDING WALL

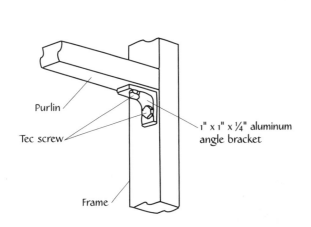

Purlin

Tec screw

Frame

1" x 1" x ¼" aluminum angle bracket

PURLIN CONNECTION TO FRAME

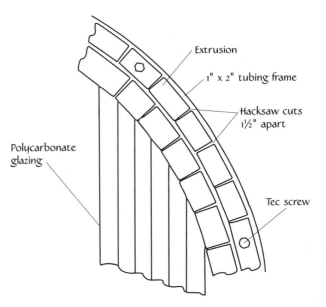

Extrusion

1" x 2" tubing frame

Hacksaw cuts 1½" apart

Polycarbonate glazing

Tec screw

METHOD OF FITTING ALUMINUM EXTRUSION TO SIDE OF CURVED EAVE

8' x 8' FREESTANDING GREENHOUSE

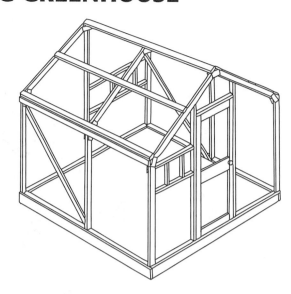

The plans for this greenhouse were originally developed for a horticulture show. The greenhouse is a good size for a hobbyist who has limited space or limited time. It is easy to build for someone with a few woodworking tools and basic construction knowledge. This plan was adapted from University of Connecticut plan number SP631.

Materials List

Quantity	Item	Location
☐ 8 pieces	3' 4x4 (pressure-treated)	Foundation posts
☐ 26 pieces	8' 2x4	Base, door frames, benches, purlins
☐ 10 pieces	10' 2x4	Frames
☐ 18 pieces	8' 1x8 (pressure-treated)	Bases, benches
☐ 1 sheet	4' x 8' x ⅜" exterior plywood	Gussets
☐ 2 sheets	52"-wide x 10' clear, corrugated polycarbonate or fiberglass glazing	Roof
☐ 1 roll	4'-wide x 50' clear, flat polycarbonate or fiberglass	Sidewalls and endwalls
☐ 1 piece	8'-long corrugated aluminum ridge	
☐ 100	#10 x 1" aluminum nails with neoprene washers	
☐ 100	#10 x 1¾" aluminum nails with neoprene washers	
☐ 32 feet	Corrugated filler strip (either wood or foam)	
☐ 5 pounds	6d galvanized nails	
☐ 5 pounds	16d galvanized nails	
☐ 1 gallon	White latex paint	
☐ 1 gallon	Copper naphthanate for treating wood in contact with the ground	

Ventilation:

☐ 1	12" shutter-mounted exhaust fan	
☐ 1	16" motorized intake louver	
☐ 1	Thermostat for fan	

Heat Requirement to Maintain 60°F Inside at 0°F Outside Temperature

Single glazing — 20,000 Btu/hour

Double glazing — 12,000 Btu/hour

8' x 8' FREESTANDING GREENHOUSE
(continued)

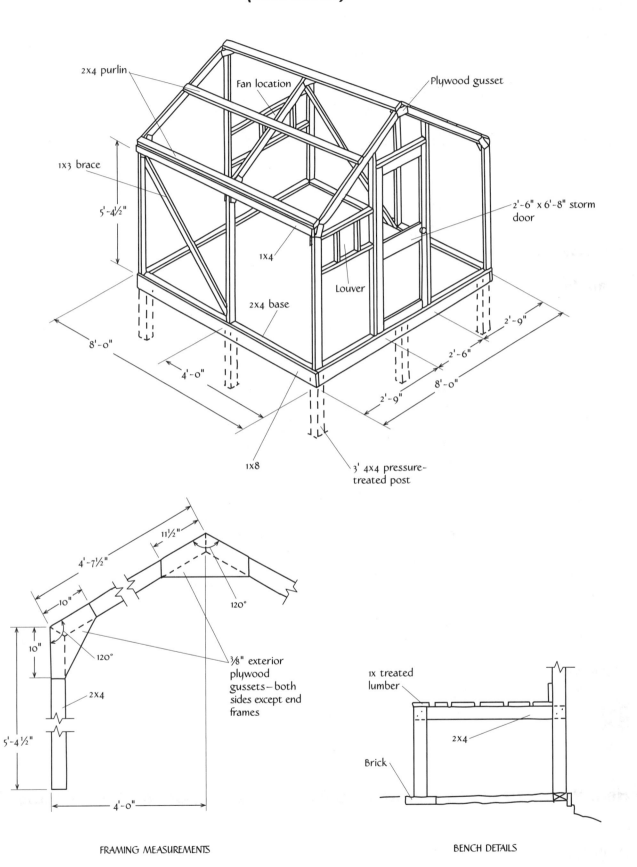

2x4 purlin

Fan location

Plywood gusset

1x3 brace

5'-4½"

2'-6" x 6'-8" storm door

1X4

Louver

2x4 base

2'-9"

2'-6"

8'-0"

4'-0"

8'-0"

2'-9"

1x8

3' 4x4 pressure-treated post

11½"

4'-7½"

120°

10"

10"

120°

120°

⅜" exterior plywood gussets—both sides except end frames

2x4

5'-4½"

4'-0"

FRAMING MEASUREMENTS

1x treated lumber

2x4

Brick

BENCH DETAILS

10' x 10' A-FRAME GREENHOUSE

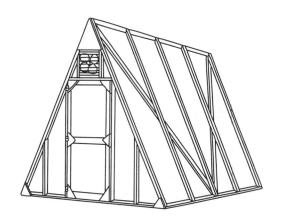

This is a simple, easy-to-build greenhouse that is good for starting annual plants in the spring or holding ornamentals and herbs during the winter. It is made from straight lumber with plywood gussets. It can be made portable or can be attached to a post foundation. Low-cost poly works well for glazing. This plan was adapted from University of Connecticut plan number 238.

Materials List

Quantity	Item	Location
4 pieces	10' 2x6 (pressure-treated)	Base
15 pieces	10' 2x3	Rafters, endwalls, door frame
4 pieces	10' 1x4	Ridge and doors
4 pieces	12' 1x3	Diagonal brace
2 sheets	4' x 8' x ½" pressure-treated plywood	Batten strips, gussets
3	3" butt hinges	Door
1	Door latch	Door
1 gallon	White exterior latex paint	Frame
6	3"-diameter x 15"-long screw-type fence anchors	Anchor base
1 roll	10' x 100' x 6-mil greenhouse-grade polyethylene	Glazing
3 pounds	4d galvanized nails	
2 pounds	6d galvanized nails	
2 pounds	20d galvanized nails	

Construction Notes

General

1. Select a level, well-drained site near water and electricity.

2. Screw anchors into ground, slot base, and tighten anchor to base.

Frame

1. Use construction-grade lumber.

2. Paint frame with exterior white paint.

10' x 10' A-FRAME GREENHOUSE
(continued)

Construction Notes *(continued)*

Covering

1. For year-round use, place plastic on both outside and inside of frame to get insulation effect. Inner layer can be attached with battens or ⅜" staples over heavy twine.

2. For spring use, a single layer on the outside is sufficient.

3. Use a greenhouse-grade plastic to get 4–5 years of service.

Walks and Benches

1. Remove topsoil and replace with sand or peastone for drainage. A weed barrier can be placed below or above drainage material.

2. A center walk of stones or bricks laid in sand can be added after the greenhouse is built.

3. Benches 30–32" high can be added for convenience.

Ventilation

1. A 10"-diameter fan with an automatic louver should be place in the endwall opposite the door. Locate a 12"-square motorized louver in the opposite endwall. Place a thermostat in the center of the greenhouse near plant level.

Heat

1. A small gas or electric heater can keep the greenhouse temperature at the desired night temperature. See the table below for sizes.

Heat requirements — 10'x10' A-frame greenhouse

		Single-layer glazing (Btu/hour)			Double-layer glazing (Btu/hour)		
		Minimum inside night temperature					
		50°	60°	70°	50°	60°	70°
Minimum	30	6,800	10,200	13,600	3,800	5,700	7,600
outside	20	10,200	13,800	17,000	5,700	7,600	9,500
temperature	10	13,600	17,000	22,040	7,600	9,500	11,400
(°F)	0	17,000	20,400	23,800	9,500	11,400	13,300
	−10	20,400	23,800	27,100	11,400	13,300	15,200

10' x 10' A-FRAME GREENHOUSE
(continued)

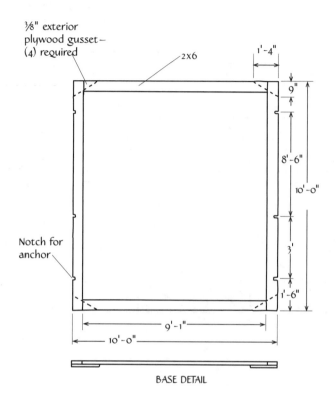

3/8" exterior plywood gusset— (4) required

2x6

1'-4"

9"

8'-6"

10'-0"

3'

1'-6"

Notch for anchor

9'-1"

10'-0"

BASE DETAIL

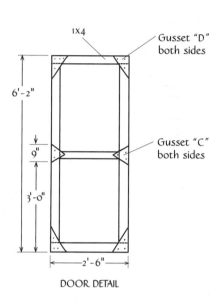

1X4

Gusset "D" both sides

6'-2"

9"

Gusset "C" both sides

3'-0"

2'-6"

DOOR DETAIL

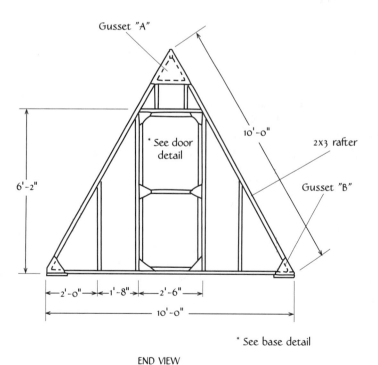

Gusset "A"

10'-0"

* See door detail

2x3 rafter

Gusset "B"

6'-2"

2'-0" 1'-8" 2'-6"

10'-0"

* See base detail

END VIEW

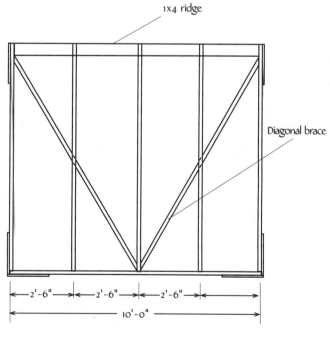

1x4 ridge

Diagonal brace

2'-6" 2'-6" 2'-6"

10'-0"

SIDE VIEW

10' x 10' A-FRAME GREENHOUSE
(continued)

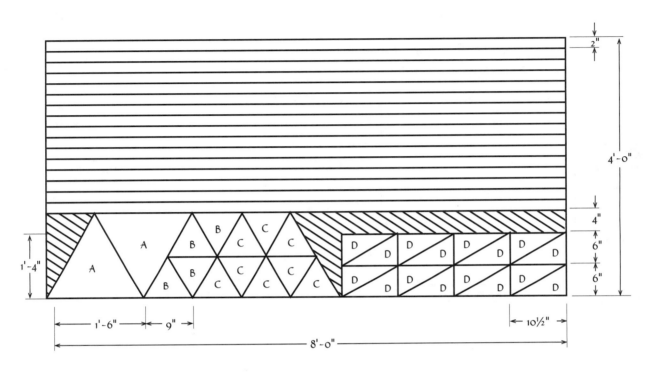

Note: Use ⅜" exterior plywood. Cut one sheet
into 2" strips and one as shown.

PLYWOOD CUTTING DIAGRAM

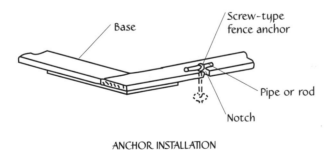

ANCHOR INSTALLATION

12' x 15' GOTHIC GREENHOUSE

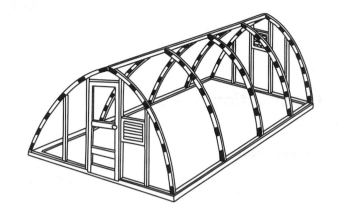

This pleasantly shaped structure is easy to build and assemble. The frames are made using a form. The glazing can be any of the standard materials except acrylic or glass. Double-layer glazing will reduce heating costs if the greenhouse is operated all winter. This plan was adapted from Virginia Polytechnic Institute and State University plan number N3:15E.

Materials List

Quantity	Item	Location

Lumber

☐ 1 piece .... 14' 2x4 .... Guide blocks for form
☐ 7 pieces .... 10' 2x4 .... Strips for rafters
☐ 4 pieces .... 12' 2x4 .... Rafter spacers, diagonal braces, door jambs
☐ 2 pieces .... 16' 1x4 .... Ridgeboard
☐ 10 pieces .... 8' 2x4 .... Endwall
☐ 4 pieces .... 12' 4x4 (pressure-treated) .... Posts
☐ 2 pieces .... 16' 2x8 (pressure-treated) .... Foundation
☐ 2 pieces .... 12' 2x8 (pressure-treated) .... Foundation
☐ 2 pieces .... 16' 2x4 (pressure-treated) .... Side sills
☐ 2 pieces .... 12' 2x4 (pressure-treated) .... End sills

Hardware

☐ 5 pounds .... 6d cement-coated nails
☐ 1 quart .... Water-resistant glue
☐ 1 gallon............... White exterior latex paint
☐ 2 pounds .... 16d galvanized box nails

Glazing

☐ 1 roll.................... 16' x 100' x 6-mil greenhouse-grade polyethylene
☐ 50 pieces .... ⅜" x 1½" x 10' lath or cut from ⅜" exterior plywood
☐ 4 pounds .... 4d galvanized box nails

12′ x 15′ GOTHIC GREENHOUSE
(continued)

Construction Notes

Foundation

1. Select a level site with good drainage and sunlight.

2. Lay out foundation so that the building is square.

3. Locate posts and dig holes. Posts should be set on solid ground.

4. Attach 2x8 foundation boards.

Frame

1. Make a rafter form on a wood floor or plywood sheets using guide blocks (see detail on page 155). Cut 20 guide blocks, 1½″ x 3½″ x 8″ and 6 spacer guide blocks, ⅜″ x 1″ x 3″. Be sure blocks are securely fastened with nails or sheet rock screws. They should be located so that they are not in the way of nailing.

2. The following are needed for each rafter:

4 pieces	½″ x 1½″ x 10′	Rafter strips
2 pieces	1½″ x 1½″ x 18″	End blocks
5 pieces	1½″ x 1½″ x 6″	Spacer blocks

   Cut 10′ 2x4 into ½″-thick strips. Cut the end blocks and spacer blocks from 12′ 2x4.

   Place two rafter strips inside the form and separate them with the end blocks and spacer blocks. Slide the next two rafter strips into place, one inside and one outside. Glue can be used between the strips and spacer blocks to increase strength. Nail the strips with 6d nails using three or more nails on each side of block. Cut the rafter ends to the right shape.

3. Mark off the rafter locations on the sills and ridge boards. Nail the rafters in place using 16d box nails. Stand the assemblies in place and attach to the foundation posts. Fasten the ridges together.

4. Weave the diagonal braces through the rafters from the peak at each end of the house down to the bottom of the center rafter. Fasten in place.

5. Frame the endwalls using 2x4 lumber. Install the door.

6. Cover the structure with poly, making sure it is attached securely.

12′ x 15′ GOTHIC GREENHOUSE
(continued)

Construction Notes (continued)

Ventilation

1. A 16″-diameter shutter-mounted fan will provide summer ventilation. If provided with a two-speed motor, two stages of ventilation can be obtained. Use a two-stage thermostat. The endwall opposite the fan should have an 18″-square motorized louver installed. This can also be connected to the thermostat.

Heat

1. A propane, natural gas, or electric heater can supply the heat for winter operation. See the table below for sizing.

Heat requirements — 12′x15′ Gothic greenhouse

		Single-layer glazing (Btu/hour)			Double-layer glazing (Btu/hour)		
				Minimum inside night temperature			
		50°	60°	70°	50°	60°	70°
Minimum	30	8,400	15,700	21,000	6,720	10,080	13,450
outside	20	15,750	21,000	26,250	10,080	13,450	16,800
temperature	10	21,000	26,250	31,500	13,450	16,800	20,150
(°F)	0	26,250	31,500	36,750	16,800	20,160	23,500
	−10	31,500	36,750	42,000	20,160	23,500	26,850

12' x 15' GOTHIC GREENHOUSE
(continued)

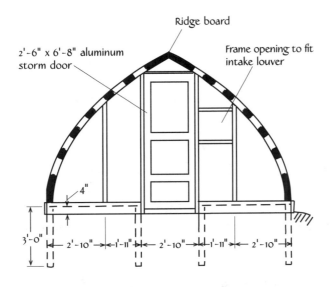

Ridge board

2'-6" x 6'-8" aluminum storm door

Frame opening to fit intake louver

4"

3'-0"

2'-10"   1'-11"   2'-10"   1'-11"   2'-10"

FRONT ELEVATION

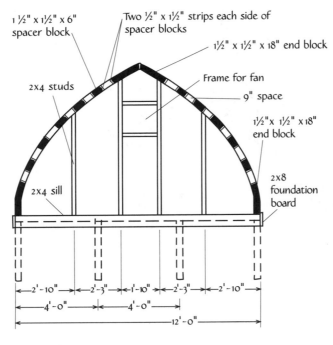

1 ½" x 1½" x 6" spacer block

Two ½" x 1½" strips each side of spacer blocks

½" x 1½" x 18" end block

2x4 studs

Frame for fan

9" space

½" x 1½" x 18" end block

2x8 foundation board

2x4 sill

2'-10"   2'-3"   1'-10"   2'-3"   2'-10"

4'-0"   4'-0"

12'-0"

BACK ELEVATION

12' x 15' GOTHIC GREENHOUSE
(continued)

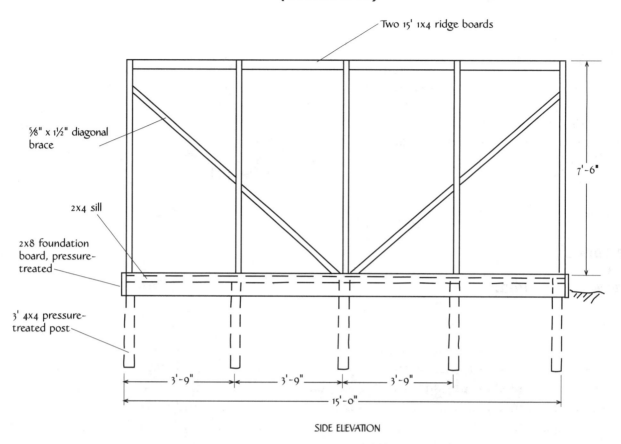

Two 15' 1x4 ridge boards

⅝" x 1½" diagonal brace

2x4 sill

2x8 foundation board, pressure-treated

3' 4x4 pressure-treated post

7'-6"

3'-9"   3'-9"   3'-9"

15'-0"

SIDE ELEVATION

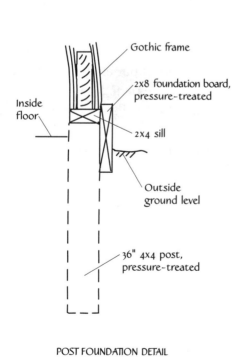

Gothic frame

2x8 foundation board, pressure-treated

2x4 sill

Inside floor

Outside ground level

36" 4x4 post, pressure-treated

POST FOUNDATION DETAIL

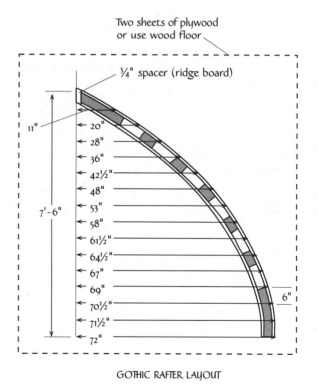

Two sheets of plywood or use wood floor

¾" spacer (ridge board)

11"

20"
28"
36"
42½"
48"
53"
58"
61½"
64½"
67"
69"
70½"
71½"
72"

7'-6"

6"

GOTHIC RAFTER LAYOUT

10′ x 12′ SLANT-LEG GREENHOUSE

This is a strong-framed greenhouse that will support a crop of tomatoes, cucumbers, or hanging baskets. The post foundation gives good support. Glazing can be corrugated fiberglass or polycarbonate, rigid structured-sheet polycarbonate, or film plastic. This plan was adapted from U.S. Department of Agriculture plan number 6181.

Materials List

Quantity	Item	Location

Lumber

☐ 8 pieces	10′ 2x4	Frames
☐ 2 pieces	10′ 2x4 (pressure-treated)	End sills
☐ 2 pieces	12′ 2x4 (pressure-treated)	Side sills
☐ 2 pieces	16′ 2x4	Endwalls
☐ 8 pieces	12′ ⁵⁄₄x4	Purlins and door
☐ 2 pieces	16′ 4x4 (pressure-treated)	Posts
☐ 2 pieces	12′ 1x12 (pressure-treated)	Foundation
☐ 2 pieces	10′ 1x12 (pressure-treated)	Foundation
☐ 1 sheet	¼″ x 4′ x 8′ exterior CC plywood	Gussets

Glazing — corrugated fiberglass or polycarbonate

☐ 3 sheets	4′ x 10′ (cut in half)	Roof panels
☐ 3 sheets	4′ x 12′ (one cut lengthwise in half)	Side panels
☐ 1 roll	4′ x 50′ flat fiberglass or polycarbonate	Endwalls
☐ 1 piece	Ridge cap — 12′ long	Ridge
☐ 75 linear feet	Closure strip	Edge of glazing
☐ 25	Anti-drip spacers	Under roof glazing
☐ 150	1¾″ aluminum ring nail w/rubber gasket	Corrugated glazing
☐ 100	1″ aluminum ring nail w/rubber gasket	Flat glazing
☐ 2 tubes	Clear silicone caulking	

Glazing — double layer film poly

☐ 1 roll	12′ x 50′ x 6-mil greenhouse-grade plastic
☐ 200 linear feet	1x2 furring strips
☐ 3 pounds	6d duplex-head nails
☐ 1	60–100 cfm squirrel cage blower

10' x 12' SLANT-LEG GREENHOUSE
(continued)

Materials List (continued)

Quantity	Item	Location
Quantity	**Item**	**Location**

Other

- ☐ 1 gallon............... White latex exterior paint .... Frame
- ☐ 3 pounds .... 6d galvanized nails
- ☐ 3 pounds .... 8d galvanized nails
- ☐ 3 pounds .... 20d galvanized nails

Construction Notes

General

1. Select a level, well-drained site with good sunlight.

2. Remove topsoil and replace it with 4–6" of gravel or stone. The floor in the greenhouse should be higher than the outside ground level to prevent water from entering.

Frame

1. Use construction-grade lumber.

2. Construct frames on a level floor. Mark out dimensions and location of gussets.

3. Use specified number of nails in gussets for strength.

4. Paint frame with exterior white paint.

Covering

1. Corrugated material is placed on roof with corrugations running vertical. On the sidewalls, the corrugations run horizontal. Flat glazing is used on the endwalls. Follow recommendations for attaching glazing.

2. Both layers of poly are placed over the outside of the frame.

3. Poly glazing should be attached securely to avoid leaks.

4. Endwalls can be covered with poly. Flat fiberglass or polycarbonate is easier to work with and will last many years.

10' x 12' SLANT-LEG GREENHOUSE
(continued)

Construction Notes *(continued)*

Ventilation

1. A shutter-mounted, two-speed fan having a capacity of 1,000 cubic feet per minute is placed in the endwall opposite the door.

2. A 16"-square motorized louver can be mounted in the opposite endwall.

3. Both are controlled by a two-stage thermostat located in the center of the greenhouse at plant height.

Heat

1. If the greenhouse is attached to the home, it may be possible to provide heat from the home heating system. Otherwise, a separate propane, natural gas, or electric heater can be used. Combustion-type heaters should be vented. Heat requirements depend on the climate and the desired inside temperature (see the following table).

Heat requirements — 10'x12' slant-leg greenhouse

		Single-layer glazing (Btu/hour)			Double-layer glazing (Btu/hour)		
		Minimum inside night temperature					
		50°	60°	70°	50°	60°	70°
Minimum	30	10,000	15,000	20,000	6,000	9,000	12,000
outside	20	15,000	20,000	25,000	9,000	12,000	15,000
temperature	10	20,000	25,000	30,000	12,000	15,000	18,000
(°F)	0	25,000	30,000	35,000	15,000	18,000	21,000
	−10	30,000	35,000	40,000	18,000	21,000	24,000

10' x 12' SLANT-LEG GREENHOUSE
(continued)

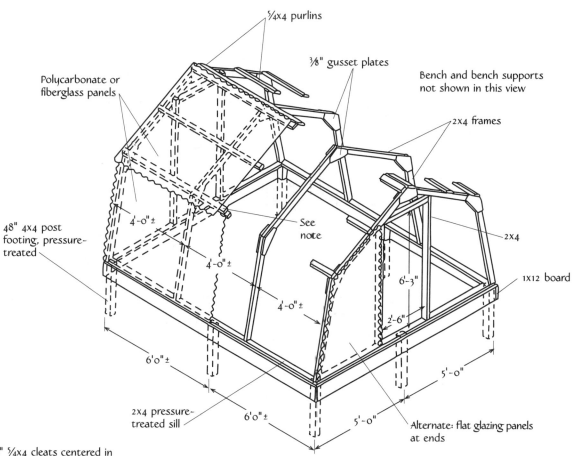

⁵⁄₄x4 purlins

⅜" gusset plates

Bench and bench supports
not shown in this view

Polycarbonate or
fiberglass panels

2x4 frames

48" 4x4 post
footing, pressure-
treated

See
note

2x4

4'-0"±

4'-0"±

4'-0"±

6'-3"

1x12 board

2'-6"

6'0"±

6'0"±

5'-0"

5'-0"

2x4 pressure-
treated sill

Alternate: flat glazing panels
at ends

Note: 6" ⁵⁄₄x4 cleats centered in
4'-0" bays and nailed to underside
of eave purlins for the purpose of
securing top edge of side glazing
panels

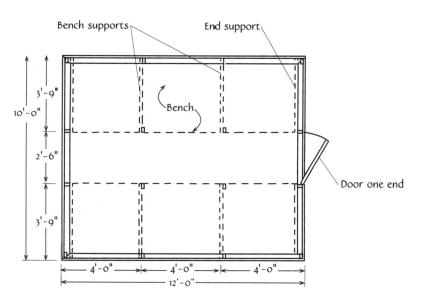

Bench supports

End support

Bench

Door one end

10'-0"

3'-9"

2'-6"

3'-9"

4'-0"

4'-0"

4'-0"

12'-0"

PLAN

10′ x 12′ SLANT-LEG GREENHOUSE
(continued)

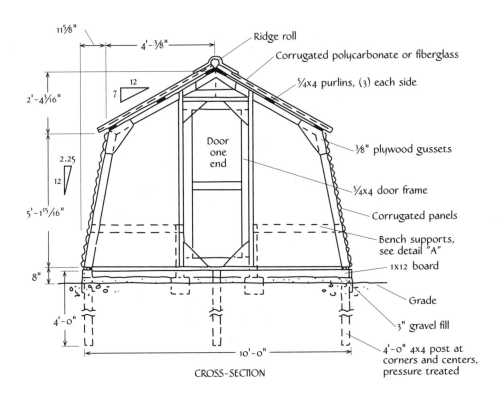

Ridge roll

Corrugated polycarbonate or fiberglass

⁵⁄₄x4 purlins, (3) each side

11⁵⁄₈″

4′-⅜″

2′-4³⁄₁₆″

7 | 12

2.25 | 12

5′-1¹⁵⁄₁₆″

Door one end

⅜″ plywood gussets

⁵⁄₄x4 door frame

Corrugated panels

Bench supports, see detail "A"

1x12 board

8″

Grade

4′-0″

3″ gravel fill

10′-0″

4′-0″ 4x4 post at corners and centers, pressure treated

CROSS-SECTION

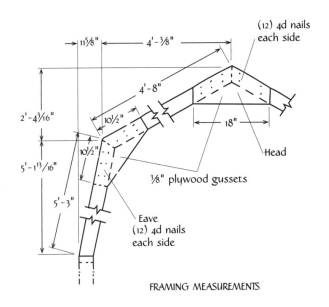

11⁵⁄₈″

4′-⅜″

(12) 4d nails each side

4′-8″

2′-4³⁄₁₆″

10½″

10½″

18″

Head

5′-1¹³⁄₁₆″

⅜″ plywood gussets

5′-3″

Eave (12) 4d nails each side

FRAMING MEASUREMENTS

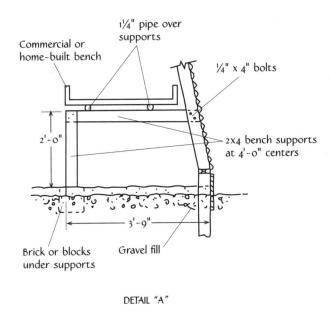

1¼″ pipe over supports

Commercial or home-built bench

¼″ x 4″ bolts

2′-0″

2x4 bench supports at 4′-0″ centers

3′-9″

Brick or blocks under supports

Gravel fill

DETAIL "A"

10' x 12' SLANT-LEG GREENHOUSE
(continued)

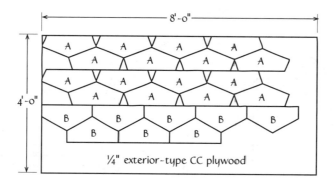

PLYWOOD SHEET CUTTING DIAGRAM

¼" exterior-type CC plywood

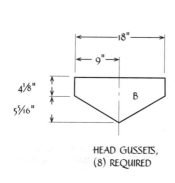

HEAD GUSSETS,
(8) REQUIRED

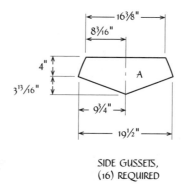

SIDE GUSSETS,
(16) REQUIRED

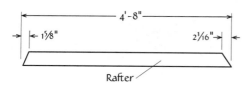

Rafter

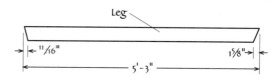

Leg

FRAME CUTTING LAYOUT [CUT FROM (8) 10' 2X4S]

10' x 12' SLANT-LEG GREENHOUSE
(continued)

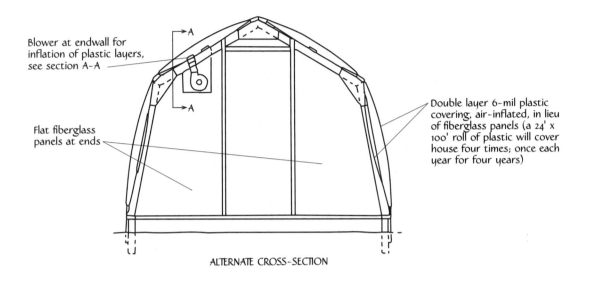

Blower at endwall for inflation of plastic layers, see section A-A

Flat fiberglass panels at ends

Double layer 6-mil plastic covering, air-inflated, in lieu of fiberglass panels (a 24' x 100' roll of plastic will cover house four times; once each year for four years)

ALTERNATE CROSS-SECTION

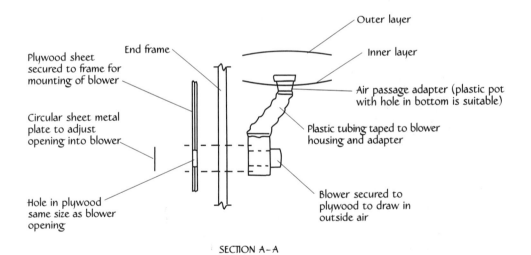

Plywood sheet secured to frame for mounting of blower

Circular sheet metal plate to adjust opening into blower

Hole in plywood same size as blower opening

End frame

Outer layer

Inner layer

Air passage adapter (plastic pot with hole in bottom is suitable)

Plastic tubing taped to blower housing and adapter

Blower secured to plywood to draw in outside air

SECTION A-A

14' x 21' VERTICAL-LEG GREENHOUSE

This is a larger home greenhouse for the grower with a lot of plants or for someone starting a small commercial business. The frame is constructed of 2x4 lumber with plywood gusset plates, making it a strong structure that will take a load of hanging baskets or support a crop of tomatoes. It is designed with double-wall, polycarbonate glazing for low maintenance but could also be covered with a single or double layer of polyethylene with air inflation. The greenhouse could be fitted with benches or beds, depending on need. This plan is adapted from University of Connecticut plan number SP 569.

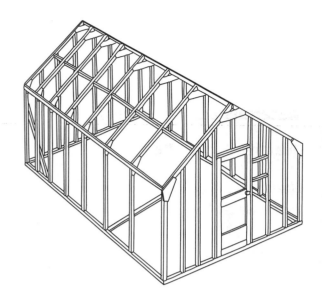

Materials List

Quantity	Item	Location

Foundation

☐ 4 pieces .... 12' 4x4 (pressure-treated) .... Posts
☐ 4 pieces .... 12' 2x4 (pressure-treated) .... Sill
☐ 2 pieces .... 14' 2x4 (pressure-treated) .... Sill
☐ 4 pieces .... 12' ⁵⁄₄x6 (pressure-treated) .... Foundation board
☐ 2 pieces .... 14' ⁵⁄₄x6 (pressure-treated) .... Foundation board
☐ 12 pieces .... Galvanized sheet metal anchor .... Frame
☐ 5 pieces .... 2' x 8' x 1" polyurethane insulation board .... Footing

Frame

☐ 16 pieces .... 14' 2x4 .... Legs/rafters
☐ 4 pieces .... 12' ⁵⁄₄x4 .... Eave girt
☐ 6 pieces .... 12' 2x4 .... Ridge/purlin
☐ 3 pieces .... 8' 2x4 .... Filler
☐ 4 pieces .... 8' 1x3 .... Diagonal brace
☐ 2 sheets .... ⅜" x 4' x 8' exterior plywood .... Gussets

Endwalls

☐ 4 pieces .... 10' 2x4
☐ 10 pieces .... 8' 2x4
☐ 1 .... 3'0" x 6'8" aluminum storm door

14' x 21' VERTICAL-LEG GREENHOUSE
(continued)

Materials List *(continued)*

Quantity	Item	Location
Glazing		
☐ 13 sheets	4' x 14' x 8mm	Polycarbonate structured sheets
☐ 3 sheets	4' x 10' x 8mm	Polycarbonate structured sheets
☐ 1 roll	Aluminum foil tape	Sealing tops of sheets
☐ 1 roll	Porous tape	Sealing bottoms of sheets
☐ 400 linear feet	Single-splice aluminum extrusion	
☐ 200 linear feet	Double-splice aluminum extrusion	
☐ 600	#12 x 1" tec screws with washer	
☐ 21 linear feet	Aluminum ridge cap	
☐ 2 tubes	Clear silicone caulk	Glazing joints
Nails		
☐ 5 pounds	6d common	
☐ 2 pounds	8d common	
☐ 2 pounds	16d common	
☐ 5 pounds	20d common	

Construction Notes

Frame

1. Lay out gusset patterns on a piece of cardboard. Mark out plywood.

2. Cut out gussets, smooth edges with rasp.

3. Mark and cut out rafters and legs.

4. Set up form on wood floor or sheet of plywood and construct half frames. Assemble full frames, leaving space for ridge board at the top.

5. Lay out base of greenhouse, providing good drainage inside and drainage away from the greenhouse outside.

6. Set posts and construct foundation.

7. Erect frames and brace and install purlins.

14' x 21' VERTICAL-LEG GREENHOUSE
(continued)

Construction Notes (continued)

Glazing

1. Place aluminum foil tape over top edges of polycarbonate sheets to seal.

2. After cutting sheets to size, place porous tape over bottom edges of sheets.

3. Attach one extrusion to one edge of greenhouse frame. Insert glazing, then slide second extrusion into place. Attach with tec screws.

4. Continue until all sheets are in place.

5. Caulk edges of extrusion to seal.

Door

1. The door can be placed at either end.

2. An aluminum storm door is easy to install and has a screen that can be opened for the summer.

Ventilation

1. A shutter-mounted fan (3,000 cubic feet per minute at ⅛" static pressure) mounted on the endwall opposite the door will provide for automatic ventilation. Frame the opening to fit the fan size. Provide a motorized intake louver on the door endwall. During the summer, the screen will provide additional air exchange. A thermostat located near the center of the house at plant height will control both the fan and louver.

Heat

1. If the greenhouse is to be heated, an electric or gas heater is best. One with a fan will circulate the heat evenly throughout the growing space. It can be located near one end.

Heat requirements — 14'x21' vertical-leg greenhouse

		Single-layer glazing (Btu/hour)			Double-layer glazing (Btu/hour)		
		Minimum inside night temperature					
		50°	60°	70°	50°	60°	70°
Minimum	30	15,000	22,500	30,000	9,000	12,500	17,000
outside	20	22,500	30,000	37,500	12,500	17,000	21,000
temperature	10	30,000	37,500	45,000	17,000	21,000	25,000
(°F)	0	37,500	45,000	52,500	21,000	25,000	29,000
	−10	45,000	52,500	60,000	25,000	29,000	34,000

14' x 21' VERTICAL-LEG GREENHOUSE
(continued)

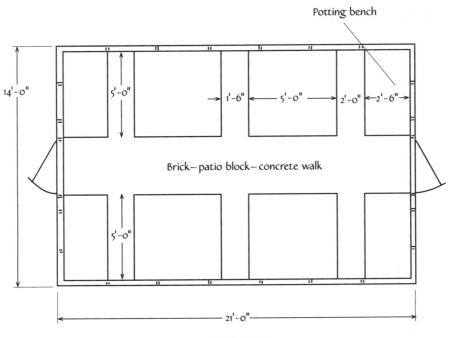

Potting bench

14'-0"

5'-0"

1'-6"

5'-0"

2'-0"

2'-6"

Brick−patio block−concrete walk

5'-0"

21'-0"

FLOOR PLAN

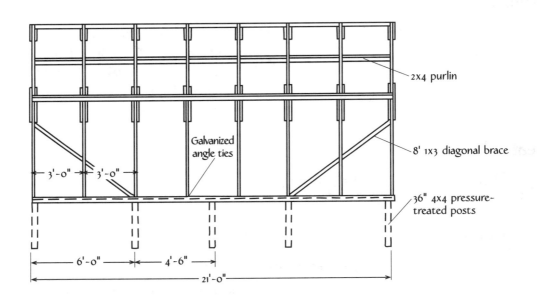

2x4 purlin

Galvanized
angle ties

8' 1x3 diagonal brace

3'-0"

3'-0"

36" 4x4 pressure-
treated posts

6'-0"

4'-6"

21'-0"

SIDE VIEW

14' x 21' VERTICAL-LEG GREENHOUSE
(continued)

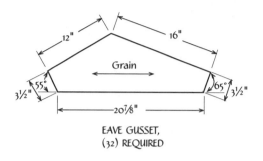

EAVE GUSSET,
(32) REQUIRED

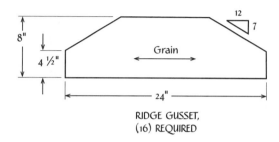

RIDGE GUSSET,
(16) REQUIRED

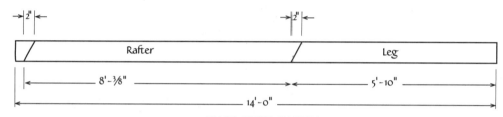

FRAME CUTTING DIAGRAM

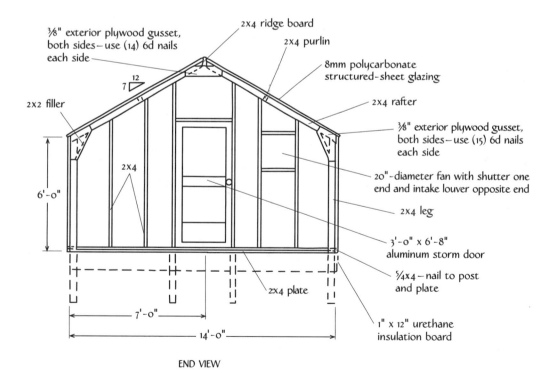

END VIEW

14' x 21' VERTICAL-LEG GREENHOUSE
(continued)

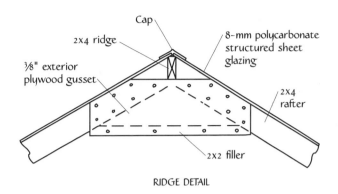

Cap

2x4 ridge

8-mm polycarbonate
structured sheet
glazing

⅜" exterior
plywood gusset

2x4
rafter

2x2 filler

RIDGE DETAIL

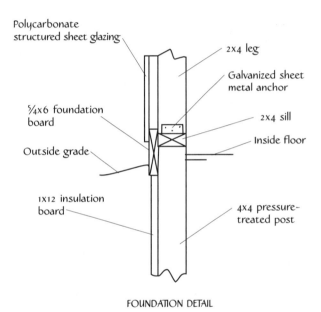

Polycarbonate
structured sheet glazing

2x4 leg

Galvanized sheet
metal anchor

⁵⁄₄x6 foundation
board

2x4 sill

Inside floor

Outside grade

1x12 insulation
board

4x4 pressure-
treated post

FOUNDATION DETAIL

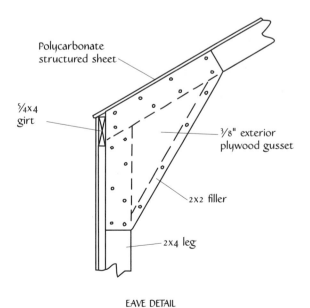

Polycarbonate
structured sheet

⁵⁄₄x4
girt

⅜" exterior
plywood gusset

2x2 filler

2x4 leg

EAVE DETAIL

10' x 16' PIT GREENHOUSE

A pit greenhouse utilizes the soil to both collect and provide heat. Only a small amount of glazing is exposed to the weather, so heating costs are less. Initial construction costs are greater than those of a conventional greenhouse, as strong walls are needed to retain the soil.

This is a traditional pit greenhouse design with the walls buried 4 feet below ground level. The walls and stairwell can be constructed of concrete blocks or poured concrete. It should be placed on a footing to keep it from settling. Adequate drainage should be installed both outside and inside to keep the floor dry.

The frame is attached to the wall with anchor bolts. A conventional 2x4 frame is erected on top of the wall. It can be covered with any glazing material desired, but polycarbonate gives good service and low maintenance. Old sash, storm window, or replacement sliding glass door glass could also be used, but the framework will have to be modified and strengthened to support this.

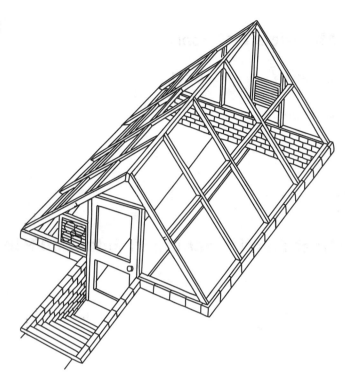

Materials List

Quantity	Item	Location
☐ 3 cubic yards	Concrete	Footing
☐ 300	8" x 8" x 16" concrete blocks	Walls
☐ 13	½" x 6" bolts	Sill anchor
☐ 2 pieces	16' 2x6 (pressure-treated)	Sill
☐ 2 pieces	10' 2x6 (pressure-treated)	Sill
☐ 5 pieces	14' 2x4	Rafter
☐ 2 pieces	16' 2x4	Purlin
☐ 5 pieces	8' 2x4	Endwall
☐ 1 piece	10' 2x12	Stairs
☐ 1 piece	16' 2x10	Stairs
☐ 1	2'6" x 6'8" aluminum storm door	
☐ 6 sheets	4' x 14' x 8mm polycarbonate structure sheets, clear	Glazing
☐ 50 linear feet	Double-splice aluminum extrusion	
☐ 120 linear feet	Single-splice aluminum extrusion	
☐ 1 roll	Aluminum foil tape	Seal tops of sheets
☐ 1 roll	Porous tape	Seal bottoms of sheets

10' x 16' PIT GREENHOUSE
(continued)

Materials List (continued)

Quantity	Item	Location

Ventilation

☐ 1 .... 16"-diameter shutter-mounted exhaust fan
☐ 1 .... 18" motorized intake louver
☐ 1 .... Thermostat

Heat Requirement to Maintain 60°F Inside at 0°F Outside

With double glazing — 13,000 Btu/hour

With single glazing — 22,500 Btu/hour

10′ x 16′ PIT GREENHOUSE
(continued)

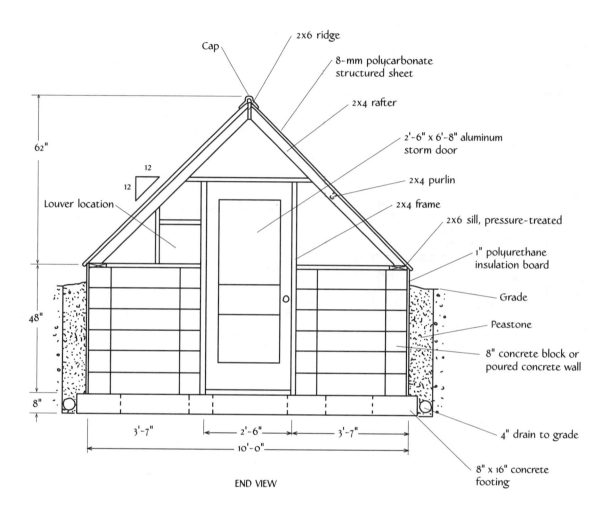

Cap

2x6 ridge

8-mm polycarbonate structured sheet

2x4 rafter

2′-6″ x 6′-8″ aluminum storm door

2x4 purlin

2x4 frame

2x6 sill, pressure-treated

1″ polyurethane insulation board

Grade

Peastone

8″ concrete block or poured concrete wall

4″ drain to grade

8″ x 16″ concrete footing

62″

12
12

Louver location

48″

8″

3′-7″

2′-6″

3′-7″

10′-0″

END VIEW

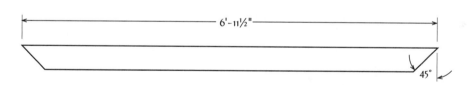

6′-11½″

45°

RAFTER DETAIL

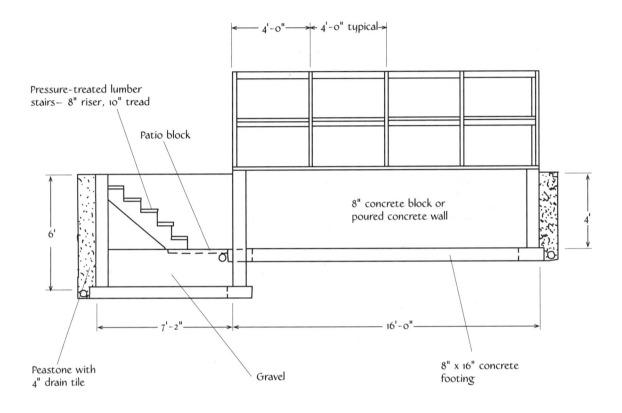

Pressure-treated lumber
stairs— 8" riser, 10" tread

Patio block

6'

Peastone with
4" drain tile

Gravel

4'-0"   4'-0" typical

8" concrete block or
poured concrete wall

4'

7'-2"

16'-0"

8" x 16" concrete
footing

10' x 12' HIGH TUNNEL

This structure works well in the garden as a high tunnel for extending the gardening season in the spring and fall. With shade material over the top, it can be used for providing sunlight modification for propagation or hardening off seedlings. In a milder climate, crops such as lettuce, carrots, and beets will grow all winter. In heavy snow areas, the plastic glazing should be removed for the winter or 2x4 posts placed under the frames to prevent collapse.

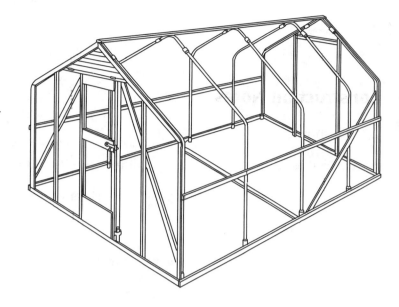

Materials List

Quantity	Item	Location
☐ 4 pieces	1" x 10' heavy-wall steel conduit (cut into 30" lengths)	Ground stakes
☐ 14 pieces	¾" x 10' heavy-wall steel conduit	Frame, roll-up side
☐ 12 pieces	¾" conduit couplings	Frame, roll-up side
☐ 5 pieces	12' 1x3	Girts
☐ 6 pieces	8' 1x3	Braces — endwall
☐ 4 pieces	10' 1x3	Endwall, footer, frame
☐ 10 pieces	8' 2x2	Endwall frame, door
☐ 180 linear feet	¼" x 1" lath	Plastic attachment
☐ 100	¼" x 3" galvanized RH stovebolts	
☐ 6	Pipe clamps for 1" conduit	Ground clamps
☐ 18	Eye screws	Roll-up side retainer
☐ 1 pair	2" tee hinges	Door
☐ 1	Door latch	
☐ 1 piece	¼" x 4' x 4' exterior plywood	Door, end vents
☐ 2 pairs	1" x 2" galvanized utility hinge	Vents
☐ 50-foot roll	12' wide x 6-mil greenhouse film plastic	Glazing
☐ 50 feet	Clothesline	Roll-up side retainer

10' x 12' HIGH TUNNEL
(continued)

Construction Notes

1. Site should be reasonably level.

2. Lay out locations for posts. Drive into ground with wood block so that tops are level.

3. Drill and insert screws for frame supports and ground purlin.

4. Bend frames.

5. Put in place — install bracing and purlins and ridge board.

6. Attach 1x3 endwall frame furring strips.

7. Build endwalls and door.

8. Attach plastic with staples and lath.

10' x 12' HIGH TUNNEL
(continued)

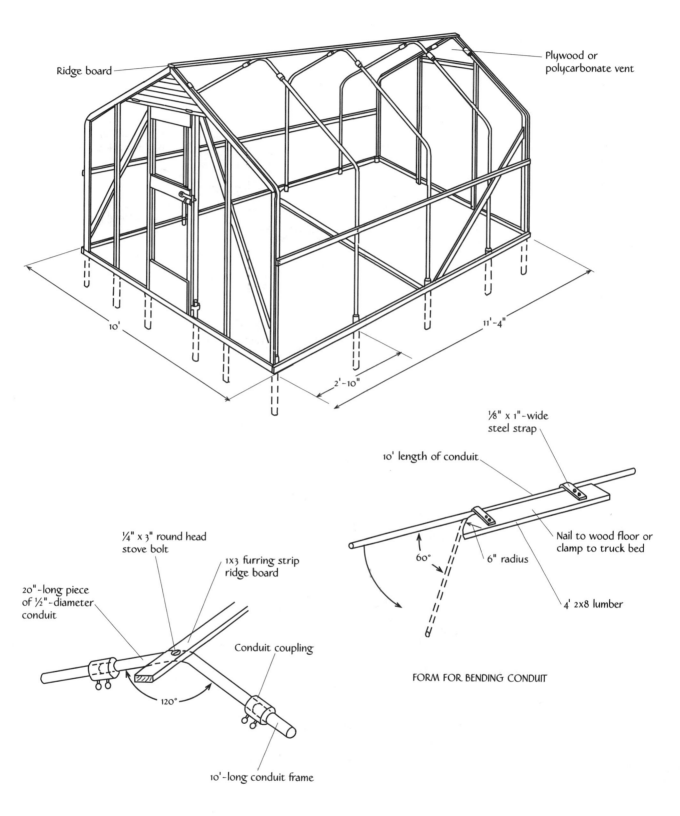

Ridge board

Plywood or polycarbonate vent

10'

11'-4"

2'-10"

⅛" x 1"-wide steel strap

10' length of conduit

Nail to wood floor or clamp to truck bed

60°

6" radius

4' 2x8 lumber

FORM FOR BENDING CONDUIT

¼" x 3" round head stove bolt

1x3 furring strip ridge board

20"-long piece of ½"-diameter conduit

Conduit coupling

120°

10'-long conduit frame

RIDGE CONSTRUCTION

10' x 12' HIGH TUNNEL
(continued)

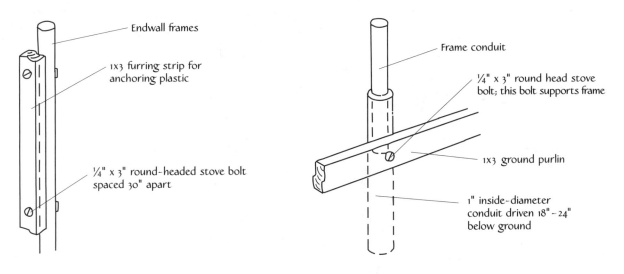

Endwall frames

1x3 furring strip for anchoring plastic

¼" x 3" round-headed stove bolt spaced 30" apart

ENDWALL FURRING STRIP FOR ATTACHING PLASTIC

Frame conduit

¼" x 3" round head stove bolt; this bolt supports frame

1x3 ground purlin

1" inside-diameter conduit driven 18"–24" below ground

GROUND PIPE INSTALLATION

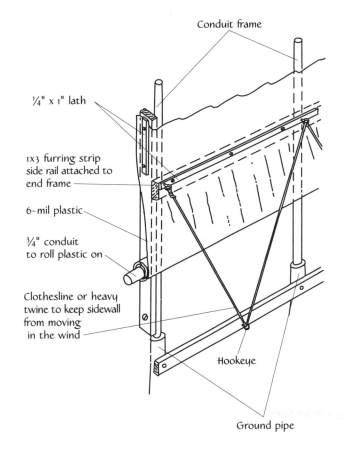

Conduit frame

¼" x 1" lath

1x3 furring strip side rail attached to end frame

6-mil plastic

¾" conduit to roll plastic on

Clothesline or heavy twine to keep sidewall from moving in the wind

Hookeye

Ground pipe

ROLL-UP SIDE INSTALLATION

3' x 6' COLD FRAME

This cold frame can be used to harden off seedlings in the spring, grow cool-season crops in spring and fall, and protect perennials and herbs over winter. By adding a heating cable, it will germinate and grow seedlings for spring planting.

The frame can be made from pressure-treated plywood or 1-inch boards for many years of service. It is easy to build and can be constructed so that it can be disassembled for storage. Film plastic or a longer-life material such as acrylic can be used for glazing. Insulation can be placed around the frame for added thermal protection.

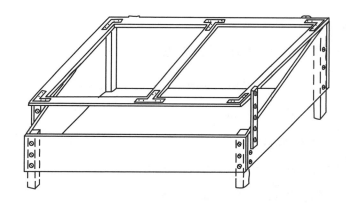

Materials List

Quantity	Item	Location
☐ 1 sheet	½" x 4' x 8' plywood (pressure-treated)	Sides
☐ 1 piece	8' 2x3 (pressure-treated)	Corner posts
☐ 2 pieces	12' 1x3 furring strips	Cover
☐ 12 linear feet	¼" x 1" lath	Plastic attachment
☐ 1 quart	Exterior white latex paint	
☐ 4 pair	3" x 3" corner plates	Cover
☐ 2 pair	3" tee hinges	Cover
☐ 32	No. 8 x 1¼" RH wood screws or deck screws	
☐ 1 piece	7' x 8' x 6-mil polyethylene plastic	
☐ 3	1½" x 3" galvanized steel hinges	

Add for hotbed

☐ 1 piece	1" x 4' x 8' polystyrene or polyurethane insulation board	
☐ 1 piece	3' x 6' galvanized hardware cloth	
☐ 1	300-watt electric heating cable with thermostat	

Construction Notes

1. Cut plywood to dimensions shown.

2. Cut corner posts.

3. Assemble with screws.

4. Construct cover from furring strips.

5. Cut lath strips for attaching plastic.

3' x 6' COLD FRAME
(continued)

Construction Notes *(continued)*

6. Cut and drill ventilation supports.

7. Paint all wood surfaces.

8. Attach plastic to cover.

9. Attach hinges and mount cover.

10. Attach ventilation supports.

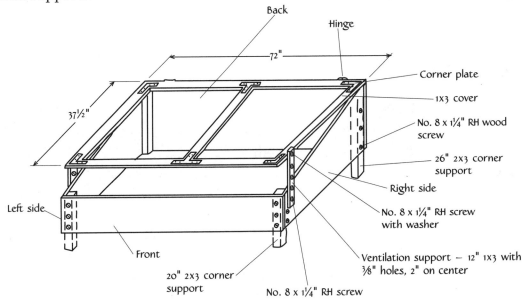

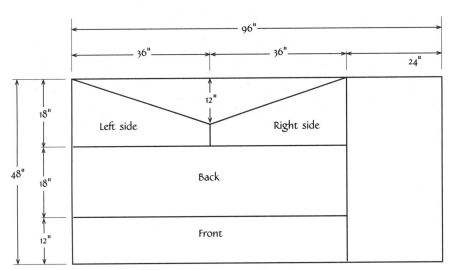

PLYWOOD CUTTING DIAGRAM

Useful Conversions

Table D-1. Conversions between Fahrenheit (°F) and Celsius (°C) temperature

Known temperature (in °C or °F)	Converted to °C	Converted to °F	Known temperature (in °C or °F)	Converted to °C	Converted to °F
−40	−40.0	−40.0	25	−3.9	77.0
−35	−37.2	−31.0	26	−3.3	78.8
−30	−34.4	−22.0	27	−2.8	80.6
−25	−31.7	−13.0	28	−2.2	82.4
−20	−28.9	−4.0	29	−1.7	84.2
−15	−26.1	5.0	30	−1.1	86.0
−10	−23.3	14.0	31	−0.6	87.8
−5	−20.6	23.0	32	0	89.6
0	−17.8	32.0	33	0.6	91.4
1	−17.2	33.8	34	1.1	93.2
2	−16.7	35.6	35	1.7	95.0
3	−16.1	37.4	36	2.2	96.8
4	−15.6	39.2	37	2.8	98.6
5	−15.0	41.0	38	3.3	100.4
6	−14.4	42.8	39	3.9	102.2
7	−13.9	44.6	40	4.4	104.0
8	−13.3	46.4	41	5.0	105.8
9	−12.8	48.2	42	5.6	107.6
10	−12.2	50.0	43	6.1	109.4
11	−11.7	51.8	44	6.7	111.2
12	−11.1	53.6	45	7.2	113.0
13	−10.6	55.4	46	7.8	114.8
14	−10.0	57.2	47	8.3	116.6
15	−9.4	59.0	48	8.9	118.4
16	−8.9	60.8	49	9.4	120.2
17	−8.3	62.6	50	10.0	122.0
18	−7.8	64.4	51	10.6	123.8
19	−7.2	66.2	52	11.1	125.6
20	−6.7	68.0	53	11.7	127.4
21	−6.1	69.8	54	12.2	129.2
22	−5.6	71.6	55	12.8	131.0
23	−5.0	73.4	56	13.3	132.8
24	−4.4	75.2	57	13.9	134.6

continued on next page

Table D-1. Conversions between Fahrenheit (°F) and Celsius (°C) temperature *(continued)*

Known temperature (in °C or °F)	Converted to °C	Converted to °F	Known temperature (in °C or °F)	Converted to °C	Converted to °F
58	14.4	136.4	84	28.9	183.2
59	15.0	138.2	85	29.4	185.0
60	15.6	140.0	86	30.0	186.8
61	16.1	141.8	87	30.6	188.6
62	16.7	143.6	88	31.1	190.4
63	17.2	145.4	89	31.7	192.2
64	17.8	147.2	90	32.2	194.0
65	18.3	149.0	91	32.8	195.8
66	18.9	150.8	92	33.3	197.6
67	19.4	152.6	93	33.9	199.4
68	20.0	154.4	94	34.4	201.2
69	20.6	156.2	95	35.0	203.0
70	21.1	158.0	96	35.6	204.8
71	21.7	159.8	97	36.1	206.6
72	22.2	161.6	98	36.7	208.4
73	22.8	163.4	99	37.2	210.2
74	23.3	165.2	100	37.8	212.0
75	23.9	167.0	105	40.6	221.0
76	24.4	168.8	110	43.3	230.0
77	25.0	170.6	115	46.1	239.0
78	25.6	172.4	120	48.9	248.0
79	26.1	174.2	125	51.7	257.0
80	26.7	176.0	130	54.4	266.0
81	27.2	177.8	135	57.2	275.0
82	27.8	179.6	140	60.0	284.0
83	28.3	181.4			

Temperature Conversion Formulas

- To convert °C to °F: (°C x 9/5) + 32 = °F

- To convert °F to °C: (°F – 32) x 5/9 = °C

Table D-2. Useful conversions

Type of measurement	To convert:	Into:	Multiply by:
Length	centimeters (cm)	inches (in)	0.394
	feet (ft)	centimeters (cm)	30.48
	feet (ft)	inches (in)	12
	feet (ft)	yards (yd)	0.33
	inches (in)	feet (ft)	0.083
	inches (in)	millimeters (mm)	25.4
	inches (in)	centimeters (cm)	2.54
	meters (m)	inches (in)	39.37
	meters (m)	feet (ft)	3.281
	meters (m)	yards (yd)	1.094
	yards (yd)	feet (ft)	3
	yards (yd)	centimeters (cm)	91.44
	yards (yd)	meters (m)	0.9144
Area	acres	square feet (ft^2)	43,560
	acres	square yards (yd^2)	4,840
	acres	hectares (ha)	0.4047
	hectares (ha)	acres	2.471
	hectares (ha)	square meters (m^2)	10,000
	square inches (in^2)	square centimeters (cm^2)	6.452
	square centimeters (cm^2)	square inches (in^2)	0.155
	square feet (ft^2)	square centimeters (cm^2)	929.09
	square feet (ft^2)	square meters (m^2)	0.0929
	square meters (m^2)	square feet (ft^2)	10.76
	square meters (m^2)	square yards (yd^2)	1.196
Weight	grams (g)	ounces (oz)	0.0353
	kilograms (kg)	pounds (lb)	2.205
	metric tons (megagrams)	short tons	1.1023
	ounces (oz)	pounds (lb)	0.0625
	ounces (oz)	grams (g)	28.35
	pounds (lb)	ounces (oz)	16
	pounds (lb)	grams (g)	453.6
	short tons	metric tons (megagrams)	0.9078
Volume, solids	bushels (bu)	cubic feet (ft^3)	1.24
	bushels (bu)	cubic meters (m^3)	0.352
	bushels (bu)	liters (L)	35.24
	cubic feet (ft^3)	liters (L)	28.32
	cubic feet (ft^3)	U.S. gallons (gal)	7.48
	cubic feet (ft^3)	cubic inches (in^3)	1,728
	cubic feet (ft^3)	cubic yards (yd^3)	0.037
	cubic feet (ft^3)	bushels (bu)	0.804
	cubic inches (in^3)	milliliters (ml)	16.39
	cubic meters (m^3)	cubic yards (yd^3)	1.308
	cubic meters (m^3)	U.S. gallons (gal)	264.2
	cubic meters (m^3)	cubic feet (ft^3)	35.3

continued on next page

Table D-2. Useful conversions *(continued)*

Type of measurement	To convert:	Into:	Multiply by:
Volume, solids (continued)	cubic yards (yd³)	cubic feet (ft³)	27
	cubic yards (yd³)	liters (L)	764.6
	cubic yards (yd³)	cubic meters (m³)	0.765
	cubic yards (yd³)	bushels (bu)	21.7
	gallons, U.S. dry (gal)	cubic inches (in³)	269
	liters (L)	cubic inches (in³)	61.02
	milliliters (mL)	cubic inches (in³)	0.0610
	quarts, dry (qt)	cubic inches (in³)	67.2
Volume, liquids	cubic centimeters (cm³ or cc)	milliliters (mL)	1
	cups (c)	fluid ounces (fl oz)	8
	gallons, U.S. (gal)	cups (c)	16
	gallons, U.S. (gal)	cubic inches (in³)	231
	gallons, U.S. (gal)	quarts (qt)	4
	gallons, U.S. (gal)	liters (L)	3.785
	gallons, U.S. (gal)	gallons, Imperial (gal)	0.833
	gallons, Imperial (gal)	cubic inches (in³)	277.42
	gallons, Imperial (gal)	liters (L)	4.546
	gallons, Imperial (gal)	gallons, U.S. (gal)	1.20
	liters (L)	pints (pt)	2.113
	liters (L)	quarts (qt)	1.057
	liters (L)	gallons, U.S. (gal)	0.2642
	milliliters (mL)	fluid ounces (fl oz)	0.0338
	pints (pt)	fluid ounces (fl oz)	16
	pints (pt)	cups (c)	2
	pints (pt)	quarts (qt)	0.5
	pints (pt)	cubic inches (in³)	28.87
	pints (pt)	liters (L)	0.4732
	fluid ounces (fl oz)	cubic inches (in³)	1.805
	fluid ounces (fl oz)	tablespoons (Tbsp)	2
	fluid ounces (fl oz)	teaspoons (tsp)	6
	fluid ounces (fl oz)	milliliters (mL)	29.57
	quarts (qt)	fluid ounces (fl oz)	32
	quarts (qt)	cups (c)	4
	quarts (qt)	pints (pt)	2
	quarts (qt)	U.S. gallons, liquid (gal)	0.25
	quarts (qt)	cubic inches (in³)	57.7
	quarts (qt)	liters (L)	0.9463
	tablespoons (Tbsp)	teaspoons (tsp)	3
	tablespoons (Tbsp)	milliliters (mL)	15
	teaspoons (tsp)	milliliters (mL)	5
Weight per volume	grams/cubic centimeter (g/cm³)	pounds/cubic foot (lbs/ft³)	62.3
	tablespoons/bushel (Tbsp/bu)	pounds/cubic yard (lbs/yd³)	1 (approx.)
	pounds/cubic yard (lbs/yd³)	ounces/cubic foot (oz/ft³)	0.6
	ounces/cubic foot (oz/ft³)	pounds/cubic yard (lbs/yd³)	1.67
	pounds/cubic yard (lbs/yd³)	grams/liter (g/L)	0.595
	kilograms/cubic meter (kg/m³)	pounds/cubic yard (lbs/yd³)	1.6821

Glossary

Acrylic glazing — Double-skin sheet with a ribbed configuration and available in several thicknesses and large-size sheets. Installation is made using extruded attachment components.

Aeroponics — A hydroponics system in which the exposed roots in an enclosed trough are fed nutrients through a fine mist or fog.

Annealed glass — Sheet glass that has been heated and slowly cooled to a flat, high-gloss surface.

Anti-condensate control film — An additive to film plastic that keeps condensed moisture in a laminar form, allowing it to run off.

Attached greenhouse — A greenhouse structure that is attached to another building. Sometimes referred to as a lean-to.

Backsiphoning — The flow of contaminated water back into the supply plumbing system through a cross-connection. A vacuum breaker or anti-siphoning valve will prevent this.

Batter board — Two boards set at a right angle and located back from the proposed corners of the greenhouse to support string that marks the location of the foundation.

Boiler — A heating system in which water is the transfer medium. Distribution can be by radiators, piping, or heat exchangers.

Calcium chloride hexahydrate — Phase-change salt used in solar greenhouses. It has a melting point of 81°F and a heat of fusion of 82 Btu/pound.

Capillary action — The force that results from the greater attraction of water to a solid surface than the internal cohesion of the water itself. This results in water being drawn up into the growing mix in a pot.

Capillary mat — Type of bottom-watering system that uses a fiber mat placed on a bench to distribute water to the bottoms of pots.

CCA — Copper chromated arsenic, a preservative used in pressure-treated wood.

Cement-asbestos board — Bench material common in older greenhouses. Because it contains asbestos, it should be removed and disposed of properly.

Certificate of Occupancy (CO) — A document issued by the building official after a greenhouse is built to denote that it complies with the building code.

CDX plywood — A type of plywood with an exterior glue used for short-term exposure to weather. For greenhouse use, an exterior grade of plywood should be used.

Cold frame — Enclosed wood frame that has a glazed top, is sloped to the south, and is located in an outside protected area. It is used to grow seedlings, propagate cuttings, or overwinter bulbs.

Combustion air — Air needed for the combustion of fuel in a furnace, boiler, or heater. A source of makeup air should be provided in a tight greenhouse.

Compressed air sprayer — A 1- to 5-gallon tank with an integral hand pump and wand with a nozzle that is used to apply pesticides.

Condensation — The change of water from the vapor state to the liquid state on a cool surface, such as the glazing of the greenhouse.

Conduction — The transfer of heat within or between solid objects. The rate depends on the area, path length, temperature difference, density, and conductivity.

Conservatory — Style of greenhouse structure built with ornate arches, flowing curves, and decorative embellishments.

Construction-grade polyethylene — A film plastic sometimes used for greenhouse glazing that has a life of about 9 months when exposed to sunlight.

Continuous feed — Feeding nutrients in dilute form every time a crop is watered.

Control joint — An indentation line in a concrete slab that controls where a crack will form when the concrete shrinks.

Controller — Solid-state control device with a sensor that integrates heating and cooling systems in the greenhouse. It takes the place of several thermostats.

Convection — Heat transfer by the physical movement of a warm gas or liquid to a colder location.

Copolymer — Polyethylene film plastic glazing that has additives to increase strength, reduce yellowing, and extend life.

Copper naphthanate — A wood preservative, safe for plant production, that protects against rot, decay, mildew, and termite damage.

Creosote — A wood preservative, formerly used on posts and telephone poles, that is now considered a health hazard. Fumes from wood treated with creosote can cause plant injury.

Day-neutral plant — A plant, such as a rose, that does not respond to the relative length of the light and dark period.

Degree-day — A measure of the heat needed to maintain temperature in a building based on the inside and outside temperature.

Dibble — A pointed dowel or metal pin or a board with the same used to preform holes in a container of growing mix before seedlings are inserted.

Drip irrigation — Also called trickle irrigation, a low-pressure system for applying water to row or potted crops at a very low flow rate.

Dry hydrant — A water hydrant used in outdoor supply systems that drains when shut off to protect it from freezing.

Ebb and flood — The periodic flooding of a water-tight bench of plants with a nutrient solution. The nutrient solution flows back to a holding tank to be recycled.

Ethylene gas — Byproduct of combustion that can cause injury to plants.

Evaporative cooling — The addition of moisture to air to reduce its dry-bulb temperature.

Evaporative pad — Wetted cellulose or synthetic fiber pad in an evaporative cooling system that allows ventilation air to pick up moisture.

Evapotranspiration rate — The quantity of water transpired by plants and evaporated from the soil. It is highly affected by the level of solar radiation.

Exhaust fan — Fan installed in the endwall of the greenhouse and controlled by a thermostat to cool the interior air. An intake louver or door is needed on the opposite endwall.

Expanded metal — Sheet metal that has been cut and stretched to form a perforated bench top with diamond-shaped holes. Usually this material is galvanized to keep it from rusting.

Far-red light — Light in the 700- to 750-nanometer range. It occurs at the limit of our visual perception.

Fascia board — The vertical board at the end of the roof overhang.

Fertilizer injector — A device that injects a concentrated nutrient solution into the supply line of an irrigation system.

Fiberglass reinforced plastic (FRP) — A glazing material made from a fiberglass mat encased in a plastic material. It is available in large sheets.

Film plastic — Plastic, usually polyethylene or poly vinyl, that is used as glazing on a greenhouse. Most common thicknesses are 0.004–0.008 inch (4–8 mil).

Flue gases — The products of combustion, including smoke, carbon dioxide, moisture, and excess air, that are vented through the stovepipe-chimney system.

Fossil fuels — Fuels, such as oil and natural gas, that were formed from decaying vegetation over millions of years.

Freestanding greenhouse — A greenhouse structure that is set apart from other structures.

Furnace — A heating system in which air is the transfer medium. Distribution is by blower or ducting.

Galvanized steel — Steel that has been dipped into a solution of zinc to prevent rust.

Germination chamber — A small insulated box or enclosed area with temperature and humidity control for germinating seed.

Girts — Longitudinal members of the framework that support the glazing material on the walls.

Glauber salt — Phase-change salt with a melting point of 90°F and a heat of fusion of 108 Btu/pound; used for solar heat storage.

Glazing — The light-transmitting material used to cover the greenhouse frame.

Ground fault interrupter (GFI) — A device in an electrical circuit that protects you against electrical shock caused by a faulty tool or appliance.

Growing bed — Ground bed in a greenhouse filled with growing mix for growing tall crops such as tomatoes or roses. It can be built to any size.

Gusset — A piece of plywood cut to join two framing members together. Gussets are usually placed on both sides of the joint and require a significant number of nails to make the joint rigid.

Header — A beam used to support roof or wall members over an opening such as a door or window.

Heating cable — Electric resistance wire covered with plastic to provide bottom heat or for hotbeds. Available in several lengths and heat outputs. May have an integral or separate thermostat.

High-intensity discharge (HID) lamp — An efficient high-output light source in which an electric current is passed through a mixture of gases under high pressure and temperature. Lamp life is 10,000 to 24,000 hours.

High-pressure sodium lamp — High-output high-intensity discharge lamp with light mostly in the yellow-orange part of the spectrum.

Hold-back clause — The statement in a contract that allows the homeowner to retain the final payment until the work is completed to satisfaction.

Horizontal air flow (HAF) — System of using one or more circulating fans in a greenhouse to create horizontal air circulation.

Hotbed — Heated cold frame for propagation or to extend the season. Thermostatically controlled heating cable provides the heat.

Hydroponics — Soilless growing system for plants that uses tanks, piping, and pumps to supply a nutrient solution.

Hygrometer — Motorized psychrometer for getting relative humidity.

Illumination — The amount of light falling on a unit area. It is measured in foot-candles (ft-c).

Infiltration — The exchange of interior and exterior air from a greenhouse through cracks around doors, vents, glazing, and other openings.

Infrared heater — Electric or gas-fired heating system that transfers heat by radiant energy.

Insect screen — A very fine mesh screen used to enclose vents and louvers to exclude insects and other pests from the greenhouse.

Interference film plastic — A greenhouse glazing with additives that can affect plant growth and pest problems.

Jamb — The vertical pieces surrounding a door or window opening.

Knapsack sprayer — A tank sprayer with a hand-operated or small engine–driven pump and wand with a nozzle used for applying pesticides.

Laminated glass — A glazing that consists of two layers of glass with a sheet of plastic between used in areas where safety protection is needed.

Lapped glass — A method of applying small panes of glass to a greenhouse to shed water.

Latitude — The angular distance north or south of the equator measured in degrees.

Leaching — Applying water in excess of the amount retained by the growing media to promote drainage of excess fertilizer residues from the root zone.

Leaf stomata — Minute pore-like openings in plant leaves for the exchange of gases.

Light spectrum — The distribution of light into wavelengths and colors.

Light transmittance — The ratio of light passing through a glazing material to the light that falls upon it from the sun.

Long-night plant — A plant that undergoes photoperiodic response, such as flowering, only when the night length is greater than a critical number of hours.

Low-emissivity (low-E) glass — Double-pane glass panels with a metallic coating on the inside face of the outer panel that reduces UV transmission and radiant heat loss.

Low-iron glass — Glass that has a low percentage of iron (0.03%) that allows greater light transmission as compared to float glass.

Manometer — A gauge that measures pressure. It is used in applying an air-inflated plastic cover to the greenhouse.

Mastic — An adhesive used to attach tile or other surface material to a greenhouse floor. The mastic should be compatible with the floor material.

Maximum-minimum thermometer — A thermometer that records the high and low temperature in the greenhouse during a 24-hour period. It also indicates current temperature.

Mesh — The size of openings in a water filter indicating the level of filtration. The greater the mesh, the smaller the particle size that can be removed. Overhead irrigation systems usually use a 100-mesh filter. Drip systems may require a 150-mesh filter.

Metal halide lamp — A high-intensity discharge lamp that uses iodides and mercury to produce a light with a spectrum near sunlight.

Mist system — An irrigation system with piping, nozzles, and control that applies a fine mist over a greenhouse bed for propagation of cuttings or germination of seedlings.

Mullion — The vertical members separating window panes.

Nanometer (nm) — The measure of the wavelengths of light. Light used by plants falls between 380 and 780 nanometers.

Natural ventilation — A method of cooling a greenhouse through roof or side vents that operates on pressure differences created and maintained by wind or temperature gradients.

Nonvented heater — A heater that does not have any provisions for exhausting the flue gases out of the greenhouse. This type of heater should generally not be used in a greenhouse, as the flue gases could cause plant damage.

Nutrient film technique (NFT) — The hydroponic growing system that supplies nutrients in a thin film of water that flows through the root system.

Nutrient solution — Fertilizer and other chemicals dissolved in water used to feed plants.

Orientation — The location of a greenhouse structure so as to capture sunlight.

Overhead irrigation — The application of water to crops from over the top of the plants.

Peastone — A graded stone from gravel used as a floor material in the greenhouse to provide good drainage.

Pellet burner — Thermostatically controlled heater that burns wood pellets.

Peninsula bench — An arrangement of greenhouse benches with a wide central aisle and narrow perpendicular side aisles. This arrangement usually results in greater space utilization in the greenhouse.

Perlite — White granules formed from heating volcanic silicate ore to 1,400°F and added to growing mix for water retention and porosity.

Pesticide persistence — The length of time that a pesticide is hazardous to human health after application.

pH — The degree of acidity or alkalinity of soil. A pH of 7.0 is neutral, while higher readings indicate alkalinity and lower readings indicate acidity. Most plants do best at a pH of 6.5–7.5.

Photometer — Meter for measuring illumination in the greenhouse and in plant growth chambers. Readings are in foot-candles.

Photomorphogenesis — The regulation by light energy of specific growth responses in plants, such as shape, orientation, and flowering.

Photoperiodism — The response of plants to the relative length of day or night. Response can be in the form of changes in leaf shape, internode length, bulb formation, or tuber formation.

Photosynthesis — The process in which a plant uses chlorophyll to trap the sun's energy in the form of sugars and produces oxygen and sugars from carbon dioxide and water.

Photosynthetically active radiation (PAR) — Light utilized in photosynthesis that comprises the wavelengths from 400 to 700 nanometers.

Pier — The vertical support for the frame of a greenhouse used to tie the structure to the ground.

Pit greenhouse — A greenhouse built over a pit in the ground to take advantage of the normal soil temperature. This reduces winter heating cost.

Polycarbonate — A ribbed or corrugated plastic glazing material available in several thicknesses and large-size sheets. Typical useful life is 15–20 years.

Polystyrene insulation board — Insulation that is available in 2-foot-by-8-foot and 4-foot-by-8-foot sheets and thicknesses from ½ to 4 inches. It is used for insulating nonglazed areas and the perimeter foundation.

Pressure-compensating emitter — A low-pressure, low-water-flow emitter that maintains a uniform flow rate over long lengths of pipe and with varying elevations.

Pressure-treated wood — Lumber that has been treated with a chemical solution of chromated copper arsenic (CCA) or other preservative to retard rotting.

Purlin — Longitudinal members of the framework that support the glazing material on the roof.

Quantum meter — Meter for measuring light energy in the 400- to 700-nanometer (PAR) range. Measurements are in micromoles/square meter-second (µmol/sq m-s).

Radiation — The transfer of heat through waves between two bodies not in direct contact. The rate depends on the capacity of the objects to transmit and absorb the rays.

Relative humidity — The amount of moisture in the air expressed as a percentage of the maximum that the air can hold at a given temperature and pressure. This is the value usually given in weather reports.

Respirator — A mask placed over the face when working in dusty conditions or when applying pesticides to filter the air that is breathed. The correct filter for the material being applied must be selected.

Rockwool — A growing media composed of finely spun fibers of rock that are formed when rock is heated to an extremely high temperature. It can be used as amendment to soilless mixes or as a support medium for hydroponics.

Root zone heat — Hot water or hot air system installed to provide heat in the floor or under the benches. It can save heating costs if room air temperature can be lowered.

Rowcover — Light, transparent fabric material placed over row crops in the garden to warm the soil and air. It can also reduce insects reaching the plants.

Sand/stone culture — The hydroponic technique for growing plants with sand or stone as a support medium.

Screed board — The form boards used around poured concrete in a walkway or floor to level the surface.

Season-extender — A low-cost, plastic-covered frame over a garden area used to lengthen the growing season in the spring and fall. Roll-up sides are used for ventilation.

Sediment trap — A device put into a sink drain or floor drain to retain soil and other material before it can enter a sewer or drain system.

Shade coefficient — The ratio of the solar gain compared to ⅛-inch clear glass.

Shade fabric — Fabric material available with different levels of light transmission that is applied to the exterior of the glazing to reduce the heat load on the greenhouse or applied over plants in the greenhouse to keep them cooler.

Shade house (lath house) — Structure with a frame covered with lath, shade fabric, or netting to reduce the intensity of sunlight reaching the plants. It is used for propagating woody plants and groundcover and overwintering sensitive plants.

Shading compound — A spray material applied to the outside of the glazing during the summer that reflects the sun's rays and reduces the heat gain inside the greenhouse.

Short-night plant — A plant that undergoes a photoperiodic response, such as flowering, only when the night length is less than a critical number of hours.

Sling psychrometer — Device with two thermometers, one with a wetted wick, that is swung like a fan. The difference in temperatures on the thermometers is a measure of relative humidity.

Snow fence — Lath held together by galvanized wire to form a flexible fence used by highway departments to prevent drifting of snow over the road. It makes an inexpensive bench top.

Soilless growing mix — A composite of peat, vermiculite, perlite, compost, or other materials and fertilizer used for growing plants. It contains no soil and is considered sterile.

Soil pasteurization — The heating of a soil or soil mix to a temperature between 140° and 200°F to kill harmful pathogens and weeds.

Solar greenhouse — An attached or freestanding greenhouse designed and located to capture maximum winter heat from the sun. Usually the north wall and part of the sidewalls are insulated to reduce heat loss.

Solar-powered vent opener — Nonelectric cylinder that contains mineral wax that expands with heat. Used for temperature control on greenhouse vents and cold frames. Has adjustable temperature settings.

Solar radiation — Solar energy from the sun that reaches the earth. Usually measured in Langleys or Btu/square foot.

Solar transmission — The percentage of solar radiation that passes through a glazing material.

Solenoid valve — An electric-controlled valve in an irrigation system. Normally a 24-volt solenoid is used to reduce electric shock potential.

Squirrel-cage blower — A small blower used for air inflation of double poly glazing on greenhouses. It should have a maximum pressure rating of ½ inch static pressure to prevent overinflation.

Static pressure — The resistance that a fan must overcome due to louvers or other obstructions. It is measured in inches of water.

Sticky cards — Small yellow or blue cards with a sticky surface that attract and catch insect pests in the greenhouse. By counting and recording the number of insects caught during a particular time period, one can determine the level of pest pressure.

Stippled glass — Glass with a pebbled surface. This tends to diffuse the light passing through.

Stock solution — The concentrated solution of fertilizer fed into irrigation water when feeding plants.

Stone dust — The fine material resulting from the crushing of quarry rock. It is used as a base for brick and stone walkways in the greenhouse or outdoors.

Submersible pump — The type of pump used in most hydroponic systems. It is located in the bottom of the nutrient tank.

Sulfur dioxide — Product of combustion that combines with water to form sulfuric acid. If this condenses on plant leaves, it can cause white burn spots.

Sunspace — A glazed structure usually built as an extension of the living space in the home.

Supplemental light — The use of artificial light to supplement natural daylight to increase plant growth.

Tec screw — A self-tapping screw used to fasten wood or metal parts of the greenhouse.

Tempered glass — Annealed glass that has been reheated and cooled rapidly to increase strength by four times. This allows larger panes with less support members. If broken, it tends to form corn-kernel-size pieces without sharp edges. Panes cannot be cut.

Thermal blanket — Energy blanket installed and operated to reduce heat loss from the greenhouse at night.

Thermal loss — Heat loss due to a temperature difference between inside and outside the greenhouse.

Thermal radiation — Heat energy radiated by objects inside the greenhouse. The value depends on the temperature of the object and its shape.

Thermostat — The sensor and switch for the control of a heating or ventilation system. Thermostats should be located at plant height and shaded from direct sunlight.

Time clock — A device that controls the length of time that a lighting system or other devices operate. The length of time is easily adjusted.

Transpiration — The loss of water from plant tissue in the form of vapor.

Trap rock — Crushed, graded stone from a quarry that is used as floor material in a greenhouse to provide drainage.

Tunnel — Frame structure placed in the garden and covered with film plastic to modify temperature and extend the growing season. Low tunnels are covered hoops of wire. High tunnels are pipe frames tall enough to walk in.

Ultraviolet (UV) light — Light with wavelengths less than 400 nanometers. It can be harmful to plants in large quantities and also breaks down plastic.

U-value — Insulating value of materials used in the greenhouse. The lower the U-value, the less the heat loss.

Vacuum breaker — A device attached to a hose bibb or end of a water line to prevent backflow of contaminated water should a break occur in a water line or hose.

Vapor barrier — An impervious plastic barrier placed over the warm side of a wall to keep moisture from getting into the insulation underneath.

Venturi principle — The principle by which some fertilizer injectors work: As water travels through a restricted section of pipe, the velocity increases and the pressure decreases. This allows the injection of a concentrated nutrient solution into the irrigation water.

Vermiculite — Gray, expanded mica ore heated to 1,800°F to create small pieces that are added to growing mix for porosity and water retention.

Visible light transmission — A measure of that portion of total solar radiation visible to the human eye.

Water filter — A screen or mesh filter in an irrigation system that removes sand, soil, organic matter, and other solid particles to prevent clogging of nozzles. They are available in many sizes and levels of filtration.

Water-soluble fertilizer — Fertilizer that will dissolve in water used in irrigation systems.

Weed barrier — A plastic sheet material placed over the soil to prevent weeds from growing but still allow water to flow through. It is used in landscaping plantings and under benches in the greenhouse.

Welded glass — Two panes of glass with an air space between that are welded together around the edges to form a thermopane.

Wetting agent — A surfactant on glazing that reduces surface tension of condensation, allowing it to run off rather than form droplets.

Window greenhouse — Small greenhouse structure fitted over a window. Care of the plants is from inside the home.

Wire glass — Molded glass that has an integral wire fabric that is used in areas subject to physical damage. The wire reduces light transmission.

Wood float — Piece of board with a handle used to create a level but rough surface when finishing a concrete floor or walkway.

Working drawings — A set of plans used by a builder to construct the greenhouse. They may also be required by the building official to check safety features.

References

Publications

Abraham, G. and K. 1975. Organic Gardening Under Glass. Rodale Press, Inc. Emmaus, PA.

Aldrich, R.A. and J.W. Bartok, Jr. 1994. Greenhouse Engineering. NRAES–33. Natural Resource, Agriculture, and Engineering Service (NRAES). Ithaca, NY.

Bartok, J.W., Jr. et al. 1994. Solar Greenhouses for the Home. NRAES–2. (Out of print.) Natural Resource, Agriculture, and Engineering Service (NRAES). Ithaca, NY.

Blaustein, J. 1979. How to Build and Use Greenhouses. Ortho Books. San Francisco, CA.

Bracken, J. 1977. Your Window Greenhouse. Thomas Y. Crowell Co. New York, NY.

Clegg P. and D. Watkins. 1979. The Complete Greenhouse Book. Garden Way Publishing. Charlotte, VT.

Coleman, E. 1993. The New Organic Grower. Chelsea Green. Chelsea, VT.

Coleman, Eliot. The Winter-Harvest Manual. Available from Four Season Farm, RR Box 14, Harborside, ME 04642.

Cooper, A. 1979. The ABC of NFT (Nutrient Film Technique). Grower Books. London.

Elwood, C. 1977. How to Build and Operate Your Greenhouse. H.P. Books. Tucson, AZ.

Jones, T. 1978. How to Build Greenhouses, Garden Shelters, and Sheds. Popular Science. Harper Row. New York.

Kramer, J. 1978. The Underground Gardener. Thomas Y. Crowell Co. New York, NY.

Martin, T. 1988. Greenhouses and Garden Rooms. Brooklyn Botanic Garden. Record 44:2.

McCullagh, J.C. et al. 1978. The Solar Greenhouse Book. Rodale Press. Emmaus, PA.

Pierce, J.H. 1977. Greenhouse Grow How. Plants Alive Books. Seattle, WA.

Resh, H.C. 1995. Hydroponic Food Production: A Definitive Guidebook of Soilless Food-Growing Methods. Woodbridge Press Publishing Co. Santa Barbara, CA.

Smith, S. 1992. Greenhouse Gardener's Companion. Fulcrum Publishing. Golden, CO.

Sunset Books. 1979. Greenhouse Gardening Lane. Publishing Co. Menlo Park, CA.

Tresidder, J. and S. Cliff. 1986. Living Under Glass. Clarkson N. Potter, Inc., Publishers. New York, NY.

Yanda, B. and R. Fisher. 1980. The Food and Heat Producing Solar-Greenhouse. John Muir Publications, Inc. Santa Fe, NM.

Organizations

The Hobby Greenhouse Association

The Hobby Greenhouse Association (HGA), 8 Glen Terrace, Bedford, MA 01730-2048, is a nonprofit organization that promotes greenhouse gardening as a hobby or avocation and disseminates practical information relative to the erection, maintenance, and operation of a greenhouse. They publish a quarterly magazine. Other member benefits include round robin letters, help and advice on greenhouse gardening, a seed exchange, video and book libraries, and discounts on certain print materials. Contact them for current dues rates.
Web site: WWW.HOBBYGREENHOUSE.ORG

The Hydroponics Society of America

The Hydroponics Society of America (HSA), P.O. Box 1183, El Cerrito, CA 94530, is a nineteen-year-old nonprofit organization dedicated to the exchange of information in the field of hydroponics. Educators, researchers, vendors, commercial growers, and hobbyists are all welcome. By joining the HSA, you will receive the *Soilless Grower* (a bimonthly newsletter), have access to the main archives of the society, get discounted prices on books available through the HSA bookstore, and get a reduced rate for the annual conference registration.
Web site: WWW.HSA.HYDROPONICS.ORG

Other Publications from NRAES

The following publications may be of interest to readers of *Greenhouses for Homeowners and Gardeners*. All are available from NRAES. Before ordering, contact NRAES for current prices and shipping and handling charges. Books can be ordered on the NRAES web site (see address below).

Currently, NRAES has published more than 95 publications and distributes a total of more than 160 publications; contact NRAES for a free catalog. Read more about NRAES on the inside back cover of this book.

NRAES (Natural Resource, Agriculture, and Engineering Service)
Cooperative Extension • 152 Riley-Robb Hall
Ithaca, New York 14853-5701

Phone: (607) 255-7654 • *Fax:* (607) 254-8770
E-mail: NRAES@CORNELL.EDU • *Web site:* WWW.NRAES.ORG

Home

Home*A*Syst: An Environmental Risk-Assessment Guide for the Home (NRAES–87)

*Home*A*Syst* helps homeowners and renters in rural and suburban areas assess their homes and properties for pollution and health risks. Eleven chapters cover topics that every resident should understand: site assessment, stormwater management, drinking water well management, household wastewater, hazardous household products, lead sources and management, yard and garden care, liquid fuels management, indoor air quality, heating and cooling systems, and household waste management. Each chapter provides key information and assessment questions to help readers evaluate their situations and management practices. How to take action toward improving practices and preventing health and environmental hazards is discussed in each chapter. (1997)

Home Buyers' Guide: Financing and Evaluating Prospective Homes (NRAES–50)

This publication explores the home-buying process. Six major areas are covered—getting information and assistance, financing a home, choosing a location, evaluating a floor plan, inspecting a home, and assessing environmental safety. This guide was designed for adult education classes, individuals planning to buy a home, and professionals who offer advice to prospective home buyers. (1991)

Home Storage of Fruits and Vegetables (NRAES–7)

This guide helps gardeners save money by preserving their own produce. It covers when to harvest, how to can and freeze, and where to store preserved foods. Specific storage conditions for 32 different fruits and vegetables are included. The handbook also provides plans for simple facilities to store homegrown produce all year round. (1979)

Home Water Treatment (NRAES–48)

This guide helps homeowners decide if water treatment is necessary and, if it is, which treatment device or system is appropriate for a particular problem. Homeowners on a public water system may find the information useful for improving the taste, smell, or appearance of their water or for treating contaminants that may leach from household plumbing. Included, in appendixes, are U.S. Environmental Protection Agency primary and secondary drinking water contaminants, their uses and/or sources, their possible chronic health effects, and potential treatment devices or methods for their removal. Also included are 41 illustrations, 30 tables, a glossary, and a list of references. (1995)

Home and Yard Improvements Handbook (MWPS–21)

A complete do-it-yourself guide to home improvement. Easy-to-follow instructions show how to add storage and recreational areas; build closets, kitchen cabinets, or a garage; build a deck; repair a damp basement; or add attic storage. A special section about adapting a home for wheelchair access is included. Ninety-one figures and 22 tables supplement the text. (1978)

Onsite Domestic Sewage Disposal Handbook (MWPS–24)

This handbook explains how to plan, design, install, and maintain a private sewage treatment and disposal system. For those with no access to municipal sewer systems, it covers septic tanks, gravity and pressure systems, and pump selection. (1982)

Private Drinking Water Supplies: Quality, Testing, and Options for Problem Waters (NRAES–47)

This general reference on drinking water quality will be useful for cooperative extension and water treatment professionals, people who supply their own water, and people who are dissatisfied with the quality of their public water supplies. It reviews standards for drinking water and activities that may affect water quality. Information on testing for contamination is provided and options for improving the quality of problem waters and developing new supplies are discussed. (1991)

Private Water Systems Handbook (NRAES–14)

Homeowners who operate and maintain their own water supply as well as contractors, pump installers, and plumbers will benefit from this handbook. Topics covered include system design, correcting problems in existing systems, water quality and quantity, water sources, pumps, pressure tanks, piping, and water treatment. (1979)

Greenhouse

Energy Conservation for Commercial Greenhouses (NRAES–3)

This publication helps greenhouse operators evaluate management options and reduce energy costs. The effects of windbreaks and structure orientation on energy use, properties of various glazing materials, and the benefits and drawbacks of retractable blankets and other insulation systems are explained. This publication will assist those planning to construct a greenhouse as well as those wishing to renovate an existing greenhouse for more efficient energy use. (1989)

Greenhouse Engineering (NRAES–33)

This manual contains information needed to plan, construct, and control the commercial greenhouse. Major sections describe various structures, methods of materials handling, the greenhouse environment, and energy conservation. Other topics include plans for noncommercial greenhouses, access for the handicapped, and remodeling existing greenhouses. (1994)

Water and Nutrient Management for Greenhouses (NRAES–56)

Preparing stock solutions for proportioners; selecting substrate; interpreting leaf, substrate, and water tests; and estimating crop nutrient needs are necessary skills in managing a greenhouse for zero runoff. This publication will help greenhouse managers learn these skills. The book begins with discussions on general crop needs, balancing nutrient applications with demand, and fertilizer measuring units. Subsequent chapters detail specific components of the root zone. How to use a fertilizer proportioner is discussed as well. (1996)

Fruit and Vegetable Production

Bramble Production Guide (NRAES–35)

In response to rising interest, this guide provides detailed information about all aspects of bramble production for both potential and established growers. Topics discussed include site selection and preparation, plant selection, pruning and trellising, pests and diseases, spray technology, harvesting and handling, and marketing. The guide contains over 115 full-color photos and a disease diagnostic key. (1989)

Highbush Blueberry Production Guide (NRAES–55)

This book covers all aspects of blueberry production, including site selection and preparation, plant selection, blueberry growth and development, maintenance, pest management, harvesting, and marketing. Topics that other fruit-production guides rarely address, such as nuisance wildlife management, water management, spray technology, and budgeting, are discussed as well. The guide features 168 full-color photos, 27 tables, 24 figures and charts, and a key to problems. (1992)

The Real Dirt: Farmers Tell about Organic and Low-Input Practices in the Northeast (NOSFaN–1)

Prepared by the Northeast Organic and Sustainable Farmers Network (NOSFaN) — a collaborative group of farmers, farm organization representatives, northeastern extension agents, and university researchers —*The Real Dirt* provides a snapshot of organic and sustainable farming in the Northeast in the 1990s. Based on interviews with over 60 farmers in eight states, the book offers a farmer's-eye view of how to design rotations, select crops, and survive economically in an increasingly chemical-dependent and industrialized agricultural system. (1994)

Strawberry Production Guide for the Northeast, Midwest, and Eastern Canada (NRAES–88)

This book provides in-depth, up-to-date coverage of every aspect of strawberry culture—from site preparation to harvesting and marketing. Topics covered include: the history and biology of the cultivated strawberry; site selection and preparation; plant selection; production systems; temperature regulation; water management; nutrient management; insect, mite, mollusc, and vertebrate scouting and management; disease management and physiological disorders; weed management; spray application technology; harvesting, handling, and transporting fresh fruit; marketing; and budgeting. Supplementing the text are 37 figures, 47 tables, and 115 full-color photographs. (1998)

Sustainable Vegetable Production from Start-Up to Market (NRAES–104)

Successful vegetable farmers do much more than produce vegetables; they also manage money, people, and natural resources effectively. For aspiring and beginning vegetable growers, experienced growers, extension personnel, classroom educators, and serious gardeners, this book introduces the full range of processes for moderate-scale vegetable production using ecological practices that minimize the need for synthetic inputs and maximize stewardship of resources. Individual chapters address principles and practices essential to planning, launching, and managing a vegetable production business: the practical implications of sustainability; getting started; farm business management; marketing; soil fertility; composting; crop rotation; cover crops; tillage equipment and field preparation; seeds and transplants; irrigation and spraying systems; harvest and postharvest handling; season extension; integrated pest management; and environmentally friendly strategies for managing insects, diseases, weeds, and wildlife. Thirty-two profiles detail the experiences of individual vegetable growers and provide enterprise budgets for a number of crops. The book includes 91 illustrations, 36 sidebars, 20 tables, six appendixes, a glossary, and extensive references. (1999)

Perennials Production

Herbaceous Perennials: Diseases and Insect Pests (IB–207)

This publication outlines strategies for the prevention and control of diseases and pests of herbaceous perennials. Forty-four full-color photographs help in identifying insects and diseases. An index to plant names will help readers locate information about a particular perennial. (1987)

Herbaceous Perennials Production: A Guide from Propagation to Marketing (NRAES–93)

This publication considers the diversity of situations encountered by perennial growers in businesses of all sizes. Key chapters in the book discuss production systems and schedules; propagation (including media, nutrients, environmental requirements, and methods); plug production; transplant and seedling care; nursery and field production; pest control (including deer and small animals); and forcing out-of-season bloom. Practical discussions about starting a business, marketing and customer service, setting prices for plants, and designing a production facility are also included. Appendixes discuss propagation methods and requirements for hundreds of species, optimum germination conditions for specific perennials and biennials, pests and diseases, and useful calculations and conversions. (1998)

Direct Marketing

Facilities for Roadside Markets (NRAES–52)

This publication is valuable for those considering a roadside market or looking to improve or expand a current one. Three chapters cover site considerations (visibility and accessibility, utilities, drainage, zoning, and building ordinances); market layout (areas for sales, preparation, and shipping and receiving); and market structure and facilities (parking, lighting, fire protection, security, and more). Also included are 26 illustrations and two sets of plans. (1992)

Produce Handling for Direct Marketing (NRAES–51)

This publication is valuable for growers who sell seasonal produce at farmers' markets or roadside markets. It describes postharvest physiology, food safety, produce handling from harvest to storage, refrigerated storage, produce displays, and specific handling and display recommendations for over 40 types of fruits and vegetables. Eleven tables and eight figures are included. (1992)

Composting

Composting to Reduce the Waste Stream: A Guide to Small Scale Food and Yard Waste Composting (NRAES–43)

This publication promotes small-scale composting of yard, garden, and vegetative food waste. Topics covered are the composting process, composting methods and alternatives, making and maintaining a compost pile, using compost, and using the guide as an educational resource. Seventeen figures, six tables, and plans for constructing nine different types of compost bins are included as well. (1991)

Field Guide to On-Farm Composting (NRAES–114)

To assist in day-to-day compost management, this book covers operations and equipment; raw materials and recipe making; process control and evaluation; site considerations, environmental management, and safety; composting livestock and poultry mortalities; and compost utilization on the farm. It includes an equipment identification table, diagrams showing windrow formation and shapes, examples and equations for recipe making and compost use estimation, a troubleshooting guide, and 24 full-color photos. (1999)

On-Farm Composting Handbook (NRAES–54)

A perennial favorite among NRAES customers (we've sold over 18,000 copies since 1992), the *On-Farm Composting Handbook* contains everything you ever wanted to know about composting on the farm — why to compost (the benefits and drawbacks), what to compost (raw materials), how to compost (the methods), and what to do if something goes wrong (management). The ten chapters also discuss site and environmental considerations, using compost, and marketing compost. Highlighting the text are 55 figures, 32 tables, and sample calculations for determining a recipe and sizing a compost pad. This book is so informative and comprehensive, it is used as a college textbook. (1992)

Other Publications of Interest

Enhancing Wildlife Habitats: A Practical Guide for Forest Landowners (NRAES–64)

This publication contains recommendations and field exercises for landowners who want to ensure quality habitats for wildlife in the region. It includes sections on forest wildlife ecology, understanding wildlife habitats, and wetlands, as well as specific guidelines for enhancing habitats of woodcock, ruffed grouse, white-tailed deer, wild turkey, and other upland and wetland animals. The book contains over 100 figures, many of which are black-and-white photographs; 11 tables; and a glossary. (1993)

Farm and Home Concrete Handbook (MWPS–35)

The many uses for concrete around farms and homes include walls, floors, drives, and other masonry construction. This compilation is a current reference for concrete users. Learn how to select a concrete mix and order ready-mix concrete. Details include forming, reinforcing, placing, finishing, and curing concrete. Selection and design recommendations for numerous practical applications are included. A major section covers the basics and preparations, weather precautions, and slip-resistant surfaces. (1989)

Index

A

Acrylic plastic 42, 44–45, 183
Air circulation 102–103
Alarm system 35

B

Beds 50
Benches
    Construction 17, 18, 49, 51–53
    Height 17, 18, 51–52
    Layout 33, 48–49
    Potting, portable 51
    Racks and shelves 49
Building permit 14–15

C

Cold frame 118–122, 183
    Construction 118–119
    Location 119
    Plans 177–178
Computer 104
Conservatory 5–6, 184
Contractor-built greenhouse 19–20
    Contract 20
Controller 104, 184
Cooling 93–100
    Evaporative 98–100, 184
    Fans 97–98, 184
    Humidification 99
    Natural ventilation 96, 186
    Shading 93–95
Cooling system maintenance 130
Covering. See glazing.
Custom designs 15–16

D

Degree-days (55° base) 76–77, 184

E

Electric supply 33–35
    Backup power 34–35
Energy conservation 33, 87–93
    Exterior cover 88–89
    Interior liner 87–88
    Thermal blanket installation 89–92
    Thermal blanket materials 89
Environmental control 17, 103–104
Equipment 55–60
    Carts 57
    Mixer 56
    Screen 56
    Seeders 19, 57
    Soil shredder 56
    Soil sterilizer 56
    Storage bins 57
    Thermometers 59–60
    Time clocks 60–61, 189
Evaporative cooling 98–100, 184

F

Fans 97–98
Fertilizer system 67–70
    Proportioner (injector) 67–70, 185
Fiberglass 42, 44, 185
Flashing, ridge 31–32
Floor
    Construction 53–55
    Drainage 55
    Materials 54–55

Foundation 25–32
   Concrete slab 26–27
   Layout 30–32
   Mounting to a deck 29–30
   No foundation 29
   Pier 27–28
   Post 28–29
   Poured concrete — concrete block 27

G

Germination cabinet 114–115, 185
   Plans 115
Glass 40–41, 43–44
   Annealed 40, 183
   Double-pane 41
   Installation 43–44
   Single-pane 40–41
Glazing 38–47, 185
   Basics 39–40
   Comparison of types (table) 39
   Glass 40–41
   Installation 43–47
   Light transmission 39–40
   Maintenance 129
   Polycarbonate 41–42
   Shade coefficient 39, 188
   U-value 39, 189
Greenhouses
   Attached (lean-to) 9, 183
     Plans 135, 140
   Cost 7–8
   For physically challenged 16–19
   Freestanding 10–11, 185
     Plans 145, 147, 151, 156, 163
   Kit 20–23
   Layout 17, 48–49
   Orientation 12, 82–82, 187
   Parts, nomenclature 3
   Pit 11–12, 187
     Plans 169
   Selection 9–13
   Size 13
   Solar 12, 82–84, 188
   Space utilization 48–53
   Styles 12–13
   Types 9–12
   Upgrading 33
   Year-round 4
Growth chamber 114, 116
   Cart 116
   Light-support frame 114, 116
   Rack 116–117

H

Handicap accessibility 16–17
Heaters
   Electric 79–80
   Gas 77–79
   Kerosene — fuel oil 80–81
   Wood 81–82
Heating cost 75–77
Heating system 33–34, 71–86
   Fuel 74–75
   Maintenance 130
   Root zone 85–87, 188
   Sizing 72–74
Heat transfer coefficients 73
High tunnel 127–128, 189
   Construction 127
   Plans 173
   Ventilation 127
Hiring a contractor 19
Hotbed 119–122, 185
   Costs 122
   Operation 121
   Plans 120
Humidifier 99
Humidity
   Control 100
   Decreasing 102
   Increasing 101–102
   Measurement 100–101
Hydroponic systems 65–67, 185

I

Instruction manual 20–22
Irrigation systems. See watering systems.

K

Kit greenhouse 20–23

L

Lath house. See shade house.
Light garden 6–7
Lighting 105–110
   Basics 105–106
   Cost 110
   Measuring 109–110
   Supplemental 105–110
   Timers, time clocks 60–61
   Under benches 53

Lighting sources   106–109
    Choosing   108–109
    Comparison (table)   108
    Fluorescent   107
    High-intensity discharge   107, 185
    Incandescent   106
    Quartz-halogen   106–107
Lumber   24, 37–38

M

Maintenance   129–130
Mist system   61–62, 186

P

Paint   25, 33
Personal protective equipment   58–59
Pesticide applicators   57–58
Plants — light requirements   38–39
Plastic glazing   41–43, 44–47
    Air inflation   46
Plot plan   14–15
Polycarbonate   41–42, 44–45, 187

R

Racks and shelves   49
Rowcover   123, 125–126, 188
    Covering material   125
    Plans   125, 126

S

Season-extender   4–5
Shade house   122–123
    Construction   123
    Plans   123, 124
    Uses   122
Shading — greenhouse   93–95
Solar heating   12, 82–84
    Heat storage   83–84
Sunspace   6, 189

T

Thermal blankets
    Installation   89–92
    Materials   89
Thermostats   104, 189
Tools   17, 19, 23, 57, 59–61
Tunnel. See high tunnel.

U

Used greenhouse   24–25

V

Ventilation. See cooling.

W

Walkways   53–55
Water
    Filters   35–36
    Quality   35–36
    Supply   35–36
Watering devices   17, 19
Watering systems   61–67
    Capillary mats   64–65
    Mist   61–62
    Overhead   62–63, 187
    Trickle, drip   63–64, 184
Window greenhouse   6, 111–114, 190
    Heating and cooling   113
    Installation   113
    Moisture control   113
    Operation   114
    Selection   111–112
Work areas   50

Z

Zoning permit   14

About the Author

John W. Bartok, Jr. is an extension professor emeritus and agricultural engineer with the Department of Natural Resources Management and Engineering at the University of Connecticut–Storrs. He was a member of the Cooperation Extension system from 1966 to 1997 and provided technical support and educational programs to the greenhouse and nursery industries in the United States and Canada. His expertise is in greenhouse design, environment control, mechanization, and energy conservation.

Bartok is author of over 400 technical papers, bulletins, and magazine articles. He is co-author of *Greenhouse Engineering*, NRAES–33, which was published by NRAES (Natural Resource, Agriculture, and Engineering Service — formerly the Northeast Regional Agricultural Engineering Service). Mr. Bartok is also a consultant on greenhouse and nursery design, environment control, and mechanization to universities, schools, manufacturers, and commercial growers.